Unit 6   Geometry

Unit Overview 141

6-1   Area of Triangles 143

6-2   Area of Quadrilaterals 147

6-3   Area of Polygons 151

6-4   Polygons in the Coordinate Plane 155

6-5   Volume of Prisms 159

6-6   Nets and Surface Area 163

       Problem Solving Connections 167

       Test Prep 171

Unit 7   Statistics

Unit Overview 173

7-1   Displaying Numerical Data 175

7-2   Measures of Center 179

7-3   Measures of Variability 183

       Problem Solving Connections 187

       Test Prep 191

Learning the Common Core State Standards

Has your state adopted the Common Core standards? If so, then students will be learning both mathematical content standards and the mathematical practice standards that underlie them. The supplementary material found in *On Core Mathematics Grade 6* will help students succeed with both.

> Here are some of the special features you'll find in *On Core Mathematics Grade 6*.

INTERACTIVE LESSONS

Students actively participate in every aspect of a lesson. They carry out an activity in an Explore and complete the solution of an Example. This interactivity promotes a deeper understanding of the mathematics.

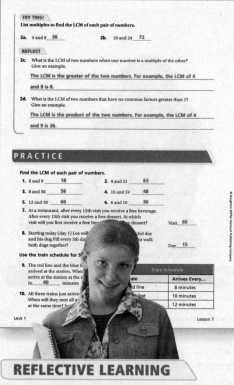

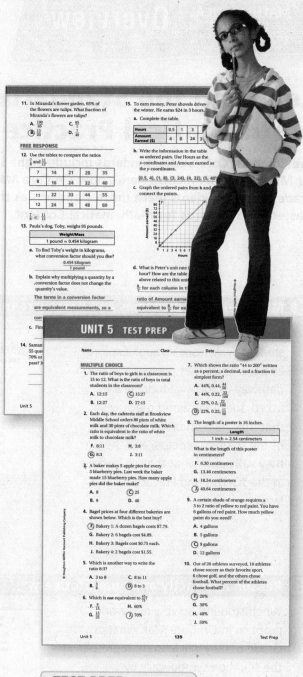

REFLECTIVE LEARNING

Students learn to be reflective thinkers through the follow-up questions after each Explore and Example in a lesson. The Reflect questions challenge students to really think about the mathematics they have just encountered and to share their understanding with the class.

TEST PREP

At the end of a unit, students have an opportunity to practice the material in multiple choice and free response formats common on standardized tests.

PROBLEM SOLVING CONNECTIONS

Special features that focus on problem solving occur near the ends of units. These features help students pull together the mathematical concepts and skills taught in a unit and apply them to real-world situations.

Learning the Standards for Mathematical Practice

The Common Core State Standards include eight Standards for Mathematical Practice. Here's how *On Core Mathematics Grade 6* helps students learn those standards as they master the Standards for Mathematical Content.

1 Make sense of problems and persevere in solving them.

In *On Core Mathematics Grade 6*, students will work through Explores and Examples that present a solution pathway to follow. Students are asked questions along the way so that they gain an understanding of the solution process, and then they will apply what they've learned in the Try This and Practice for the lesson.

> **2 EXAMPLE** Using Exponents to Write Expressions
>
> Use exponents to write each expression.
>
> A $6 \times 6 \times 6 \times 6 \times 6 \times 6 \times 6$
>
> What number is being multiplied? __6__ This number is the base.
>
> How many times does the base appear in the product? __7__ This number is the exponent.
>
> $6 \times 6 \times 6 \times 6 \times 6 \times 6 \times 6 = $ __6^7__
>
> B $\frac{2}{3} \times \frac{2}{3} \times \frac{2}{3}$
>
> What number is being multiplied? __$\frac{2}{3}$__ This number is the base.
>
> How many times does the base appear in the product? __3__ This number is the exponent.
>
> $\frac{2}{3} \times \frac{2}{3} \times \frac{2}{3} = $ __$\left(\frac{2}{3}\right)^3$__

2 Reason abstractly and quantitatively.

When students solve a real-world problem in *On Core Mathematics Grade 6*, they will learn to represent the situation symbolically by translating the problem into a mathematical expression or equation. Students will use these mathematical models to solve the problem and then state the answer in terms of the problem context. Students will reflect on the solution process in order to check their answers for reasonableness and to draw conclusions.

> B **Matthew throws a discus 58.7 meters. Zachary throws the discus 56.12 meters. How much farther did Matthew throw the discus?**
>
> **Step 1** Align the decimal points.
> **Step 2** Add zeros as placeholders when necessary.
> **Step 3** Subtract from right to left, regrouping when necessary.
>
> | | 5 | 8 | . | 7 | 0 |
> |---|---|---|---|---|---|
> | − | 5 | 6 | . | 1 | 2 |
> | | | 2 | . | 5 | 8 |
>
> Matthew threw the discus __2.58__ meters farther than Zachary.
>
> To check that your answer is reasonable, you can estimate. Round each decimal to the nearest whole number.
>
> 58.7 ⟶ 59
> − 56.12 ⟶ − 56
> 2.58 ⟶ 3   Check that your answer is close to your estimate.

> **2 EXAMPLE** Writing an Equation
>
> Mark scored 17 points in a basketball game. His teammates scored a total of p points, and the team as a whole scored 46 points. Write an equation to represent this situation.
>
> | Mark's points | + | Teammates' points | = | Total points |
> |---|---|---|---|---|
> | 17 | + | p | = | 46 |
>
> **REFLECT**
>
> **2a.** Write an equation containing an operation other than addition that also represents the situation.
>
> Sample answer: $46 - p = 17$

On Core
Mathematics

Middle School Grade 6

HOUGHTON MIFFLIN HARCOURT

Table of Contents Grade 6

COMMON CORE

▶ Unit 1 The Number System: Fractions and Decimals

Unit Overview 1
1-1 Dividing Multi-Digit Numbers 3
1-2 Dividing Fractions 7
1-3 Adding and Subtracting Decimals 11
1-4 Multiplying Decimals 15
1-5 Dividing Decimals 19
1-6 Greatest Common Factor 23
1-7 Least Common Multiple 27
     Problem Solving Connections 29
     Test Prep 33

▶ Unit 2 The Number System: Positive and Negative Numbers

Unit Overview **35**
2-1 The Number Line 37
2-2 Comparing and Ordering Numbers 39
2-3 Absolute Value 43
2-4 The Coordinate Plane 45
2-5 Distance in the Coordinate Plane 49
     Problem Solving Connections 51
     Test Prep 55

▶ Unit 3 Expressions

Unit Overview **57**
3-1 Exponents 59
3-2 Writing Expressions 63
3-3 Parts of an Expression 67
3-4 Evaluating Expressions 69
3-5 Equivalent Expressions 73
     Problem Solving Connections 77
     Test Prep 81

© Houghton Mifflin Harcourt Publishing Company

Unit 4 Equations

Unit Overview 83

4-1 Equations and Solutions 85

4-2 Addition and Subtraction Equations 89

4-3 Multiplication and Division Equations 93

4-4 Equations, Tables, and Graphs 97

4-5 Solutions of Inequalities 101

Problem Solving Connections 105

Test Prep 109

Unit 5 Ratios and Proportional Relationships

Unit Overview 111

5-1 Ratios 113

5-2 Ratios, Tables, and Graphs 117

5-3 Unit Rates 119

5-4 Percents 123

5-5 Percent Problems 127

5-6 Converting Measurements 131

Problem Solving Connections 135

Test Prep 139

© Houghton Mifflin Harcourt Publishing Company

③ Construct viable arguments and critique the reasoning of others.

Throughout *On Core Mathematics Grade 6*, students will be asked to make conjectures, construct mathematical arguments, explain their reasoning, and justify their conclusions. Reflect questions offer opportunities for cooperative learning and class discussion. Students will have additional opportunities to critique reasoning in Error Analysis problems.

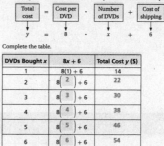

3b. Error Analysis Marisol said, "Bailey's lemonade is stronger because it has more lemon juice. Bailey's lemonade has 3 cups of lemon juice, and Anna's lemonade has only 2 cups of lemon juice." Explain why Marisol is incorrect.

Sample answer: It is not enough to compare the amounts of lemon juice. You also need to know the amount of water in which the lemon juice is diluted.

a. Will this object's length in centimeters be greater than x or less than x? Explain.

Greater than; sample answer: centimeters are smaller than inches, so it will take more centimeters than inches to measure the object.

b. Will this object's length in meters be greater than x or less than x? Explain.

Less than; sample answer: meters are larger than inches, so it will take fewer meters than inches to measure the object.

④ Model with mathematics.

On Core Mathematics Grade 6 presents problems in a variety of contexts such as science, business, and everyday life. Students will use mathematical models such as expressions, equations, tables, and graphs to represent the information in the problem and to solve the problem. Then students will interpret their results in the problem context.

Essential question: *How can you use equations, tables, and graphs to represent relationships between two variables?*

CORE
CC.6.EE.9

1 EXPLORE Equations in Two Variables

Tina is buying DVDs from an online store. Each DVD costs $8, and there is a flat fee of $6 for shipping.

Let x represent the number of DVDs that Tina buys. Let y represent Tina's total cost. An equation in two variables can represent the relationship between x and y.

Total cost	=	Cost per DVD	·	Number of DVDs	+	Cost of shipping
y	=	8	·	x	+	6

Complete the table.

DVDs Bought x	$8x + 6$	Total Cost y ($)
1	8(1) + 6	14
2	8(2) + 6	22
3	8(3) + 6	30
4	8(4) + 6	38
5	8(5) + 6	46
6	8(6) + 6	54
7	8(7) + 6	62

REFLECT

1a. Look at the y-values in the right column of the table. What pattern do you see? What does this pattern mean in the problem?

Each y-value is 8 greater than the previous y-value. Each additional DVD increases the total cost by $8 (the cost per DVD).

1b. A **solution of an equation in two variables** is an ordered pair (x, y) that makes the equation true. The ordered pair (1, 14) is a solution of $y = 8x + 6$. Write the other solutions from the table as ordered pairs.

(2, 22), (3, 30), (4, 38), (5, 46), (6, 54), (7, 62)

⑤ Use appropriate tools strategically.

Students will use a variety of tools in *On Core Mathematics Grade 6*, including manipulatives, paper and pencil, and technology. Students might use manipulatives to develop concepts, paper and pencil to practice skills, and technology (such as graphing calculators, spreadsheets, or geometry software) to investigate more complicated mathematical ideas.

⑥ Attend to precision.

Precision refers not only to the correctness of arithmetic calculations, algebraic manipulations, and geometric reasoning but also to the proper use of mathematical language, symbols, and units to communicate mathematical ideas. Throughout *On Core Mathematics Grade 6* students will demonstrate their skills in these areas when asked to calculate, describe, show, explain, prove, and predict.

x

In *On Core Mathematics Grade 6*, students will look for patterns or regularity in mathematical structures such as expressions, equations, operations, geometric figures, and diagrams. Students will use these patterns to generalize beyond a specific case and to make connections between related problems.

---

4 EXPLORE Solving Problems Using Exponents

Judah had two children. When those children grew up, each one also had two children, who later each had two children as well. If this pattern continues, how many children are there in the 7th generation?

You can use a diagram to model this situation. The first point at the top represents Judah. The other points represent children. Complete the diagram to show the 3rd generation.

Judah

1st generation →

2nd generation →

3rd generation →

A How many children are in each generation?

1st __2__   2nd __4__   3rd __8__

B Do you see a pattern in the numbers above? Try to find a pattern using exponents.

increasing powers of 2: 2^1, 2^2, 2^3

C How is the number of children in a generation related to the generation number?

It is 2 raised to the power of the generation number.

D How many children will be in the 7th generation?

$2^7 = 128$

TRY THIS!

4. A female guinea pig has about 4 litters per year, and a typical litter consists of 4 baby guinea pigs. How many baby guinea pigs would a typical female have in 4 years?

$4^3 = 64$

---

1 EXPLORE Using Variables to Describe Patterns

Look at the pattern of squares below.

Stage 1   Stage 2   Stage 3

A What is the pattern? At each stage, add 3 more squares.

How many squares will be in stage 4? _____ 12

B What is the relationship between the stage number and the number of squares?

The number of squares is 3 times the stage number.

Use this relationship to complete the table below.

Stage	1	2	3	4	5	6	7	8	n
Squares	3	6	9	12	15	18	21	24	$3 \times n$

C Let n represent any stage number. How many squares are in stage n?

$3 \times n$

Add a column to the end of the table in **B** for stage n.

REFLECT

1. When might it be useful to know how many squares are in stage n?

H&S Graphics, Inc/

The Number System: Fractions and Decimals

Unit Vocabulary

greatest common factor (1-6)

least common multiple (1-7)

reciprocals (1-2)

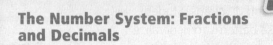

UNIT 1

The Number System: Fractions and Decimals

Unit Focus

You have already learned how to multiply and divide whole numbers. In this unit, you will learn how to divide multi-digit numbers and fractions. You will also learn how to add, subtract, multiply, and divide decimals. You will then learn how to find the greatest common factor and least common multiple of two numbers.

Unit at a Glance

COMMON CORE

Lesson		Standards for Mathematical Content
1-1	Dividing Multi-Digit Numbers	CC.6.NS.2
1-2	Dividing Fractions	CC.6.NS.1
1-3	Adding and Subtracting Decimals	CC.6.NS.3
1-4	Multiplying Decimals	CC.6.NS.3
1-5	Dividing Decimals	CC.6.NS.3
1-6	Greatest Common Factor	CC.6.NS.4
1-7	Least Common Multiple	CC.6.NS.4
	Problem Solving Connections	
	Test Prep	

Unit 1   1   The Number System: Fractions and Decimals

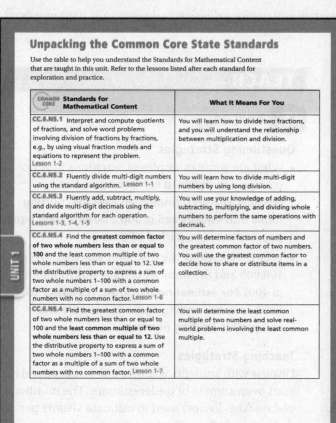

Unpacking the Common Core State Standards

Use the table to help you understand the Standards for Mathematical Content that are taught in this unit. Refer to the lessons listed after each standard for exploration and practice.

COMMON CORE Standards for Mathematical Content	What It Means For You
CC.6.NS.1 Interpret and compute quotients of fractions, and solve word problems involving division of fractions by fractions, e.g., by using visual fraction models and equations to represent the problem. Lesson 1-2	You will learn how to divide two fractions, and you will understand the relationship between multiplication and division.
CC.6.NS.2 Fluently divide multi-digit numbers using the standard algorithm. Lesson 1-1	You will learn how to divide multi-digit numbers by using long division.
CC.6.NS.3 Fluently add, subtract, multiply, and divide multi-digit decimals using the standard algorithm for each operation. Lessons 1-3, 1-4, 1-5	You will use your knowledge of adding, subtracting, multiplying, and dividing whole numbers to perform the same operations with decimals.
CC.6.NS.4 Find the greatest common factor of two whole numbers less than or equal to 100 and the least common multiple of two whole numbers less than or equal to 12. Use the distributive property to express a sum of two whole numbers 1–100 with a common factor as a multiple of a sum of two whole numbers with no common factor. Lesson 1-6	You will determine factors of numbers and the greatest common factor of two numbers. You will use the greatest common factor to decide how to share or distribute items in a collection.
CC.6.NS.4 Find the greatest common factor of two whole numbers less than or equal to 100 and the **least common multiple of two whole numbers less than or equal to 12**. Use the distributive property to express a sum of two whole numbers 1–100 with a common factor as a multiple of a sum of two whole numbers with no common factor. Lesson 1-7	You will determine the least common multiple of two numbers and solve real-world problems involving the least common multiple.

Unpacking the Common Core State Standards

This page lists and explains the Standards for Mathematical Content that are addressed in this unit. For information about the Standards for Mathematical Practice, which are integrated throughout the text, see Teacher Edition pages vii–xiii.

UNIT 1

Notes

_____

_____

_____

_____

_____

_____

_____

_____

Dividing Multi-Digit Numbers

Essential question: *How can you use long division to divide multi-digit numbers?*

© Houghton Mifflin Harcourt Publishing Company

⬤ **COMMON** **Standards for**
CORE **Mathematical Content**

CC.6.NS.2 Fluently divide multi-digit numbers using the standard algorithm.

Prerequisites
Model and find quotients

Math Background
Division can be a confusing process for many students. When adding, subtracting, or multiplying, start at the ones place and move to the left. With division, however, start with the greatest place value and move to the right. Just as multiplication is a way of adding the same number many times, dividing can be described as a subtracting the same number many times.

INTRODUCE

Connect to prior learning by asking students to divide using multiples of ten; for example, $800 \div 4 = 200$, $800 \div 40 = 20$, and $800 \div 400 = 2$. Tell students that they will be dividing by numbers that have multiple digits in this lesson.

TEACH

1 EXPLORE

Questioning Strategies
- What are some examples of situations in which you need to divide to solve the problem? **Possible answers: finding an average, putting items into equal-sized groups, determining equal payments over a period of time**
- Why do you think the dividend was rounded to 100,000 and the number of days was rounded to 400? **For estimating purposes, it's easier to have as many ending zeros as possible and compatible leading numbers.**

Teaching Strategies
Discuss with students whether 250 visitors per day is an overestimate or underestimate. The number of days (the divisor) used to estimate visitors per day is rounded up. The total number of visitors was actually spread over fewer days (divided by a smaller number), so the actual number of visitors per day would be higher. Thus, 250 visitors per day is an underestimate.

2 EXAMPLE

Questioning Strategies
- What does finding the average mean? **finding the sum of a list of numbers and dividing the sum by the number of items in the list**
- What is the first step when dividing? **Possible answer: Estimate to decide where to put the first digit in the quotient.**
- How do you know whether the first digit you choose in the quotient is correct? **When you multiply the digit with the divisor and subtract the product, the difference should be smaller than the divisor. If not, the number chosen was too small.**

Avoid Common Errors
Students sometimes misalign the digits during calculation. Suggest that students use graph paper to align digits in the correct place-value positions.

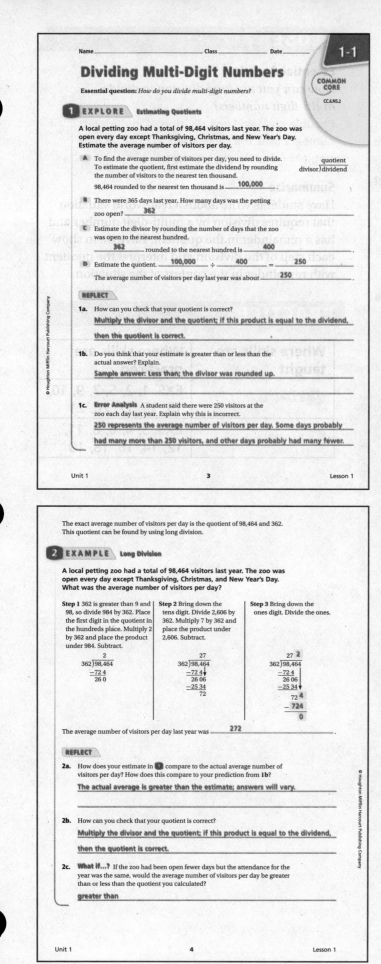

Name _____ Class _____ Date _____

1-1

COMMON
CORE
CC.6.NS.2

Dividing Multi-Digit Numbers

Essential question: *How do you divide multi-digit numbers?*

1 EXPLORE   Estimating Quotients

A local petting zoo had a total of 98,464 visitors last year. The zoo was open every day except Thanksgiving, Christmas, and New Year's Day. Estimate the average number of visitors per day.

A To find the average number of visitors per day, you need to divide. To estimate the quotient, first estimate the dividend by rounding the number of visitors to the nearest ten thousand.

98,464 rounded to the nearest ten thousand is ___100,000___

quotient
divisor)dividend

B There were 365 days last year. How many days was the petting zoo open? ___362___

C Estimate the divisor by rounding the number of days that the zoo was open to the nearest hundred.

___362___ rounded to the nearest hundred is ___400___

D Estimate the quotient. ___100,000___ ÷ ___400___ = ___250___

The average number of visitors per day last year was about ___250___

REFLECT

1a. How can you check that your quotient is correct?

Multiply the divisor and the quotient; if this product is equal to the dividend,

then the quotient is correct.

1b. Do you think that your estimate is greater than or less than the actual answer? Explain.

Sample answer: Less than; the divisor was rounded up.

1c. **Error Analysis** A student said there were 250 visitors at the zoo each day last year. Explain why this is incorrect.

250 represents the average number of visitors per day. Some days probably

had many more than 250 visitors, and other days probably had many fewer.

Unit 1   3   Lesson 1

The exact average number of visitors per day is the quotient of 98,464 and 362. This quotient can be found by using long division.

2 EXAMPLE   Long Division

A local petting zoo had a total of 98,464 visitors last year. The zoo was open every day except Thanksgiving, Christmas, and New Year's Day. What was the average number of visitors per day?

Step 1 362 is greater than 9 and 98, so divide 984 by 362. Place the first digit in the quotient in the hundreds place. Multiply 2 by 362 and place the product under 984. Subtract.

$$\begin{array}{r} 2 \\ 362\overline{)98,464} \\ -72\ 4 \\ \hline 26\ 0 \end{array}$$

Step 2 Bring down the tens digit. Divide 2,606 by 362. Multiply 7 by 362 and place the product under 2,606. Subtract.

$$\begin{array}{r} 27 \\ 362\overline{)98,464} \\ -72\ 4\downarrow \\ \hline 26\ 06 \\ -25\ 34 \\ \hline 72 \end{array}$$

Step 3 Bring down the ones digit. Divide the ones.

$$\begin{array}{r} 27\ 2 \\ 362\overline{)98,464} \\ -72\ 4 \\ \hline 26\ 06 \\ -25\ 34\downarrow \\ \hline 72\ 4 \\ -724 \\ \hline 0 \end{array}$$

The average number of visitors per day last year was ___272___

REFLECT

2a. How does your estimate in **1** compare to the actual average number of visitors per day? How does this compare to your prediction from **1b**?

The actual average is greater than the estimate; answers will vary.

2b. How can you check that your quotient is correct?

Multiply the divisor and the quotient; if this product is equal to the dividend,

then the quotient is correct.

2c. **What if...?** If the zoo had been open fewer days but the attendance for the year was the same, would the average number of visitors per day be greater than or less than the quotient you calculated?

greater than

Unit 1   4   Lesson 1

© Houghton Mifflin Harcourt Publishing Company

Questioning Strategies

- How would you estimate the solution?
  Possible answer: 1900 ÷ 10 = 190

- Would 154 boxes be enough to hold all her books? Why or why not? No; there would be two books that would not be packaged.

- How can you check that your quotient is correct? Multiply the quotient and the divisor and then add the remainder. The answer should be the dividend.

Avoid Common Errors

Students sometimes finish with a remainder that is larger than the divisor. Remind students to circle the divisor and the remainder and compare them. If the remainder is larger than the dividend, the quotient is too small.

MATHEMATICAL PRACTICE · **Highlighting the Standards**

This example is an opportunity to address Standard 2 (Reason abstractly and quantitatively). Students are asked to determine how many boxes are needed to pack the books. The students need to reason and interpret the quotient in terms of the context. The quotient 154 R2 actually indicates that 155 boxes are needed.

CLOSE

Essential Question

How can you use long division to divide multi-digit numbers?

Possible answer: Long division of multi-digit numbers uses the same steps as division by a single- or double-digit number.

Summarize

Have students write about a real-world situation that requires division by a multi-digit number and has a remainder in the quotient. Have them show each step of the division and interpret the quotient with remainder in the context of the situation.

PRACTICE

Where skills are taught	Where skills are practiced
2 EXAMPLE	EXS. 1, 2, 5, 7, 9, 10, 13, 15, 17, 20, 21
3 EXAMPLE	EXS. 3, 4, 6, 8, 11, 12, 14, 16, 18, 19

3 EXAMPLE Long Division with a Remainder

Callie has 1,850 books. She must pack them into boxes to ship to a bookstore. Each box holds 12 books. How many boxes will she need to pack all of the books?

Divide 1,850 by 12.

$$
\begin{array}{r}
154\ \text{R }2 \\
12\overline{)1{,}850} \\
-12 \\
\hline
65 \\
-60 \\
\hline
50 \\
-48 \\
\hline
2
\end{array}
$$

Notice that the numbers do not divide evenly. There is a remainder. What does the remainder mean in this situation?

After packing 154 boxes, there will be 2 books left over.

How many boxes does Callie need to pack the books? **155** boxes
Explain.

An extra box is needed for the 2 books left over.

TRY THIS!

3a. Divide 5,796 by 28. **207**   **3b.** $67\overline{)3{,}098}$ **46 R16**

PRACTICE

Divide.

1. $2{,}226 \div 53$ **42**   2. Divide 4,514 by 74. **61**

3. $83\overline{)2{,}001}$ **24 R9**   4. $3{,}493 \div 37$ **94 R15**

5. Divide 18,156 by 267. **68**   6. $438\overline{)35{,}506}$ **81 R28**

7. $23{,}712 \div 247$ **96**   8. $313\overline{)39{,}760}$ **127 R9**

Divide.

9. $1{,}643 \div 53$ **31**   10. Divide 578 by 34. **17**

11. $134\overline{)3{,}685}$ **27 R67**   12. $423 \div 12$ **35 R3**

13. Divide 819 by 117. **7**   14. $92\overline{)598}$ **6 R46**

15. $10{,}626 \div 21$ **506**   16. $24\overline{)6{,}339}$ **264 R3**

17. A theater has 1,120 seats in 35 equal rows. How many seats are in each row? **32** seats

18. At a wedding reception, there will be 1,012 guests. A round table will seat 12 guests. How many tables will be needed? **85** tables

19. Emilio has 8,450 trees to plant in rows on his tree farm. He will plant 115 trees per row. How many rows of trees will he have? **74** rows

20. Camila has 1,296 beads to make bracelets. Each bracelet will contain 24 beads. How many bracelets can she make? **54** bracelets

21. The table shows the number of miles that Awan drove over six months. Find the average number of miles per day for each month.

January: **62** miles

February: **105** miles

March: **115** miles

April: **121** miles

May: **78** miles

June: **117** miles

Month	Number of Days	Miles Traveled
January	31	1,922
February	28	2,940
March	31	3,565
April	30	3,630
May	31	2,418
June	30	3,510

22. **Reasoning** How is the quotient $80{,}000 \div 2{,}000$ different from the quotient $80{,}000 \div 200$ or $80{,}000 \div 20$?

The number of zeros in the quotient will be different depending on the

number of zeros in the divisor.

23. **Reasoning** Given that $9{,}554 \div 562 = 17$, how can you find the quotient $95{,}540 \div 562$?

The quotient is 10 times greater because the dividend is 10 times greater.

$95{,}540 \div 562 = 170$

© Houghton Mifflin Harcourt Publishing Company

Dividing Fractions

Essential question: *How do you divide fractions?*

COMMON CORE **Standards for Mathematical Content**

CC.6.NS.1 Interpret and compute quotients of fractions, and solve word problems involving division of fractions by fractions, e.g., by using visual fraction models and equations to represent the problem.

Vocabulary
reciprocals

Prerequisites
Multiplying fractions

Math Background
When two numbers have a product of one, they are called *reciprocals*. For example, $\frac{2}{5}$ and $\frac{5}{2}$ are reciprocals because they have a product of one. To find the reciprocal of a whole number, start by writing the whole number as a fraction with a denominator of one and then invert the fraction. The reciprocal of a fraction is used when writing a division expression as a multiplication expression. Dividing fractions can be defined as multiplying by the reciprocal.

INTRODUCE

Connect to prior learning by asking students to find the product of two fractions or a fraction and a whole number. Tell students they will use skills they have already learned for multiplying fractions to divide fractions.

TEACH

1 EXPLORE

Questioning Strategies
- What do the solid vertical segments in the diagram show? What does the shading represent? **They show the bar divided into fourths. 3 of the fourths are shaded to represent $\frac{3}{4}$ cup of salsa.**
- What do the dotted vertical segments in the diagram show? **They show each fourth divided in two to represent $\frac{1}{8}$ cup.**

Differentiated Instruction
Allow students to model this situation with a strip of paper. Fold the strip of paper into 4 equal sections and then open the paper and lightly shade 3 of the 4 sections to represent three-fourths. Then, fold the paper to divide the same strip into eight equal sections. Direct students to discover the number of eighths that are shaded.

2 EXAMPLE

Questioning Strategies
- When finding the reciprocal of a number, what do you interchange? **numerator and denominator**
- What is the product of any number and its reciprocal? **1**
- How can you find the reciprocal of a mixed number? **Change the mixed number to an improper fraction first.**

Teaching Strategies
Review with students how to write a mixed number as an improper fraction. Have students write the multiplication and addition symbols within the fraction as a visual reminder. $2\frac{+4}{\times 7} = \frac{2 \cdot 7 + 4}{7} = \frac{18}{7}$

1-2

Name_____ Class_____ Date_____

Dividing Fractions

Essential question: *How do you divide fractions?*

COMMON CORE
CC.6.NS.1

1 EXPLORE Modeling Fraction Division

You have $\frac{3}{4}$ cup of salsa for making burritos. Each burrito requires $\frac{1}{8}$ cup of salsa. How many burritos can you make?

To find the number of burritos that can be made, you need to determine how many $\frac{1}{8}$s are in $\frac{3}{4}$.

How many $\frac{1}{8}$s are there in $\frac{3}{4}$? _____ 6

$\frac{3}{4}$

$\frac{1}{8}$

You have enough salsa to make _____ 6 burritos.

REFLECT

1a. Division can be checked by using multiplication. What would you multiply to check your answer above?

$6 \times \frac{1}{8} = \frac{3}{4}$

TRY THIS!

1b. How many burritos could you make with $\frac{1}{2}$ cup of salsa? _____ 4

$\frac{1}{2}$

$\frac{1}{8}$

1c. Five people share $\frac{1}{2}$ pound of chocolate equally. How much chocolate does each person receive? $\frac{1}{10}$ pound

$\frac{1}{2}$

$\frac{1}{10}$

Another way to divide fractions is to use *reciprocals*. Two numbers whose product is 1 are **reciprocals**. To find the reciprocal of a fraction, switch the numerator and denominator.

$\frac{numerator}{denominator} \cdot \frac{denominator}{numerator} = 1$

2 EXAMPLE Reciprocals

Find the reciprocal of each fraction or mixed number.

A $\frac{5}{8}$

Switch the numerator and denominator: $\frac{8}{5}$

The reciprocal of $\frac{5}{8}$ is $\frac{8}{5}$.

Check:

$\frac{8}{5} \times \frac{5}{8} = \frac{40}{40} = 1$

B $\frac{1}{6}$

Switch the numerator and denominator: $\frac{6}{1}$

Simplify: 6

The reciprocal of $\frac{1}{6}$ is 6.

C $1\frac{2}{7}$

Change to an improper fraction: $1\frac{2}{7} = \frac{9}{7}$

Switch the numerator and denominator: $\frac{7}{9}$

The reciprocal of $1\frac{2}{7}$ is $\frac{7}{9}$.

TRY THIS!

Find the reciprocal of each fraction or mixed number.

2a. $\frac{7}{8}$ $\frac{8}{7}$ **2b.** $\frac{9}{15}$ $\frac{15}{9}$ **2c.** $\frac{1}{11}$ 11   **2d.** $2\frac{4}{5}$ $\frac{5}{14}$

REFLECT

2e. Is any number its own reciprocal? If so, what number(s)?

yes; 1

2f. Does every number have a reciprocal? Explain.

No; 0 does not have a reciprocal.

2g. The reciprocal of a whole number is a fraction with _____ 1 in the numerator.

Questioning Strategies

- What reciprocal do you use to solve in part A? $\frac{6}{5}$
- How do you write the expression as a multiplication expression? **Multiply the first fraction by the reciprocal of the second fraction.**
- When working with fractions, what is the last step you do? **Make sure it is written in simplest form.**

Avoid Common Errors

Some students incorrectly find the reciprocal of the first number instead of the second. Have students practice and verify problems like "8 divided by 2 is the same as half of 8."

4 **EXAMPLE**

Questioning Strategies

- If the formula for area involves multiplication, why is this a division problem? **Because you are given the area and one of the dimensions; to find the area, you multiply the dimensions, but to find one of the dimensions, you divide the area by the known dimension.**

MATHEMATICAL PRACTICE — Highlighting the Standards

This example is an opportunity to address Standard 1 (Make sense of problems and persevere in solving them). Students integrate many mathematical concepts (geometry, formulas, substituting a value for a variable, relating information from words to diagrams, and fraction operations) to solve this problem. This allows students to review and apply previously learned concepts while practicing the new skill.

CLOSE

Essential Question

How do you divide fractions?
Possible answer: To divide fractions, rewrite the division problem as multiplication of the reciprocal. Multiply and simplify as needed.

Summarize

Have students explain in their journals how to divide fractions. Have them include an example of dividing a fraction by a mixed number and dividing a fraction by a whole number.

PRACTICE

Where skills are taught	Where skills are practiced
2 EXAMPLE	EXS. 1–6
3 EXAMPLE	EXS. 7–15, 17
4 EXAMPLE	EX. 16

Notice that dividing by a whole number is equivalent to multiplying by its reciprocal. This is also true when dividing by fractions. To divide by a fraction, multiply by its reciprocal.

$24 \div 3 = 8$

$24 \times \frac{1}{3} = 8$

3 EXAMPLE Using Reciprocals to Divide Fractions

Divide.

A $\frac{5}{8} \div \frac{5}{6}$

Step 1 Rewrite the problem as multiplication using the reciprocal of the second fraction.

$\frac{5}{8} \div \frac{5}{6} = \frac{5}{8} \times \frac{6}{5}$

Step 2 Multiply and simplify.

$\frac{5}{8} \times \frac{6}{5} = \frac{30}{40}$

$\frac{30}{40} = \frac{3}{4}$

$\frac{5}{8} \div \frac{5}{6} = \boxed{\frac{3}{4}}$

B $1\frac{3}{7} \div \frac{2}{5}$

Step 1 Convert the mixed number to a fraction.

$1\frac{3}{7} = \frac{10}{7}$

Step 2 Rewrite the problem as multiplication using the improper fraction and the reciprocal of the second fraction.

$1\frac{3}{7} \div \frac{2}{5} = \frac{10}{7} \div \frac{2}{5} = \frac{10}{7} \times \frac{5}{2}$

Step 3 Multiply and simplify.

$\frac{10}{7} \times \frac{5}{2} = \frac{50}{14}$

$= \frac{25}{7}, \text{ or } 3\frac{4}{7}$

$1\frac{3}{7} \div \frac{2}{5} = \boxed{3\frac{4}{7}}$

TRY THIS!

Divide.

3a. $\frac{9}{10} \div \frac{2}{5} = \boxed{2\frac{1}{4}}$

3b. $2\frac{9}{10} \div \frac{3}{5} = \boxed{4\frac{5}{6}}$

Unit 1　　　9　　　Lesson 2

4 EXAMPLE Solving Problems Involving Area

The area of a rectangular flower bed is $6\frac{1}{2}$ square feet. The width of the flower bed is $\frac{3}{4}$ feet. What is the length? (*Hint:* area = length × width)

To find the length of the flower bed, divide the area by the width.

$6\frac{1}{2} \div \frac{3}{4} = \frac{13}{2} \div \frac{3}{4}$

$= \frac{13}{2} \times \frac{4}{3} = \frac{52}{6} = 8\frac{4}{6} = 8\frac{2}{3}$

$$A = 6\frac{1}{2} \text{ ft}^2 \qquad w = \frac{3}{4} \text{ ft}$$
$$\ell = ?$$

The length of the flower bed is $\boxed{8\frac{2}{3}}$ feet.

PRACTICE

Find the reciprocal of each fraction or mixed number.

1. $\frac{2}{5}$ $\boxed{\frac{5}{2}}$　　2. $\frac{1}{9}$ $\boxed{9}$　　3. $\frac{5}{3}$ $\boxed{\frac{3}{5}}$

4. $\frac{4}{11}$ $\boxed{\frac{11}{4}}$　　5. $4\frac{1}{5}$ $\boxed{\frac{5}{21}}$　　6. $3\frac{1}{8}$ $\boxed{\frac{8}{25}}$

Divide.

7. $\frac{4}{3} \div \frac{5}{3} = \boxed{\frac{4}{5}}$　　8. $\frac{3}{10} \div \frac{4}{5} = \boxed{\frac{3}{8}}$　　9. $\frac{1}{2} \div \frac{2}{5} = \boxed{1\frac{1}{4}}$

10. $\frac{8}{9} \div \frac{1}{2} = \boxed{1\frac{7}{9}}$　　11. $4\frac{1}{4} \div \frac{3}{4} = \boxed{5\frac{2}{3}}$　　12. $4 \div 1\frac{1}{8} = \boxed{3\frac{5}{9}}$

13. A recipe for one loaf of banana bread requires $\frac{2}{3}$ cup of oil. You have 2 cups of oil. How many loaves of banana bread can you make?　　$\boxed{3}$ loaves

14. Ayita made $5\frac{1}{2}$ cups of trail mix. She wants to divide the trail mix into $\frac{3}{4}$ cup servings. How many servings will she have?　　$\boxed{7\frac{1}{3}}$ serving(s)

15. Dao has $2\frac{3}{8}$ pounds of hamburger meat. He is making $\frac{1}{4}$-pound burgers. How many hamburgers can he make?　　$\boxed{9\frac{1}{2}}$ hamburger(s)

16. A rectangular piece of land has an area of $\frac{3}{4}$ square mile and is $\frac{1}{2}$ mile wide. What is the length?　　$\boxed{1\frac{1}{2}}$ mile(s)

17. Write a real-world problem whose solution requires dividing the fractions $\frac{1}{3}$ and $\frac{3}{4}$. Then solve your problem.
Sample answer: Trinh has $\frac{3}{4}$ pound of birdseed. How many $\frac{1}{3}$-pound bags can she make? $2\frac{1}{4}$ bags

Unit 1　　　10　　　Lesson 2

© Houghton Mifflin Harcourt Publishing Company

Adding and Subtracting Decimals

Essential question: *How do you add and subtract decimals?*

© Houghton Mifflin Harcourt Publishing Company

COMMON CORE Standards for Mathematical Content

CC.6.NS.3 Fluently add, subtract, multiply, and divide multi-digit decimals using the standard algorithm for each operation.

Prerequisites
Decimal number sense
Rounding decimals

Math Background
Adding and subtracting decimals is much like adding and subtracting whole numbers. It is very important to align the decimal points in order to add and subtract tenths from tenths, hundredths from hundredths, and so on. It is helpful to add zeros to the right of the decimal as placeholders to keep corresponding place values aligned. It is also helpful to estimate the answer first so you can make sure that the placement of the decimal in the final answer is reasonable.

INTRODUCE

Decimals are used every day. Some of the most common uses of decimals involve calculating monetary amounts, tracking time, and making measurements. Tell students that they will learn to add and subtract decimals in this lesson. They will learn how the decimal point plays a key role in solving problems.

TEACH

1 EXPLORE

Questioning Strategies
- What key words indicate the operation of addition in the problem? **combines, total**
- Why are there 100 squares in the grid? **Both numbers have place value to the hundredths.**
- What would it mean if all the squares were colored? **The model would represent the whole number 1.**

MATHEMATICAL PRACTICE Highlighting the Standards

This example is an opportunity to address Standard 4 (Model with mathematics). Students solve an application problem with modeling. They use an addition statement to model the real-world situation. Then, they use 10-by-10 grids to model the addition of decimals in hundredths. In this way, students see hundredths as a unit. Then students interpret their model back to a complete mathematical addition statement and use it to answer the original question.

2 EXAMPLE

Questioning Strategies
- What key words in the problem indicate addition? **"in all"**
- Why is a zero placed in the number for Tuesday's mileage? **to fill the hundredths place like the other decimal**

Teaching Strategies
Be sure students understand that only digits in corresponding place values must be added. One way to make sure that all of the digits are aligned properly is to use zeros as placeholders at the end of a decimal to line up the corresponding place values.

Name_____ Class_____ Date_____

Adding and Subtracting Decimals

COMMON CORE
CC.6.NS.3

Essential question: *How do you add and subtract decimals?*

1 EXPLORE Modeling Decimal Addition

A chemist combines 0.17 mL of water and 0.49 mL of hydrogen peroxide in a beaker. How much total liquid is in the beaker?

You can use a decimal grid divided into 100 small squares to solve this problem. The entire decimal grid represents 1 unit, so each small square represents 0.01, or 1 one-hundredth.

Water	+	Hydrogen Peroxide	=	Total
How many squares are shaded to represent 0.17 mL of water?		How many squares are shaded to represent 0.49 mL of hydrogen peroxide?		How many total squares are shaded?
17		49		66

$0.17 + 0.49 =$ __0.66__

There are __0.66__ mL of liquid in the beaker.

TRY THIS!

Shade the grid to find each sum.

1a. $0.24 + 0.71 =$ __0.95__

1b. $0.08 + 0.65 =$ __0.73__

© Houghton Mifflin Harcourt Publishing Company

Adding and subtracting decimals are very similar to adding and subtracting whole numbers. First align the numbers by place value. Start adding or subtracting at the right and regroup when necessary. Bring down the decimal point into your answer.

2 EXAMPLE Adding Decimals

Hector rode his bicycle 3.12 miles on Monday and 4.7 miles on Tuesday. How many miles did he ride in all?

Step 1 Align the decimal points.
Step 2 Add zeros as placeholders when necessary.
Step 3 Add from right to left.

	3	.	1	2
+	4	.	7	0
	7	.	8	2

Hector rode __7.82__ miles in all.

To check that your answer is reasonable, you can estimate.
Round each decimal to the nearest whole number.

```
  3.12  ———→   3
+ 4.70  ———→ + 5
  7.82         8        Since 8 is close to 7.82, the answer is reasonable.
```

TRY THIS!

Add.

2a. $0.42 + 0.27 =$ __0.69__

2b. $0.61 + 0.329 =$ __0.939__

2c. $3.25 + 4.6 =$ __7.85__

2d. $17.27 + 3.88 =$ __21.15__

REFLECT

2e. Why can you rewrite 4.7 as 4.70?

Sample answer: 7 tenths has the same area model as 70 hundredths,

so 4.7 = 4.70.

2f. Why is it important to align the decimal points when adding?

Aligning the decimal points ensures that you are adding digits with

the same place value.

© Houghton Mifflin Harcourt Publishing Company

Questioning Strategies

- What key words in the problem indicate subtraction? **"taller . . . than"**

- Is it helpful to add zeros as placeholders in part A? Explain. **No; both numbers have the same number of digits to the right of the decimal point.**

- Is it helpful to add zeros as placeholders in part B? Explain. **Yes; the first number, 58.7, does not have a digit in the hundredths place, as 56.12 does. A zero is added as a placeholder to give 58.7 the same number of digits to the right of the decimal point as 56.12.**

Differentiated Instruction

Have students read the decimal values aloud to hear the place value of each number. If they do not have the same place value, zeros may be added as placeholders.

Technology

When using calculators to add or subtract decimals, it is not necessary to include zeros as placeholders. Calculators also do not show unneeded zeros in the answers.

Essential Question

How do you add and subtract decimals?
Possible answer: Add and subtract decimals just as if you were adding or subtracting whole numbers. Align the numbers according to place values, using zeros as placeholders to help. Start at the right and regroup when necessary. Be sure to include the decimal point in the answer, checking your answer against an estimate.

Summarize

Have students make a list of similarities and differences for subtracting whole numbers and decimals. Include them in a table like the one below. **Possible answer:**

Adding and Subtracting Decimals	
Similar to Whole Numbers	**Different from Whole Numbers**
1. Align the numbers by place value.	1. Decimal point placement
2. Regroup when necessary.	2. Use of zeros as placeholders to equalize place values
3. Estimation is a good way to check the solution.	

PRACTICE

Where skills are taught	Where skills are practiced
1 EXPLORE	EXS. 1–2
2 EXAMPLE	EXS. 3–10, 19–20, 23, 25–26
3 EXAMPLE	EXS. 11–18, 21–22, 24–26

3 EXAMPLE Subtracting Decimals

A Mia is 160.2 centimeters tall. Rosa is 165.1 centimeters tall. How much taller is Rosa than Mia?

Step 1 Align the decimal points.
Step 2 Add zeros as placeholders when necessary.
Step 3 Subtract from right to left, regrouping when necessary.

Rosa is __4.9__ centimeters taller than Mia.

	1	6	5	.	1
−	1	6	0	.	2
			4	.	9

To check that your answer is reasonable, you can estimate.
Round each decimal to the nearest whole number.

$$165.1 \longrightarrow 165$$
$$- 160.2 \longrightarrow - 160$$
$$4.9 \longrightarrow 5$$

Check that your answer is close to your estimate.

B Matthew throws a discus 58.7 meters. Zachary throws the discus 56.12 meters. How much farther did Matthew throw the discus?

Step 1 Align the decimal points.
Step 2 Add zeros as placeholders when necessary.
Step 3 Subtract from right to left, regrouping when necessary.

Matthew threw the discus __2.58__ meters farther than Zachary.

	5	8	.	7	0
−	5	6	.	1	2
		2	.	5	8

To check that your answer is reasonable, you can estimate.
Round each decimal to the nearest whole number.

$$58.7 \longrightarrow 59$$
$$- 56.12 \longrightarrow - 56$$
$$2.58 \longrightarrow 3$$

Check that your answer is close to your estimate.

TRY THIS!

Subtract.

3a. $0.91 - 0.45 =$ __0.46__   3b. $4.7 - 0.83 =$ __3.87__

3c. $12.17 - 9.49 =$ __2.68__   3d. $16.04 - 5.716 =$ __10.324__

REFLECT

3e. How can you check a subtraction problem?

__Add your answer to the number being subtracted; if your answer is__
__correct, this sum will be the number that is subtracted from.__

3f. Use the decimals 2.47, 9.57, and 7.1 to write two different addition facts and two different subtraction facts.

__$2.47 + 7.1 = 9.57$; $7.1 + 2.47 = 9.57$; $9.57 - 2.47 = 7.1$; $9.57 - 7.1 = 2.47$__

© Houghton Mifflin Harcourt Publishing Company

PRACTICE

Shade the grid to find each sum.

1. $0.72 + 0.19 =$ __0.91__

2. $0.38 + 0.4 =$ __0.78__

Add or subtract.

3. $54.87 + 7.48 =$ __62.35__   4. $2.19 + 34.92 =$ __37.11__

5. $0.215 + 3.74 =$ __3.955__   6. $28.341 + 37.5 =$ __65.841__

7. $5.623 + 4.19 =$ __9.813__   8. $7.03 + 33.006 =$ __40.036__

9. $0.24 + 1.36 + 7.005 =$ __8.605__   10. $2.25 + 65.47 + 2.333 =$ __70.053__

11. $9.73 - 7.16 =$ __2.57__   12. $18.419 - 6.47 =$ __11.949__

13. $5.006 - 3.2 =$ __1.806__   14. $504.6 - 398.42 =$ __106.18__

15. $25.36 - 2.004 =$ __23.356__   16. $123.8 - 26.42 =$ __97.38__

17. $28.6 - 0.975 =$ __27.625__   18. $5.6 - 0.105 =$ __5.495__

19. $25.68 + 12 =$ __37.68__   20. $57.42 + 4 + 1.602 =$ __63.022__

21. $150.25 - 78 =$ __72.25__   22. $83 - 12.76 =$ __70.24__

Use the café menu to answer each question.

23. What is the cost of a muffin and coffee?

$ __5.29__

24. How much more does coffee cost than tea?

$ __0.71__

25. Isaac buys 2 bagels. He has a coupon for $1.75 off. How much must Isaac pay? $ __2.75__

26. Karen buys a pastry and a cup of tea. She pays with a $10 bill. How much change does she receive?

$ __4.86__

Café Menu	
Muffin	$2.79
Bagel	$2.25
Pastry	$3.35
Coffee	$2.50
Tea	$1.79

© Houghton Mifflin Harcourt Publishing Company

Multiplying Decimals

Essential question: *How do you multiply decimals?*

COMMON CORE   Standards for Mathematical Content

CC.6.NS.3 Fluently add, subtract, multiply, and divide multi-digit decimals using the standard algorithm for each operation.

Prerequisites

Decimal number sense

Rounding decimals

Math Background

Multiplying decimals is similar to multiplying whole numbers with the exception of correctly placing the decimal point in the product. To place the decimal point in the product, first count the total number of places to the right of the decimal in all of the factors of the multiplication problem. Then, place the decimal point in the product so that the total number of decimal places you counted in the factors equals the number of decimal places in the product.

Examples:

$$3 \times 1.5 = 4.5$$
$$0.3 \times 1.5 = 0.45$$
$$0.03 \times 1.5 = 0.045$$

INTRODUCE

Connect to prior learning by telling students that they will once again be using grid paper to model the multiplication of decimals. Keeping track of place value is the key to operating with decimals. When adding and subtracting decimals, keep the place value positions aligned. When multiplying decimals, ignore the place value during calculation and place the decimal point at the end.

TEACH

1 EXPLORE

Questioning Strategies

- How many unit squares are shaded for 0.3? **30 out of 100, which equals 3 out of 10**
- How many unit squares are shaded for 0.5? **50 out of 100, which equals 5 out of 10, or $\frac{1}{2}$**
- How many unit squares are in the overlapping shaded area? **15 out of 100**
- How is the part B product different from the part A product? **Product B has mixed number factors.**
- How is the product in part B modeled? **With square units for wholes and rectangular units for tenths**

Differentiated Instruction

Working with decimal grids offers a visual and kinesthetic learning approach. Another kinesthetic opportunity is given in the following activity: Have 10 students stand in front of the class. Ask 3 students to step forward. Ask: *What part of the group do the students represent as a decimal?* **(0.3)** Ask another group of three students to step forward. Write the problem $2 \times 0.3 = 0.6$ on the board.

2 EXAMPLE

Questioning Strategies

- Will Dwight pay more or less than $1.95? How do you know? **More; he bought more than 2 pounds.**
- How do you know the number of decimal places in the answer? **Add the number of decimal places in each factor (2 + 1 = 3).**

Avoid Common Errors

When multiplying decimals, students sometimes try to place decimal points in the partial products. Remind students to wait and place the decimal point in the final answer.

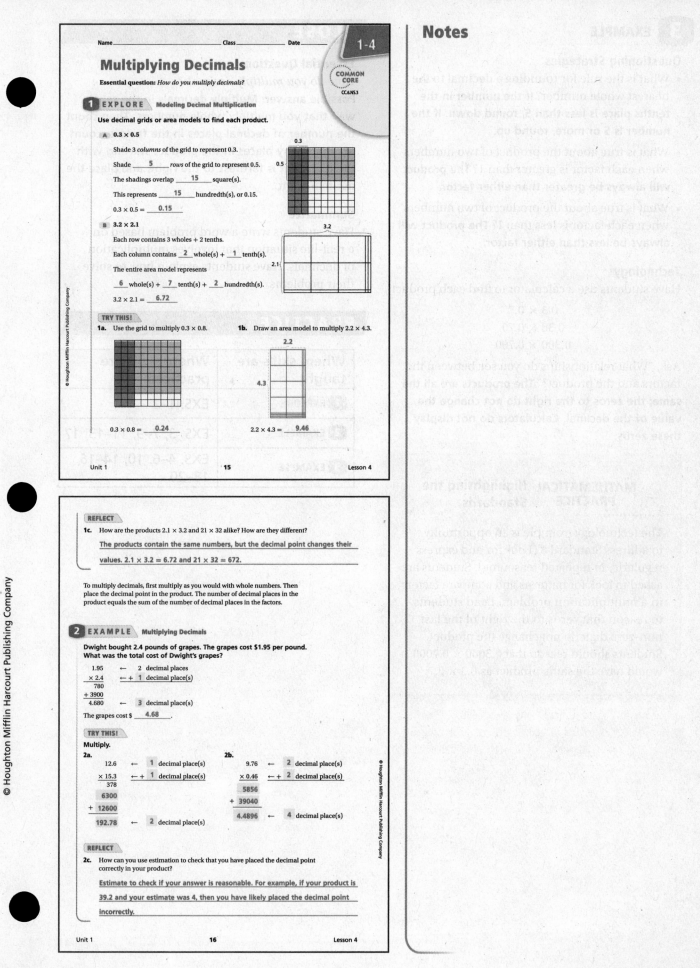

Name _____ Class _____ Date _____

1-4

Multiplying Decimals

Essential question: *How do you multiply decimals?*

COMMON CORE
CC.6.NS.3

1 EXPLORE Modeling Decimal Multiplication

Use decimal grids or area models to find each product.

A 0.3 × 0.5

Shade 3 *columns* of the grid to represent 0.3.

Shade ___5___ *rows* of the grid to represent 0.5.

The shadings overlap ___15___ square(s).

This represents ___15___ hundredth(s), or 0.15.

0.3 × 0.5 = ___0.15___

B 3.2 × 2.1

Each row contains 3 wholes + 2 tenths.

Each column contains __2__ whole(s) + __1__ tenth(s).

The entire area model represents

__6__ whole(s) + __7__ tenth(s) + __2__ hundredth(s).

3.2 × 2.1 = ___6.72___

TRY THIS!

1a. Use the grid to multiply 0.3 × 0.8.

0.3 × 0.8 = ___0.24___

1b. Draw an area model to multiply 2.2 × 4.3.

2.2 × 4.3 = ___9.46___

REFLECT

1c. How are the products 2.1 × 3.2 and 21 × 32 alike? How are they different?

The products contain the same numbers, but the decimal point changes their

values. 2.1 × 3.2 = 6.72 and 21 × 32 = 672.

To multiply decimals, first multiply as you would with whole numbers. Then
place the decimal point in the product. The number of decimal places in the
product equals the sum of the number of decimal places in the factors.

2 EXAMPLE Multiplying Decimals

**Dwight bought 2.4 pounds of grapes. The grapes cost $1.95 per pound.
What was the total cost of Dwight's grapes?**

```
   1.95    ←    2  decimal places
 × 2.4     ← +  1  decimal place(s)
  780
+ 3900
 4.680     ←    3  decimal place(s)
```

The grapes cost $ ___4.68___ .

TRY THIS!

Multiply.

2a.
```
   12.6    ←    1  decimal place(s)
 × 15.3    ← +  1  decimal place(s)
   378
  6300
+ 12600
 192.78    ←    2  decimal place(s)
```

2b.
```
   9.76    ←    2  decimal place(s)
 × 0.46    ← +  2  decimal place(s)
   5856
+ 39040
 4.4896    ←    4  decimal place(s)
```

REFLECT

2c. How can you use estimation to check that you have placed the decimal point
correctly in your product?

Estimate to check if your answer is reasonable. For example, if your product is

39.2 and your estimate was 4, then you have likely placed the decimal point

incorrectly.

Questioning Strategies

- What is the rule for rounding a decimal to the nearest whole number? **If the number in the tenths place is less than 5, round down. If the number is 5 or more, round up.**

- What is true about the product of two numbers when each factor is greater than 1? **The product will always be greater than either factor.**

- What is true about the product of two numbers when each factor is less than 1? **The product will always be less than either factor.**

Technology

Have students use a calculator to find each product.

$$0.3 \times 0.7$$
$$0.30 \times 0.70$$
$$0.300 \times 0.700$$

Ask, "What relationships do you see between the factors and the product?" **The products are all the same; the zeros to the right do not change the value of the decimal. Calculators do not display these zeros.**

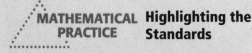 MATHEMATICAL PRACTICE **Highlighting the Standards**

The technology example is an opportunity to address Standard 8 (Look for and express regularity in repeated reasoning). Students are asked to look for patterns and compare factors in a multiplication problem. Lead students to reason that zeros to the right of the last non-zero digit do not change the product. Students should reason that 0.3000×0.7000 would have the same product as 0.3×0.7.

Essential Question

How do you multiply decimals?
Possible answer: Multiply decimals in the same way that you multiply whole numbers. Then count the number of decimal places in the factors, count off that many places in the product starting with the digit that is farthest to the right, and place the decimal point.

Summarize

Have students write a word problem based on a real-life situation that involves multiplication of decimals. Have students explain how to solve their problems.

PRACTICE

Where skills are taught	Where skills are practiced
1 EXPLORE	EXS. 1–2
2 EXAMPLE	EXS. 3, 7–9, 11–13, 17
3 EXAMPLE	EXS. 4–6, 10, 14–16, 18–20

3 EXAMPLE Multiplying Decimals

A tree grows 9.25 inches per year. If the tree continues to grow at this rate, how much will the tree grow in 3.75 years?

$$
\begin{array}{r}
9.25 \quad \leftarrow \quad \underline{2} \text{ decimal place(s)} \\
\times 3.75 \quad \leftarrow + \; \underline{2} \text{ decimal place(s)} \\
\hline
4625 \\
64750 \\
+ \; 277500 \\
\hline
34.6875 \quad \leftarrow \quad \underline{4} \text{ decimal place(s)}
\end{array}
$$

The tree will grow __34.6875__ inches in 3.75 years.

Estimate to check whether your answer is reasonable:

Round 9.25 to the nearest whole number. __9__

Round 3.75 to the nearest whole number. __4__

Multiply the whole numbers. __36__

Is the answer reasonable? Explain. __Yes; 36 is close to 34.6875.__

TRY THIS!

Multiply.

3a.
$$
\begin{array}{r}
7.14 \\
\times 6.78 \\
\hline
5712 \\
49980 \\
+ 428400 \\
\hline
48.4092
\end{array}
$$

3b.
$$
\begin{array}{r}
11.49 \\
\times 8.27 \\
\hline
8043 \\
22980 \\
+ 919200 \\
\hline
95.0223
\end{array}
$$

3c. Rico bicycles at an average speed of 15.5 miles per hour. What distance will Rico bicycle in 2.5 hours? __38.75__ miles

3d. Use estimation to show that your answer to **3c** is reasonable.

__Sample answer: Round 15.5 to 15 and 2.5 to 3; 15 × 3 = 45; 45 is close to 38.75.__

REFLECT

3e. Compare the products 6.95 × 38.3 and 69.5 × 3.83. What do you notice? Explain.

__The products are the same because the factors contain the same numbers__

__and the total number of decimal places in the factors is the same.__

Unit 1　　17　　Lesson 4

PRACTICE

1. Use the grid to multiply 0.4 × 0.7.

0.4 × 0.7 = __0.28__

2. Draw an area model to multiply 1.1 × 2.4.

1.1 × 2.4 = __2.64__

Place the decimal point in each product.

3. 3.9 × 4.6 = 1 7, 9 4

4. 0.219 × 6.2 = 1 , 3 5 7 8

5. 14.9 × 0.092 = 1 , 3 7 0 8

6. 5.546 × 8.14 = 4 5 , 1 4 4 4 4

Multiply.

7. 0.18 × 0.06 = __0.0108__

8. 35.15 × 3.7 = __130.055__

9. 0.96 × 0.12 = __0.1152__

10. 62.19 × 32.5 = __2,021.175__

11. 3.4 × 4.37 = __14.858__

12. 3.762 × 0.66 = __2.48292__

13. 11.89 × 41 = __487.49__

14. 73.8 × 19.85 = __1,464.93__

15. 12.7 × 1.83 = __23.241__

16. 44.1 × 24.66 = __1,087.506__

17. Chan Hee bought 3.4 pounds of coffee that cost $6.95 per pound. How much did he spend on coffee?

$ __23.63__

18. Adita earns $9.40 per hour working at an animal shelter. How much money will she earn for 18.5 hours of work?

$ __173.90__

Catherine tracked her gas purchases for one month.

19. How much did Catherine spend on gas in week 2?

$ __29.21__

20. How much more did she spend in week 4 than in week 1?

$ __1.06__

	Gallons	Cost per gallon ($)
Week 1	10.4	2.65
Week 2	11.5	2.54
Week 3	9.72	2.75
Week 4	10.6	2.70

Unit 1　　18　　Lesson 4

© Houghton Mifflin Harcourt Publishing Company

Dividing Decimals

Essential question: *How do you divide decimals?*

COMMON CORE **Standards for Mathematical Content**

CC.6.NS.3 Fluently add, subtract, multiply, and divide multi-digit decimals using the standard algorithm for each operation.

Prerequisites
Decimal number sense
Rounding decimals

Math Background
Long division with decimals is similar to dividing whole numbers with the additional step of multiplying the dividend and the divisor by a power of 10 to create a whole number divisor. Some students struggle with division by decimals that are between 0 and 1 because the quotient is larger than the dividend.

INTRODUCE

Connect to prior learning by reviewing division of whole numbers. Review the different ways in which a division problem can be represented.

$$8 \div 4 \qquad \frac{8}{4} \qquad 4\overline{)8}$$

Tell students that now they will be using division to divide decimals. This skill is used in real-world situations like shopping, income, taxes, and unit rates.

TEACH

1 EXPLORE

Questioning Strategies
- Why are there 6 full grids shaded? The 6 full grids represent the whole number 6 in the dividend 6.39.

- What operation is used when separating into groups? Division

Teaching Strategies
Review the vocabulary associated with division. Include the words *quotient*, *dividend*, and *divisor*.

$$\text{dividend} \div \text{divisor} = \text{quotient}$$

$$\text{divisor} \overline{)\text{dividend}}^{\text{quotient}}$$

Have students create and share ways to help them memorize the different parts of a division expression. For example, the division symbol can be imagined as a house. A den is a room in a house, and the word "den" is found in "dividend," so the dividend goes inside the division symbol.

2 EXAMPLE

Questioning Strategies
- How do you know that the quotient will be greater than 1? The dividend, 9.76, is greater than the divisor, 8. You can estimate that 8 goes into 9.76 a little more than 1 time.

- Why is it important to align your numbers when you are dividing? The numbers need to be aligned to help place the decimal point correctly in the quotient.

Avoid Common Errors
Some students align digits incorrectly when dividing. Have students use grid paper (or lined paper turned sideways) to help align the digits correctly at each step in the division process.

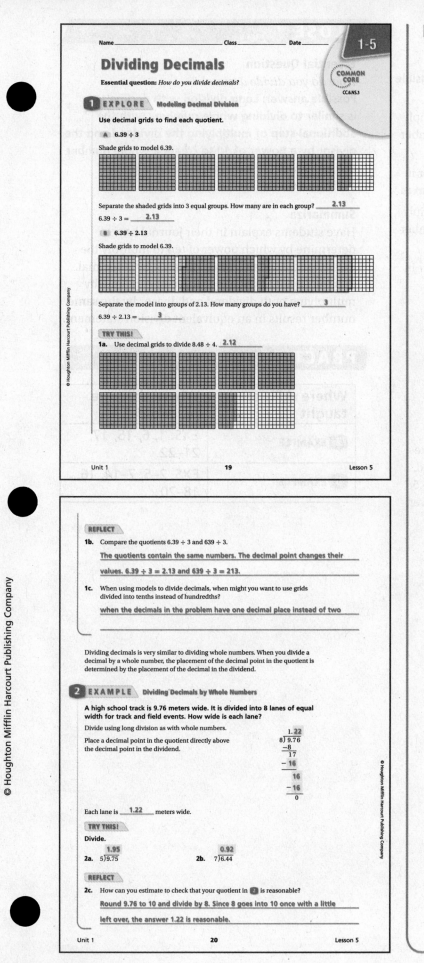

Dividing Decimals

Name_____ Class_____ Date_____

1-5
COMMON CORE
CC.6.NS.3

Essential question: *How do you divide decimals?*

1 EXPLORE Modeling Decimal Division

Use decimal grids to find each quotient.

A 6.39 ÷ 3

Shade grids to model 6.39.

Separate the shaded grids into 3 equal groups. How many are in each group? **2.13**

6.39 ÷ 3 = _____**2.13**_____

B 6.39 ÷ 2.13

Shade grids to model 6.39.

Separate the model into groups of 2.13. How many groups do you have? **3**

6.39 ÷ 2.13 = _____**3**_____

TRY THIS!

1a. Use decimal grids to divide 8.48 ÷ 4. **2.12**

Unit 1   19   Lesson 5

REFLECT

1b. Compare the quotients 6.39 ÷ 3 and 639 ÷ 3.

The quotients contain the same numbers. The decimal point changes their

values. 6.39 ÷ 3 = 2.13 and 639 ÷ 3 = 213.

1c. When using models to divide decimals, when might you want to use grids
divided into tenths instead of hundredths?

when the decimals in the problem have one decimal place instead of two

Dividing decimals is very similar to dividing whole numbers. When you divide a
decimal by a whole number, the placement of the decimal point in the quotient is
determined by the placement of the decimal in the dividend.

2 EXAMPLE Dividing Decimals by Whole Numbers

A high school track is 9.76 meters wide. It is divided into 8 lanes of equal
width for track and field events. How wide is each lane?

Divide using long division as with whole numbers.

Place a decimal point in the quotient directly above
the decimal point in the dividend.

$$
\begin{array}{r}
1.22 \\
8\overline{)9.76} \\
-8 \\
\hline
17 \\
-16 \\
\hline
16 \\
-16 \\
\hline
0
\end{array}
$$

Each lane is _____**1.22**_____ meters wide.

TRY THIS!

Divide.

2a. **1.95** 5)9.75

2b. **0.92** 7)6.44

REFLECT

2c. How can you estimate to check that your quotient in **2** is reasonable?

Round 9.76 to 10 and divide by 8. Since 8 goes into 10 once with a little

left over, the answer 1.22 is reasonable.

Unit 1   20   Lesson 5

Questioning Strategies

- In part A, what is a reasonable estimate? **Possible answer: 30 ÷ 5 = 6**

- In part A, by what power of 10 will you multiply the divisor and dividend to get a whole-number divisor? **10^1, or 10**

- Why is a whole number a reasonable answer in part A? **We assume she makes only whole cakes.**

- In part B, by what power of 10 will you multiply the divisor and dividend to get a whole-number divisor? **10^2, or 100**

- Why is a whole number a reasonable answer in part B? **You can only buy whole pens.**

MATHEMATICAL PRACTICE Highlighting the Standards

This example is an opportunity to address Standard 1 (Make sense of problems and persevere in solving them). Students are asked to analyze real-world problems and determine that division is needed. Then, the solution to the problem must be interpreted. For example, in part A, without context, 6.5 would round up to 7; in this context, however, it makes sense to round down. Students must recognize that there are not enough raspberries to make 7 cakes and that only 6 cakes can be made.

CLOSE

Essential Question

How do you divide decimals?

Possible answer: Long division with decimals is similar to dividing whole numbers with the additional step of multiplying the dividend and the divisor by a power of 10 to create a whole number divisor. Divide and place the decimal point in the quotient.

Summarize

Have students explain in their journal how to determine by which power of ten to multiply the divisor and dividend when dividing by a decimal. You may want to challenge them to explain why multiplying both dividend and divisor by the same number results in an equivalent division statement.

PRACTICE

Where skills are taught	Where skills are practiced
2 EXAMPLE	EXS. 1, 6, 15, 17, 21–22
3 EXAMPLE	EXS. 2–5, 7–14, 16, 18–20

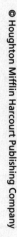

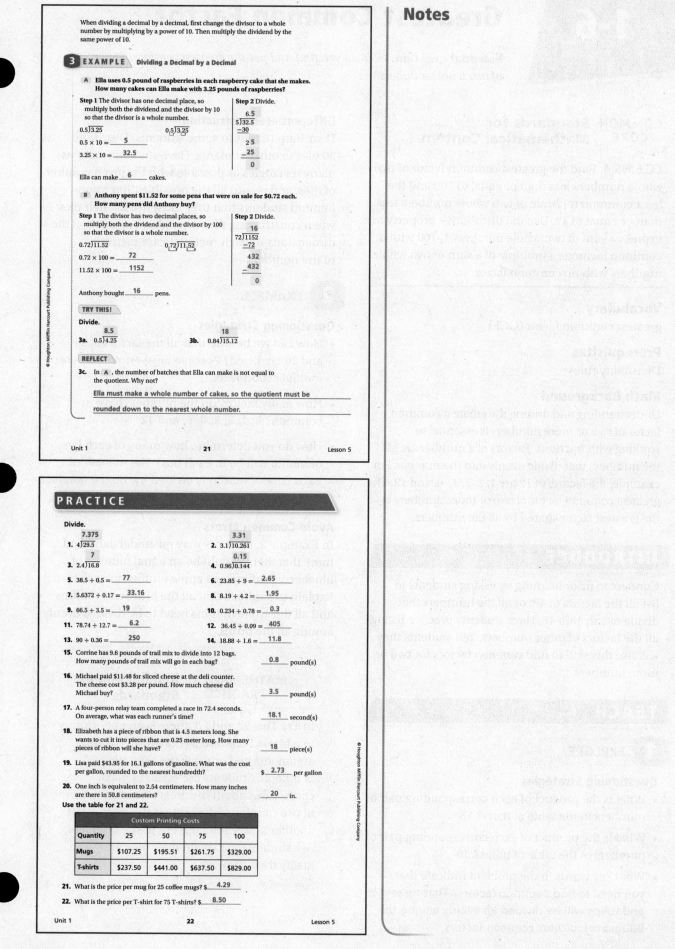

When dividing a decimal by a decimal, first change the divisor to a whole number by multiplying by a power of 10. Then multiply the dividend by the same power of 10.

3 EXAMPLE Dividing a Decimal by a Decimal

A Ella uses 0.5 pound of raspberries in each raspberry cake that she makes. How many cakes can Ella make with 3.25 pounds of raspberries?

Step 1 The divisor has one decimal place, so multiply both the dividend and the divisor by 10 so that the divisor is a whole number.

$0.5\overline{)3.25}$ $\qquad$ $0.5_{\wedge}\overline{)3.25_{\wedge}}$

$0.5 \times 10 =$ __5__

$3.25 \times 10 =$ __32.5__

Step 2 Divide.

```
    6.5
5)32.5
  −30
    2 5
   −2 5
       0
```

Ella can make __6__ cakes.

B Anthony spent $11.52 for some pens that were on sale for $0.72 each. How many pens did Anthony buy?

Step 1 The divisor has two decimal places, so multiply both the dividend and the divisor by 100 so that the divisor is a whole number.

$0.72\overline{)11.52}$ $\qquad$ $0.72_{\wedge}\overline{)11.52_{\wedge}}$

$0.72 \times 100 =$ __72__

$11.52 \times 100 =$ __1152__

Step 2 Divide.

```
      16
72)1152
   −72
    432
   −432
      0
```

Anthony bought __16__ pens.

TRY THIS!

Divide.

3a. $0.5\overline{)4.25}$ → 8.5

3b. $0.84\overline{)15.12}$ → 18

REFLECT

3c. In **A**, the number of batches that Ella can make is not equal to the quotient. Why not?

Ella must make a whole number of cakes, so the quotient must be rounded down to the nearest whole number.

PRACTICE

Divide.

1. $4\overline{)29.5}$ → 7.375

2. $3.1\overline{)10.261}$ → 3.31

3. $2.4\overline{)16.8}$ → 7

4. $0.96\overline{)0.144}$ → 0.15

5. $38.5 \div 0.5 =$ __77__

6. $23.85 \div 9 =$ __2.65__

7. $5.6372 \div 0.17 =$ __33.16__

8. $8.19 \div 4.2 =$ __1.95__

9. $66.5 \div 3.5 =$ __19__

10. $0.234 \div 0.78 =$ __0.3__

11. $78.74 \div 12.7 =$ __6.2__

12. $36.45 \div 0.09 =$ __405__

13. $90 \div 0.36 =$ __250__

14. $18.88 \div 1.6 =$ __11.8__

15. Corrine has 9.6 pounds of trail mix to divide into 12 bags. How many pounds of trail mix will go in each bag? __0.8__ pound(s)

16. Michael paid $11.48 for sliced cheese at the deli counter. The cheese cost $3.28 per pound. How much cheese did Michael buy? __3.5__ pound(s)

17. A four-person relay team completed a race in 72.4 seconds. On average, what was each runner's time? __18.1__ second(s)

18. Elizabeth has a piece of ribbon that is 4.5 meters long. She wants to cut it into pieces that are 0.25 meter long. How many pieces of ribbon will she have? __18__ piece(s)

19. Lisa paid $43.95 for 16.1 gallons of gasoline. What was the cost per gallon, rounded to the nearest hundredth? $ __2.73__ per gallon

20. One inch is equivalent to 2.54 centimeters. How many inches are there in 50.8 centimeters? __20__ in.

Use the table for 21 and 22.

Custom Printing Costs				
Quantity	25	50	75	100
Mugs	$107.25	$195.51	$261.75	$329.00
T-shirts	$237.50	$441.00	$637.50	$829.00

21. What is the price per mug for 25 coffee mugs? $ __4.29__

22. What is the price per T-shirt for 75 T-shirts? $ __8.50__

Greatest Common Factor

Essential question: *How do you find and use the greatest common factor of two whole numbers?*

COMMON CORE Standards for Mathematical Content

CC.6.NS.4 Find the greatest common factor of two whole numbers less than or equal to 100 and the least common multiple of two whole numbers less than or equal to 12. Use the distributive property to express a sum of two whole numbers 1–100 with a common factor as a multiple of a sum of two whole numbers with no common factor.

Vocabulary

greatest common factor (GCF)

Prerequisites

Divisibility rules

Math Background

Understanding and finding the greatest common factor of two or more numbers is essential to working with fractions. Factors of a number are all the numbers that divide evenly into the number. For example, the factors of 12 are 1, 2, 3, 4, 6, and 12. The greatest *common* factor of two or more numbers is the greatest factor shared by all the numbers.

INTRODUCE

Connect to prior learning by asking students to list all the factors of 48, or all the numbers that divide evenly into 48. Have students practice listing all the factors of other numbers. Tell students they will use this skill to find *common* factors for two or more numbers.

TEACH

1 EXPLORE

Questioning Strategies

• What is the product of each corresponding pair of numbers in the table of roses? **18**

• What is the product of each corresponding pair of numbers in the table of tulips? **30**

• What key words in the problem indicate that you need to find common factors? **That roses and tulips will be divided up evenly among the bouquets indicates common factors.**

Differentiated Instruction

Distribute 18 tiles to some students. Distribute 30 tiles to other students. Have students make as many rectangles as possible with the given number of tiles, and record all the possible dimensions. Remind students that they must use all their tiles when constructing the rectangles. Explain that the dimensions of each rectangle are factors of the number.

2 EXAMPLE

Questioning Strategies

• How can we be sure that all the factors of 24 and 36 are listed? **Possible answer: We can use multiplication facts.**

• How many factors do the numbers have in common? **6; 1, 2, 3, 4, 6, and 12**

• How do you determine how many of each type of muffin will be in each box? **The number of each type of muffin is divided by 12, the greatest common factor.**

Avoid Common Errors

In Example 2, students may misunderstand and think that there should be an equal number of blueberry muffins and apple muffins in each box. Explain to students that all the blueberry muffins and all the apple muffins need to be divided evenly among all the boxes.

MATHEMATICAL PRACTICE Highlighting the Standards

In Try This 2c and 2d, there is an opportunity to address Standard 3 (Construct viable arguments and critique the reasoning of others). Students are asked to make conjectures about the greatest common factor of two numbers when one is the multiple of another and when both are prime numbers. Ask students to explain their reasoning and justify their answers.

Name_____ Class_____ Date_____

Greatest Common Factor

COMMON CORE
CC.6.NS.4

Essential question: *How do you find and use the greatest common factor of two whole numbers?*

1 EXPLORE   Greatest Common Factor

A florist plans to make bouquets of roses and tulips. She has 18 roses and 30 tulips. Each bouquet must have the same number of roses and the same number of tulips. She wants to use all of the flowers. What are the possible bouquets she can make?

A   Complete the tables below.

Roses

Number of bouquets	1	2	3	6	9	18
Number of roses in each bouquet	18	9	6	3	2	1

Tulips

Number of bouquets	1	2	3	5	6	10	15	30
Number of tulips in each bouquet	30	15	10	6	5	3	2	1

B   Can the florist make five bouquets? Why or why not?

No; 18 (the number of roses) is not divisible by 5.

If a number is a factor of two or more counting numbers, it is called a *common factor* of those numbers.

C   What are the common factors of 18 and 30? What do they represent in this situation?

1, 2, 3, and 6; the possible numbers of bouquets

The **greatest common factor (GCF)** of two or more counting numbers is the greatest factor shared by the numbers.

D   What is the GCF of 18 and 30?   6

If the florist wants the number of bouquets to be as large as possible, how many bouquets can she make?   6

How many roses will be in each bouquet?   3

How many tulips will be in each bouquet?   5

One way to find the GCF of two numbers is to list all of their factors.

2 EXAMPLE   Greatest Common Factor

A baker has 24 blueberry muffins and 36 apple muffins to divide into boxes for sale. Each box must have the same number of blueberry muffins and the same number of apple muffins. What is the greatest number of boxes that the baker can make using all of the muffins? How many blueberry muffins and how many apple muffins will be in each box?

A   List the factors of 24 and 36. Then circle the common factors.

Factors of 24: (1) (2) (3) (4) (6) 8 (12) 24

Factors of 36: (1) (2) (3) (4) (6) 9 (12) 18 36

B   What do the common factors represent in this situation?

the possible numbers of boxes the baker can make

C   What is the GCF of 24 and 36?   12

D   The greatest number of boxes that the baker can make is   12   . There will be   2   blueberry muffin(s) and   3   apple muffin(s) in each box.

TRY THIS!

List the factors to find the GCF of each pair of numbers.

2a. 14 and 35   7

14: 1, 2, 7, 14

35: 1, 5, 7, 35

2b. 20 and 28   4

20: 1, 2, 4, 5, 10, 20

28: 1, 2, 4, 7, 14, 28

2c. The sixth-grade class is competing in the school field day. There are 32 girls and 40 boys who want to participate in the relay race. Each team must have the same number of girls and the same number of boys. What is the greatest number of teams that can be formed? How many boys and how many girls will be on each team?

8 teams; 4 girls, 5 boys

REFLECT

2d. What is the GCF of two numbers when one number is a multiple of the other? Give an example.

The GCF is the lesser of the numbers. For example, the GCF of 4 and 8 is 4.

2e. What is the GCF of two prime numbers? Give an example.

1; for example, the GCF of 11 and 13 is 1.

Questioning Strategies

- Why must area models of products be rectangles? **You must have two whole-number factors, so a rectangle is the only shape that works.**

- How do you know when your figure can be a square? **Possible answer: The dimensions, or factors, must be equal.**

- List some numbers that could be modeled by squares. **Possible answer: 25, 36, 49**

Differentiated Instruction

Using cooperative learning with students in groups, give each group 105 counters—45 of one color and 60 of another color. Instruct them to divide each color equally into piles. Have them record the different number of piles that can be formed with each color.

Example:

Yellow: 1 pile of 60, 2 piles of 30, 3 piles...

Red: 1 pile of 45, 3 piles of 15, 5 piles...

Ask students to find the greatest number (GCF) of the two numbers using this method.

Essential Question

How do find and use the greatest common factor of two whole numbers?

Possible answer: List the factors of each number, circle the common factors, and identify the greatest of those factors.

Summarize

Have students define the terms *factor* and *greatest common factor* and illustrate their definitions with an example.

PRACTICE

Where skills are taught	Where skills are practiced
1 EXPLORE	EXS. 1–17
2 EXAMPLE	EXS. 4–17
3 EXPLORE	EXS. 18–21

You can use the Distributive Property to rewrite a sum of two or more numbers as a product of their GCF and another number.

3 EXPLORE Distributive Property

You can use grid paper to draw area models of 45 and 60.
Here are all of the possible area models of 45.

A What do the side lengths of the area models above (1, 3, 5, 9, 15, and 45) represent? ___factors of 45___

B On your own grid paper, show all of the possible area models of 60.

C What side lengths do the area models of 45 and 60 have in common?
___1, 3, 5, 15___

What do these side lengths represent? ___common factors of 45 and 60___

D What is the greatest common side length? What does it represent?
___15; GCF of 45 and 60___

E Write 45 as a product of the GCF and another number. ___15×3___
Write 60 as a product of the GCF and another number. ___15×4___

F Use your answers above to rewrite 45 + 60.

$45 + 60 = 15 \times \boxed{3} + 15 \times \boxed{4}$

Use the Distributive Property and your answer above to write 45 + 60 as a product of the GCF and another number.

$15 \times \boxed{3} + 15 \times \boxed{4} = 15 \times \left(\boxed{3} + \boxed{4}\right) = 15 \times \boxed{7}$

TRY THIS!

Write each sum as a product of the GCF of the two numbers.

3a. $27 + 18 \; \underline{9 \times (3 + 2) = 9 \times 5}$ **3b.** $120 + 36 \; \underline{12 \times (10 + 3) = 12 \times 13}$

REFLECT

3c. Does the same process work with subtraction? For example, can you write 120 − 36 as a product of the GCF and another number? Explain.

Yes; $120 − 36 = 12 \times (10 − 3) = 12 \times 7$.

© Houghton Mifflin Harcourt Publishing Company

PRACTICE

List the factors of each number.

1. 16 ___1, 2, 4, 8, 16___

2. 39 ___1, 3, 13, 39___

3. 50 ___1, 2, 5, 10, 25, 50___

Find the GCF of each pair of numbers.

4. 40 and 48 ___8___   5. 10 and 45 ___5___

6. 6 and 21 ___3___   7. 60 and 72 ___12___

8. 21 and 40 ___1___   9. 28 and 32 ___4___

10. 28 and 70 ___14___   11. 45 and 81 ___9___

12. 30 and 45 ___15___   13. 55 and 77 ___11___

14. Mrs. Davis is sewing vests. She has 16 green buttons and 24 yellow buttons. Each vest will have the same number of yellow buttons and the same number of green buttons. What is the greatest number of vests Mrs. Davis can make using all of the buttons? ___8___ vests

15. A baker has 27 wheat bagels and 36 plain bagels that will be divided into boxes. Each box must have the same number of wheat bagels and the same number of plain bagels. What is the greatest number of boxes the baker can make using all of the bagels? ___9___ boxes

16. Lola is putting appetizers on plates. She has 63 meatballs and 84 cheese cubes. She wants both kinds of food on each plate, and each plate must have the same number of meatballs and the same number of cheese cubes. What is the greatest number of plates she can make using all of the appetizers? ___21___ plates

17. The Delta High School marching band has 54 members. The Swanton High School marching band has 90 members. The bands are going to march in a parade together. The director wants to arrange the bands into the same number of rows. What is the greatest number of rows in which the two bands can be arranged? ___18___ rows

Write each sum as a product of the GCF of the two numbers.

18. 75 + 90
    $15 \times (5 + 6) = 15 \times 11$

19. 36 and 45
    $9 \times (4 + 5) = 9 \times 9$

20. 56 + 64
    $8 \times (7 + 8) = 8 \times 15$

21. 48 + 14
    $2 \times (24 + 7) = 2 \times 31$

© Houghton Mifflin Harcourt Publishing Company

Least Common Multiple

Essential question: *How do you find the least common multiple of two numbers?*

COMMON CORE **Standards for Mathematical Content**

CC.6.NS.4 Find the greatest common factor of two whole numbers less than or equal to 100 and the least common multiple of two whole numbers less than or equal to 12. Use the distributive property to express a sum of two whole numbers 1–100 with a common factor as a multiple of a sum of two whole numbers with no common factor.

Vocabulary

least common multiple (LCM)

Prerequisites

Multiplication facts

Multiples

Math Background

The least common multiple (LCM) is used when working with fractions, most commonly to write fractions with a common denominator. You can add and subtract fractions with any common denominator, but when the LCM is used for a common denominator, the complexity of the computation involved is usually minimized because the numbers are smaller than those for greater common denominators.

INTRODUCE

Suppose you and a friend have part-time jobs. You get paid every Friday, and your friend gets paid every other Friday. Find the earliest day that you both get paid. The least common multiple of two numbers is the first shared number in ordered lists of multiples of the two numbers.

TEACH

1 EXPLORE

Questioning Strategies

- What is the first multiple of any number? **The first multiple is always the number itself.**

- Why do you not include the number 120 in your list? **Shannon is training only for the next 100 days.**

MATHEMATICAL PRACTICE **Highlighting the Standards**

This Explore is an opportunity to address Standard 5 (Use the appropriate tools strategically). Students use a table to circle and shade multiples of two numbers. They determine the least common multiple by determining the smallest number that is both shaded and circled. The table is used strategically to help them visualize and organize the information.

2 EXAMPLE

Questioning Strategies

- In what order are the multiples of 3 and 4 listed? **least to greatest**

- How do you know whether you are missing any multiples or if they are out of order? **List the numbers in order by starting with 1 times the number, 2 times, 3 times, and so on.**

CLOSE

Essential Question

How do you find the least common multiple of two numbers?
Possible answer: List the multiples of each number. Identify those multiples that are the same for both numbers and find the least (smallest) one.

Summarize

Have students find the least common multiple and the greatest common factor of two numbers. Have students compare GCF and LCM for one pair of numbers.

PRACTICE

Where skills are taught	Where skills are practiced
1 EXPLORE	EXS. 7–10
2 EXAMPLE	EXS. 1–10

Name_____ Class_____ Date_____

Least Common Multiple

Essential question: *How do you find the least common multiple of two numbers?*

1 EXPLORE Least Common Multiple

For the next 100 days, Shannon will be training for a biathlon. She will swim every 6 days and bicycle every 8 days. On what days will she both swim and bicycle?

Step 1 Shade each day Shannon will swim.

Step 2 Circle each day Shannon will bicycle.

Shannon will both swim and bicycle on days ___24, 48, 72, and 96___

The numbers of the days that Shannon will swim and bicycle are common multiples of 6 and 8.

➤ The **least common multiple (LCM)** is the least common multiple of two or more counting numbers.

1	2	3	4	5	6	7	8	9	10
11	12	13	14	15	16	17	18	19	20
21	22	23	24	25	26	27	28	29	30
31	32	33	34	35	36	37	38	39	40
41	42	43	44	45	46	47	48	49	50
51	52	53	54	55	56	57	58	59	60
61	62	63	64	65	66	67	68	69	70
71	72	73	74	75	76	77	78	79	80
81	82	83	84	85	86	87	88	89	90
91	92	93	94	95	96	97	98	99	100

What is the LCM of 6 and 8? What does it represent in this situation?

___24; the first day that Shannon will both swim and bicycle___

2 EXAMPLE Least Common Multiple

A store is holding a grand opening promotion. Every 3rd customer receives a free key chain and every 4th customer receives a free magnet. Which customer will be the first to receive both a key chain and a magnet?

List the multiples of each number. Circle the common multiples.

Multiples of 3: _3_ , 6 , 9 , ⑫ , 15 , 18 , 21 , ㉔ , 27

Multiples of 4: _4_ , 8 , ⑫ , 16 , 20 , ㉔ , 28 , 32 , 36

What is the LCM of 3 and 4? ___12___

The first customer to get both a key chain and a magnet is ___the 12th customer___

Unit 1   27   Lesson 7

TRY THIS!

List multiples to find the LCM of each pair of numbers.

2a. 4 and 9 ___36___   **2b.** 18 and 24 ___72___

REFLECT

2c. What is the LCM of two numbers when one number is a multiple of the other? Give an example.

___The LCM is the greater of the two numbers. For example, the LCM of 4___
___and 8 is 8.___

2d. What is the LCM of two numbers that have no common factors greater than 1? Give an example.

___The LCM is the product of the two numbers. For example, the LCM of 4___
___and 9 is 36.___

PRACTICE

Find the LCM of each pair of numbers.

1. 6 and 9 ___18___   **2.** 9 and 21 ___63___

3. 8 and 56 ___56___   **4.** 16 and 24 ___48___

5. 12 and 30 ___60___   **6.** 6 and 10 ___30___

7. At a restaurant, after every 12th visit you receive a free beverage. After every 15th visit you receive a free dessert. At which visit will you first receive a free beverage and a free dessert?   Visit ___60___

8. Starting today (day 1) Lee will walk his dog Fido every 3rd day and his dog Fifi every 5th day. On which day will Lee first walk both dogs together?   Day ___15___

Use the train schedule for 9 and 10.

9. The red line and the blue line trains just arrived at the station. When will they next arrive at the station at the same time? In ___40___ minutes

10. All three trains just arrived at the station. When will they next all arrive at the station at the same time? In ___120___ minutes

Train Schedule	
Train	**Arrives Every...**
Red line	8 minutes
Blue line	10 minutes
Yellow line	12 minutes

Unit 1   28   Lesson 7

© Houghton Mifflin Harcourt Publishing Company

Problem Solving Connections
Welcome Back!

COMMON CORE Standards for Mathematical Content

CC.6.NS.1 Interpret and compute quotients of fractions, and solve word problems involving division of fractions by fractions, e.g., by using visual fraction models and equations to represent the problem.

CC.6.NS.2 Fluently divide multi-digit numbers using the standard algorithm.

CC.6.NS.3 Fluently add, subtract, multiply, and divide multi-digit decimals using the standard algorithm for each operation.

CC.6.NS.4 Find the greatest common factor of two whole numbers less than or equal to 100 and the least common multiple of two whole numbers less than or equal to 12. Use the distributive property to express a sum of two whole numbers 1–100 with a common factor as a multiple of a sum of two whole numbers with no common factor.

INTRODUCE

Someday you may attend or plan a class reunion. Cost is an important part of making decisions. Ask students to imagine they are planning a class reunion. What kind of choices need to be made? You may want to record students' responses on the board. Explain that this project is going to explore some of these ideas and use mathematical concepts that they have learned in this unit.

TEACH

1 Seating

Questioning Strategies

- How many people do you need seating for? **256**

- How much would it cost to rent a covered round table? **$8.75**

- If Elizabeth purchases only 7 packages of name cards, by how many packages would she be short? **4**

Teaching Strategy

Students may have difficulty reading the given table. Ask students questions like "How many people are seated at a rectangular table? How much does it cost to rent a round table?"

2 Decorations and Favors

Questioning Strategies

- Will you use the least common multiple or the greatest common factor to find the number of bouquets of balloons? **GCF**

- Will you use the least common multiple or the greatest common factor to find which guests receive door prizes? **LCM**

Avoid Common Errors

When finding the number of banners that can be made, students must divide 87.5 by 11.25. Students might incorrectly round their answer of 7.8 up to 8 rather than down to 7. Point out to students that it is not acceptable to make the eighth banner if there isn't all of the required material. Elizabeth would not want a partial banner.

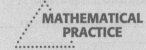

MATHEMATICAL PRACTICE | **Highlighting the Standards**

Part 2 of this project is an opportunity to address Standard 5 (Use the appropriate tools strategically). Students must decide whether to find the greatest common factor or least common multiple to solve problems. Students can use a variety of methods to solve the problems, including listing factors and multiples, making a table, or circling numbers on a grid.

Name_____ Class_____ Date_____

UNIT 1

Problem Solving Connections 🌐

COMMON
CORE
CC.6.NS.1
CC.6.NS.2
CC.6.NS.3
CC.6.NS.4

Welcome Back! Elizabeth is an event planner who has been hired to plan a class reunion. The class has 275 people and 256 will be attending. Elizabeth must plan the seating, decorations, and food. She then needs to determine how much to charge each guest so that all costs are covered.

1 Seating

The cost sheet shows the types of tables available, the cost per table, and the cost per tablecloth.

A How many round tables would be necessary to seat all of the guests?

$256 \div 8 = 32$ tables

Type of Table	Seats	Cost per Table ($)	Cost per Tablecloth ($)
Round	8	5.00	3.75
Rectangular	12	7.50	4.35

B How many rectangular tables would be necessary to seat all of the guests?

$256 \div 12 = 21.3$; 22 tables

C Which table, round or rectangular, would be cheaper for the reunion? How much cheaper?

Round: $32 \times (5 + 3.75) = \$280$

Rectangular: $22 \times (7.50 + 4.35) = \$260.70$

$\$280 - \$260.70 = \$19.30$

The rectangular tables would be cheaper by $19.30.

D A name card will be placed at each seat. Elizabeth finds that 36 name cards come in a package. How many packages will she need? Explain.

$256 \div 36 = 7.11$

8 packages; 7 packages will provide only 252 name cards.

Unit 1   29   Problem Solving Connections

© Houghton Mifflin Harcourt Publishing Company

2 Decorations and Favors

A The school colors are blue and white. Elizabeth has 84 blue balloons and 96 white balloons. How many balloon bouquets can she make if she wants to have the same number of each color in each bouquet and use all of her balloons?

84: 1, 2, 3, 4, 6, 7, 12, 14, 21, 28, 42, 84

96: 1, 2, 3, 4, 6, 8, 12, 16, 24, 32, 48, 96

12 bouquets

B How many of each color balloon will be in each bouquet?

7 blue and 8 white

C Elizabeth has 87.75 feet of banner paper. How many banners can she make that are 11.25 feet long? Explain.

$87.75 \div 11.25 = 7.8$

7 banners; she will not have enough paper to make 8 banners.

D Elizabeth plans to hand out door prizes as the guests arrive. Every 6th guest will receive a mug, and every 14th guest will receive a T-shirt. Which guest will be the first to receive both a mug and a T-shirt?

Multiples of 6: 6, 12, 18, 24, 30, 36, 42, 48

Multiples of 14: 14, 28, 42, 56

the 42nd guest

E Elizabeth has two $8\frac{1}{2}$-pound bags of mints. She plans to put $\frac{1}{12}$ pound at each place setting. Will she have enough mints?

$8\frac{1}{2} \div \frac{1}{12} = 102$ servings per bag

$102 \times 2 = 204$ servings; no

Unit 1   30   Problem Solving Connections

© Houghton Mifflin Harcourt Publishing Company

Questioning Strategies

- How much would two meats and three total sides cost? $10.25 + $0.75 + $0.75 = $11.75

- In part D, why can't you just divide 640 by 8 to get the answer? Each person is expected to have 2 servings of punch.

Teaching Strategy

Students may be unfamiliar with the term "budget." Explain the term and how it is used in the project. Be sure that students understand that each meat option comes with one side for the given price in the table, and each additional side costs $0.75. Note that a salad is not a "side."

Questioning Strategies

- Where would you find how many rectangular tables will be needed? In part A, under "seating"

- How will you determine how many T-shirts are needed? 256 ÷ 14 = 18.3; 19 T-shirts

- How can you determine the total cost per person for the reunion? Divide total cost by 256.

Technology

You may want to allow students to use calculators to check their answers and find the total cost of the reunion, but have students show all the work.

CLOSE

Journal

Have students give an example of each type of decimal operation in the project. Have them explain each step they take when performing the operation. You may also have students make notes about which decimal operations are challenging for them.

© Houghton Mifflin Harcourt Publishing Company

3 Food and Drink

A Use the price sheet to find the total cost of a basic meal of one meat and one side for each guest.

Meal Options	Price per Plate ($)
1 meat, 1 side	9.25
2 meats, 1 side	10.25
Additional sides	0.75
Salad	1.45

$$\$9.25 \times 256 = \$2,368.00$$

B How would you determine how much more it would cost to serve each guest a salad rather than an additional side?

> Sample answer:
>
> Find the difference between the cost of a salad, $1.45, and the cost of a side, $0.75, and multiply by 256, the number of guests.

C Elizabeth has budgeted $3,000 for food. If she decides to serve an additional side and a salad, can she choose the meal with two meats and stay within her budget?

> Two meat option: $10.25 × 256 = $2,624.00
>
> Additional side: $0.75 × 256 = $192.00
>
> Additional salad: $1.45 × 256 = $371.20
>
> Total cost: $3,187.20; no

D Elizabeth purchases a container of punch mix that, when mixed with water, makes 640 ounces of punch. Elizabeth has 8-ounce drinking glasses. She assumes that each person will drink 2 glasses of punch. Show how to determine how many people can be served with one container of punch.

> 2 glasses × 8 ounces = 16 ounces per person
>
> 640 ÷ 16 = 40 people

4 Answer the Question

A Elizabeth's budget for the class reunion is shown. Help her complete the budget using some of your answers from previous questions. You may also have to perform additional computations.

Class Reunion Budget			
Item	Number of Items/Packages	Cost per Item	Total Cost
Rectangular tables	22	$11.85	$260.70
Name cards	8	$5.10	$40.80
Balloons	180	$0.13	$23.40
Sign	1	$25.25	$25.25
T-shirts	19	$7.50	$142.50
Mugs	43	$5.00	$215.00
Mints	3	$5.50	$16.50
Meals	256	$11.45	$2,931.20
Punch	7	$4.25	$29.75
Pie	16	$6.75	$108.00
Cake	7	$12.00	$84.00
Elizabeth's Fee			$1,800.00
Total Cost			$5,677.10

B Based on your total cost, determine the amount each guest should pay to attend the reunion. Would $20 per person be enough to cover all of the expenses? Explain. How much would you charge? Justify your answer.

> $5,677.10 ÷ 256 ≈ $22.18; no
>
> Sample answer: I would charge $23.00 to have a little bit left over in case of unexpected expenses.

COMMON CORE CORRELATION

Standard	Items
CC.6.NS.1	3, 8, 19
CC.6.NS.2	1, 2
CC.6.NS.3	4–7, 9, 12–13, 15–17
CC.6.NS.4	10, 11, 14, 18

TEST PREP DOCTOR ⊕

Multiple Choice: Item 5

- Students who answered **A** subtracted the width from the length and then multiplied by two. The student does not understand the formula for finding the perimeter of a rectangle.
- Students who answered **B** added the length of only one side and one width. The student did not include the length and width of the other sides to find the perimeter.
- Students who answered **D** multiplied the length times the width and found the area of the figure, not the perimeter.

Multiple Choice: Item 7

- Students who answered **A** added the amounts of money Rusty had in his jar and wallet but did not subtract this total from the purchase price of the sweater. Thus, the amount needed was not found.
- Students who answered **B** subtracted the amount of money in his wallet from the purchase price of the sweater but did not subtract the amount in his jar.
- Students who answered **C** subtracted the amount of money in his jar from the purchase price of the sweater but did not subtract the amount in his wallet.

Free Response: Item 15

- Students who answered **$5.99** added the cost per pound to the weight of the bag of apples.
- Students who answered **$3.41** subtracted the cost per pound from the total weight of the apples.
- Students who answered **$6.07** did not round to the nearest cent correctly.
- Students who answered **$3.65** divided the weight of the apples by the price per pound.

Free Response: Item 18

- Students who answered **1** found the least common *factor* of 6 and 10.
- Students who answered **60** multiplied the given factors. While 60 has both 6 and 10 as factors, it is not the *smallest* number with these factors.
- Students who answered **2** may not understand how to find factors of a number. They found the least number other than 1 by which both 6 and 10 are divisible.

© Houghton Mifflin Harcourt Publishing Company

UNIT 1 TEST PREP

Name _____ Class _____ Date _____

MULTIPLE CHOICE

1. The Harrison family traveled 2,112 miles in four days on their last vacation. The family traveled the same distance each day. How many miles did the Harrisons travel each day?

   A. 506 miles (C) 528 miles

   B. 542 miles D. 844 miles

2. Margaret borrowed $2,597 from her parents for a foreign exchange trip. She plans to repay her parents $175 each month. How much will Margaret's last payment be?

   F. $123 H. $168

   (G) $147 J. $175

3. Cedric made 30 cups of soup. How many $1\frac{1}{4}$-cups servings does he have?

   (A) 24 servings C. 30 servings

   B. 28 servings D. 35 servings

4. A snail travels 0.03 mile per hour. How far will the snail travel in 36.8 hours?

   F. 0.1104 miles H. 11.04 miles

   (G) 1.104 miles J. 110.4 miles

5. A rectangular garden has the dimensions shown in the figure.

   7.48 meters

   15.6 meters

   What is the perimeter of the garden?

   A. 16.24 meters (C) 46.16 meters

   B. 23.08 meters D. 116.688 meters

6. Adam drove from his house directly to one of the destinations shown in the table. Adam's trip odometer read 248.9 miles when he left home and 316.3 miles when he reached his destination. What was his destination?

Destination	Distance from Adam's House
Museum	64.6 miles
Baseball stadium	67.4 miles
Theater	70.4 miles
Historical landmark	66.4 miles
Mall	71.4 miles

   F. Mall

   G. Theater

   H. Historical landmark

   (J) Baseball stadium

7. Rusty has $25.45 in the bank and $16.18 in his wallet. He wants to purchase a sweater that costs $49.99. How much more money does he need?

   A. $41.63 C. $24.54

   B. $33.81 (D) $8.36

8. Josie has $24\frac{1}{2}$ pounds of birdseed. She puts $1\frac{3}{4}$ pounds of seed in her feeders each day. How many days will she be able to fill her feeders?

   F. $10\frac{1}{2}$ days H. 16 days

   (G) 14 days J. $18\frac{1}{2}$ days

9. Which of the following quotients has the greatest value?

   A. $0.075 \div 6$ C. $0.75 \div 0.06$

   (B) $7.5 \div 0.006$ D. $0.75 \div 0.6$

Unit 1   33   Test Prep

---

10. For a soccer clinic, 15 coaches and 35 players will be split into groups. Each group must have the same number of players and the same number of coaches. At most, how many groups can there be?

    F. 3 groups H. 7 groups

    (G) 5 groups J. 15 groups

11. Two cruise ships set sail from Florida on the same day. One makes a round trip every 12 days, and the other makes a round trip every 16 days. In how many days will both cruise ships be in Florida again?

    A. 32 days (C) 48 days

    B. 40 days D. 192 days

FREE RESPONSE

12. You deposited $45.25 in your checking account, but instead of adding $45.25 to your balance, the bank accidentally subtracted $45.25. How much money should the bank add to your account to correct the mistake? Explain.

    $90.50; Add $45.25 twice, once for the

    accidental subtraction and once for

    the actual deposit.

13. Is the quotient $4.5 \div 0.9$ greater or less than 4.5? Why?

    Greater than; when the divisor is

    less than 1, the quotient is

    greater than the dividend.

14. The greatest common factor of 18 and a mystery number is 6. Give three possible values for the mystery number.

    6, 12, 24

15. Apples cost $1.29 per pound. How much would a bag of apples weighing 4.7 pounds cost? (Round your answer to the nearest cent.)

    $6.06

16. A bridge is 21.6 kilometers long. A nearby tunnel is 2.3 times as long as the bridge. How long is the tunnel?

    49.68 kilometers

17. Explain how to draw a model to find the quotient of $2.4 \div 3$. What is this quotient?

    Use 3 decimal grids divided into

    tenths. Shade 2 whole grids and

    4 tenths of the 3rd grid. Divide the

    shaded sections into 3 equal

    groups to show that $2.4 \div 3 = 0.8$.

18. What is the least number that has both 6 and 10 as factors?

    30

19. Tyler has a piece of ribbon that is $\frac{3}{4}$ yard long. How many $\frac{1}{8}$-yard pieces can he cut? Draw and label a diagram to support your answer.

    6 pieces

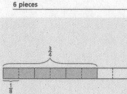

Unit 1   34   Test Prep

UNIT 2

The Number System: Positive and Negative Numbers

Unit Vocabulary

absolute value	(2-3)
axis	(2-4)
coordinate plane	(2-4)
coordinates	(2-4)
inequality	(2-2)
integers	(2-1)
negative numbers	(2-1)
opposites	(2-1)
ordered pair	(2-4)
origin	(2-4)
positive numbers	(2-1)
quadrant	(2-4)
x-axis	(2-4)
x-coordinate	(2-4)
y-axis	(2-4)
y-coordinate	(2-4)

UNIT 2

UNIT 2

The Number System: Positive and Negative Numbers

Unit Focus

You have learned that integers are the set of whole numbers and their opposites. In this unit, you will learn more about integers as well as other positive and negative rational numbers. You will learn real-world applications of positive and negative numbers, such as temperatures above and below 0. You will compare and order positive and negative numbers, and you will learn about opposites and absolute value. Finally, you will learn about the coordinate plane and how to find the distance between two points in the coordinate plane.

COMMON CORE

Unit at a Glance

Lesson		Standards for Mathematical Content
2-1	The Number Line	CC.6.NS.5, CC.6.NS.6a, CC.6.NS.6c
2-2	Comparing and Ordering Numbers	CC.6.NS.7a, CC.6.NS.7b
2-3	Absolute Value	CC.6.NS.7c, CC.6.NS.7d
2-4	The Coordinate Plane	CC.6.NS.6b, CC.6.NS.6c, CC.6.NS.8
2-5	Distance in the Coordinate Plane	CC.6.NS.8
	Problem Solving Connections	
	Test Prep	

UNIT 2

Unit 2   **35** The Number System: Positive and Negative Numbers

© Houghton Mifflin Harcourt Publishing Company

Unpacking the Common Core State Standards

Use the table to help you understand the Standards for Mathematical Content that are taught in this unit. Refer to the lessons listed after each standard for exploration and practice.

COMMON CORE Standards for Mathematical Content	What It Means For You
CC.6.NS.5 Understand that positive and negative numbers are used together to describe quantities having opposite directions or values; use positive and negative numbers...in real-world contexts... Lesson 2-1	You will represent positive and negative numbers on a number line and use them to describe situations in the real world, such as temperatures above and below 0.
CC.6.NS.6a Recognize opposite signs of numbers as indicating locations on opposite sides of 0 on the number line; recognize that the opposite of the opposite of a number is the number itself... Lesson 2-1	You will learn that numbers with opposite signs (+ and −) are located on opposite sides of 0 on the number line. You will identify the opposite of a number.
CC.6.NS.6b Understand signs of numbers in ordered pairs as indicating quadrants of the coordinate plane... Lesson 2-4	You will learn to graph ordered pairs of positive and negative numbers on the coordinate plane and identify the quadrant in which a point is located.
CC.6.NS.6c Find and position...rational numbers on a ...number line diagram; find and position pairs of ...rational numbers on a coordinate plane. Lessons 2-1, 2-4	You will use a number line to order a set of positive and negative numbers. You will graph an ordered pair of rational numbers in a coordinate plane.
CC.6.NS.7a Interpret statements of inequality as statements about the relative position of two numbers on a number line. Lesson 2-2	You will learn the relative positions on a number line of two unequal numbers. You will also learn how to write a statement of inequality.
CC.6.NS.7b Write, interpret, and explain statements of order for rational numbers in real-world contexts. Lesson 2-2	You will use your knowledge of rational numbers to describe and explain real-world situations.
CC.6.NS.7c Understand absolute value of a rational number as its distance from 0 on the number line... Lesson 2-3	You will learn that absolute value is a distance on the number line. You will apply absolute value to real-world situations.
CC.6.NS.8 Solve...problems by graphing points in all four quadrants of the coordinate plane. Lesson 2-4	You will graph points on the coordinate plane to solve real-world and mathematical problems.

Unpacking the Common Core State Standards

This page lists and explains the Standards for Mathematical Content that are addressed in this unit. For information about the Standards for Mathematical Practice, which are integrated throughout the text, see Teacher Edition pages vii–xiii.

Notes

© Houghton Mifflin Harcourt Publishing Company

Essential question: *How are positive and negative numbers represented on a number line?*

© Houghton Mifflin Harcourt Publishing Company

COMMON CORE Standards for Mathematical Content

CC.6.NS.5 Understand that positive and negative numbers are used together to describe quantities having opposite directions or values; use positive and negative numbers to represent quantities in real-world contexts, explaining the meaning of 0 in each situation.

CC.6.NS.6a Recognize opposite signs of numbers as indicating locations on opposite sides of 0 on the number line; recognize that the opposite of the opposite of a number is the number itself and that 0 is its own opposite.

CC.6.NS.6c Find and position integers and other rational numbers on a horizontal number line diagram.

Vocabulary

positive numbers
negative numbers
opposites
integers

Prerequisites

Graphing numbers on a number line
Ordering numbers

Math Background

Positive numbers consist of any number on the right side zero on the number line. Each positive number has an opposite, a corresponding negative number that is the same distance away from zero on the left side of zero. Negative numbers are always written with a negative sign, such as −3. Positive numbers may be written with a plus sign (+3) or without a plus sign (3). The opposite of any positive number is negative, and the opposite of any negative number is positive. The sum of a number and its opposite is zero, which is neither positive nor negative.

INTRODUCE

Connect to prior learning by asking students whether they have ever experienced temperatures below zero. Ask them whether they can think of other real-world situations involving positive and negative numbers, such as altitude (above or below sea level) and financial information (having or owing money).

TEACH

1 EXPLORE

Questioning Strategies

- How does plotting numbers on a number line help you put them in order? **On a number line, points are arranged from least to greatest as you read from left to right.**

- On a number line, how do the values change as you move farther left away from zero? **They decrease.**

2 EXPLORE

Questioning Strategies

- How can you tell which temperature is the greatest? **It is the one at the farthest right on the number line.**

- On the number line, what numbers are opposites? **Numbers that are the same distance from zero and on opposite sides of zero on the number line; for example, −7 and 7.**

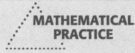

MATHEMATICAL PRACTICE **Highlighting the Standards**

This Explore is an opportunity to address Standard 5 (Use appropriate tools strategically). Students use a number line showing negative and positive numbers to understand measures in a real-world context. Using the number line allows students to see the numbers in terms of their relationship to zero and to each other.

CLOSE

Essential Question

How are positive and negative numbers represented on a number line?
Possible answer: Points on the number line left of zero represent negative numbers and points right of zero represent positive numbers.

Name_____ Class_____ Date_____

2-1

COMMON
CORE
CC.6.NS.5
CC.6.NS.6a
CC.6.NS.6c

The Number Line

Essential question: *How are positive and negative numbers represented on a number line?*

Positive numbers are numbers greater than 0. They are located to the right of 0 on a number line. Positive numbers can be written with or without a plus sign; for example, 3 is the same as +3.

Negative numbers are numbers less than 0. They are located to the left of 0 on the number line. Negative numbers must always be written with a negative sign.

The number 0 is neither positive nor negative.

1 EXPLORE Positive and Negative Numbers

The elevation of a location describes its height above or below sea level, which has elevation 0. Elevations below sea level are represented by negative numbers, and elevations above sea level are represented by positive numbers.

A The table shows the elevations of several locations in a state park. Graph the locations on the number line according to their elevations.

Location	Little Butte A	Cradle Creek B	Dinosaur Valley C	Mesa Ridge D	Juniper Trail E
Elevation (ft)	5	−5	−8.5	8	−3

B What point on the number line represents sea level? _____0_____

C Which location is closest to sea level? How do you know?

Juniper Trail; its elev. is closest to 0 on the number line.

D Is the location in C above or below sea level? _____below_____

E Which two locations are the same distance from sea level? Are these locations above or below sea level?

Little Butte (above) and Cradle Creek (below)

F Which location has the least elevation? How do you know?

Dinosaur Valley; its elev. is farthest left on the number line.

Unit 2   37   Lesson 1

TRY THIS!

1. The table shows winter temperatures of several world cities. Graph the cities on the number line according to their temperatures.

City	Anchorage, AK, USA F	Fargo, ND, USA G	Oslo, Norway H	St. Petersburg, Russia I	Helsinki, Finland J	Budapest, Hungary K
Temperature (°F)	−4	9	−6	−10	7	6

Two numbers are **opposites** if, on a number line, they are the same distance from 0 but on different sides of 0. For example, 5 and −5 are opposites; 2.15 and −2.15 are also opposites. 0 is its own opposite.

Integers are the set of all whole numbers and their opposites.

2 EXPLORE Opposites

On graph paper, use a ruler or straightedge to draw a number line. Label the number line with each integer from −10 to 10. Fold your number line in half so that the crease goes through 0. Numbers that line up after folding the number line are opposites.

A Use your number line to find the opposites of 7, −4, 1, and 9. −7; 4; −1; −9

B How does your number line show that 0 is its own opposite?

The crease goes through 0, so 0 lines up with itself.

C What is the opposite of 8.5? −8.5

D What is the opposite of the opposite of 3? 3

TRY THIS!

2a. Graph and label the following points on the number line.

A. −2   **B.** 9.5   **C.** −8   **D.** −9.5   **E.** 5   **F.** 8

2b. Which points represent integers? A, C, E, and F

2c. Which pairs of points represent opposites? B and D; C and F

Unit 2   38   Lesson 1

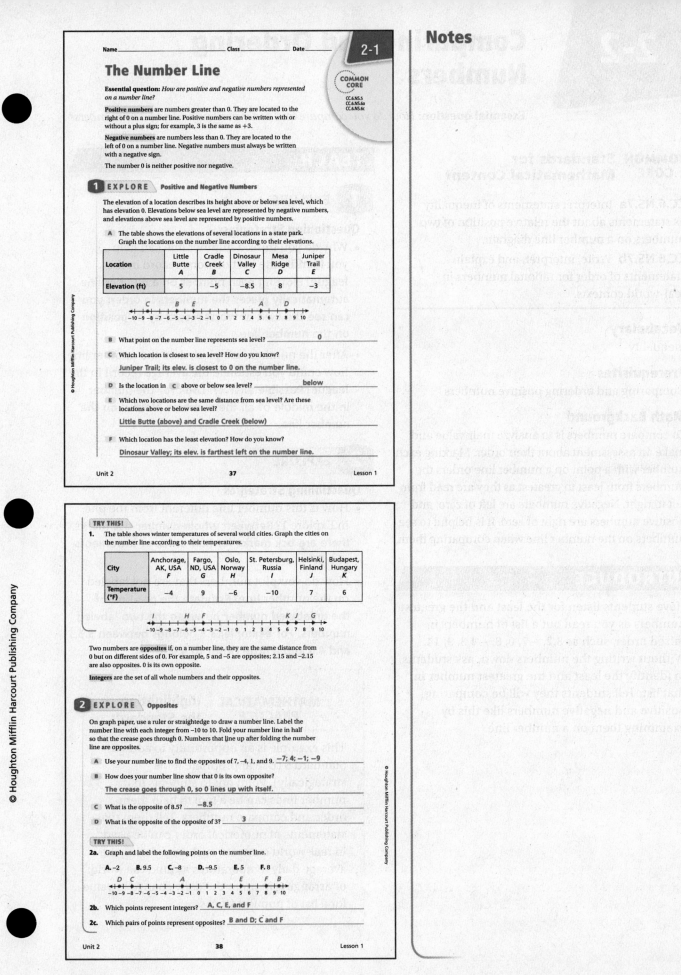

Comparing and Ordering Numbers

Essential question: *How do you compare and order positive and negative numbers?*

COMMON CORE Standards for Mathematical Content

CC.6.NS.7a Interpret statements of inequality as statements about the relative position of two numbers on a number line diagram.

CC.6.NS.7b Write, interpret, and explain statements of order for rational numbers in real-world contexts.

Vocabulary
inequality

Prerequisites
Comparing and ordering positive numbers

Math Background
To compare numbers is to analyze their value and make an assessment about their order. Marking each number with a point on a number line orders the numbers from least to greatest as they are read from left to right. Negative numbers are left of zero, and positive numbers are right of zero. It is helpful to see numbers on the number line when comparing them.

INTRODUCE

Have students listen for the least and the greatest numbers as you read out a list of numbers in mixed order, such as 3.2, −7, 0, 8, −4.3, 9, 14. Without writing the numbers down, ask students to identify the least and the greatest number in that list. Tell students they will be comparing positive and negative numbers like this by examining them on a number line.

TEACH

1 EXPLORE

Questioning Strategies
- Why do you think a number line can help you identify the best or worst record in the league? **Plotting each number on a number line automatically places the numbers in order; you can see the best or worst record by its position on the number line.**

- After the numbers are plotted on the number line, how could you estimate the average record in the league? **Possible answer: Look for the number in the middle of all the numbers plotted on the number line.**

2 EXPLORE

Questioning Strategies
- How is this number line different from the one in Explore 1? **Between whole-number tick marks, there are tick marks for half-units, or increments of 0.5.**

- How do you plot numbers that are not labeled on the number line? **Estimate the position of the unlabeled number between the two labeled numbers. For example, 3.8 belongs between 3.5 and 4.0 and a little closer to 4.0.**

> **MATHEMATICAL PRACTICE**
> **Highlighting the Standards**
>
> This example is an opportunity to address Standard 5 (Use appropriate tools strategically). Point out to students that number lines can be a tool to help them order and compare numbers. Tell them that statements of numerical order can be used in real-world contexts, such as ordering the average daily temperatures around the world, or arranging in order the daily change in value for a list of popular stocks.

© Houghton Mifflin Harcourt Publishing Company

Name_____ Class_____ Date_____

2-2

Comparing and Ordering Numbers

COMMON CORE
CC.6.NS.7a
CC.6.NS.7b

Essential question: *How do you compare and order positive and negative numbers?*

1 EXPLORE Comparing Positive and Negative Integers

The Westfield soccer league ranks its teams using a number called the "win/loss combined record." A team with more wins than losses will have a positive combined record, and a team with fewer wins than losses will have a negative combined record. The table shows the total win/loss combined record for each team at the end of the season.

Team	Sharks A	Jaguars B	Badgers C	Tigers D	Cougars E	Hawks F	Wolves G
Win/Loss Combined Record	−4	3	−7	−8	−1	−5	7

A On the number line, graph a point for each team according to its win/loss combined record.

B Which team had the best record in the league? How do you know?

Wolves; their record is farthest right on the number line.

C Which team had the worst record? How do you know?

Tigers; their record is farthest left on the number line.

REFLECT

1. How would you evaluate the Westfield league as a whole? Explain.

Sample answer: The league's teams are not very successful. Five of the

seven teams have neg. win/loss records, which means they lost more

games than they won.

© Houghton Mifflin Harcourt Publishing Company

When you read a number line from left to right, the numbers are in order from least to greatest.

2 EXPLORE Ordering Rational Numbers

Graph the following rational numbers on the number line:

1.6   3.8   4.9   2.0   5.3   −1.2

To list the numbers in order from least to greatest, read the numbers on the number line from left to right.

−1.2, 1.6, 2.0, 3.8, 4.9, 5.3

A Which number is third least? _____ 2.0

B Which number is second greatest? _____ 4.9

TRY THIS!

Graph each set of numbers on a number line. Then list the numbers in order from least to greatest.

2a. 5.6   −8   3.1   −4   7   −2

−8, −4, −2, 3.1, 5.6, 7

2b. −14   12   −7   11   18   −2   1   5   −8

−14, −8, −7, −2, 1, 5, 11, 12, 18

REFLECT

2c. In a given list of numbers, the greatest number is negative. What can you say about the numbers in this list?

They are all negative.

An **inequality** is a statement that two quantities are not equal. The symbols < and > are used to write inequalities.

• The symbol > means "is greater than."
• The symbol < means "is less than."

You can use a number line to help write an inequality.

© Houghton Mifflin Harcourt Publishing Company

Questioning Strategies

• How can you tell which number is greater by looking at the number line? **The number to the right of the other is the greater number.**

• What symbol is used to compare two numbers that are written in increasing order from left to right? **<**

• What symbol is used to compare two numbers that are written in decreasing order from left to right? **>**

Teaching Strategies

Students can practice comparing numbers without a number line by visualizing them on a number line. For example, ask: *Would −123 be to the left of −74?* Have students challenge one another to tell whether a number should go to the left or right of another number on the number line.

Avoid Common Errors

Students sometimes get the inequality symbols confused. Some students find it helpful to think of the inequality symbols as arrows. The point of the arrow (the smallest part) always points at the lesser number, and the opening (the largest part) always faces the greater number. Have students get used to reading the symbols aloud.

Essential Question

How do you compare and order positive and negative numbers?

Possible answer: To compare numbers, consider their positions on a number line, which orders numbers from left (least) to right (greatest).

Summarize

Have students order a given list of numbers, such as 3.2, −5, −2.1, 1, and 2.1 on a number line. Have them write at least five inequality statements involving the given numbers and practice reading them aloud when checking their answers.

PRACTICE

Where skills are taught	Where skills are practiced
1 EXPLORE	EX. 1
2 EXPLORE	EXS. 2–5
3 EXAMPLE	EXS. 6–18

3 EXAMPLE Writing Inequalities

On December 18, the high temperature in Portland, Oregon, was 42 °F.
On January 18, the high temperature was 28 °F. Which day was warmer?

Graph 42 and 28 on the number line.

25 26 27 28 29 30 31 32 33 34 35 36 37 38 39 40 41 42 43 44 45

A 42 is to the right of 28 on the number line.

This means that 42 is ~~greater than~~ / less than 28.

Use < or > to complete the inequality: 42 $>$ 28.

B 28 is to the left of 42 on the number line.

This means that 28 is greater than / ~~less than~~ 42.

Use < or > to complete the inequality: 28 $<$ 42.

The temperature was warmer on __December 18__.

C In **A** and **B**, you wrote two inequalities to compare 42 and 28.
Write two inequalities to compare −6 and 7. __−6 < 7; 7 > −6__

D Write two inequalities to compare −9 and −4. __−4 > −9; −9 < −4__

TRY THIS!
Compare. Write > or <. Use the number line to help you, if necessary.

3a. −10 $<$ −2   **3b.** −6 $<$ 6   **3c.** −7.1 $>$ −8.3

−10 −9 −8 −7 −6 −5 −4 −3 −2 −1 0 1 2 3 4 5 6 7 8 9 10

3d. Write two inequalities to compare −2 and −18. __−2 > −18; −18 < −2__

3e. Write two inequalities to compare 39 and −39. __−39 < 39; 39 > −39__

REFLECT

3f. Negative numbers are __less__ than positive numbers.

3g. 0 is __greater__ than all negative numbers.

3h. What is the greatest negative integer? __−1__

3i. Is there a greatest positive integer? If so, what is it? If not, why not?

__No; for any positive integer, you can find greater positive integers to the__
__right of it on the number line.__

3j. What is the least nonnegative number? __0__

Unit 2   41   Lesson 2

PRACTICE

1a. On the number line, graph a point for each of the following cities according to their temperatures.

City	A	B	C	D	E
Temperature (°F)	−9	10	−2	0	4

A   C   D   E   B
−10 −9 −8 −7 −6 −5 −4 −3 −2 −1 0 1 2 3 4 5 6 7 8 9 10

b. Which city was coldest? __A__

c. Which city was warmest? __B__

List the numbers in order from least to greatest.

2. 4, −6, 0, 8, −9, 1, −3

__−9, −6, −3, 0, 1, 4, 8__

3. 31, 5, 7, −0.1, 1, 1.5, −9

__−9, −0.1, 1, 1.5, 5, 7, 31__

4. −80, 88, 96, −14, 75, 59, −32

__−80, −32, −14, 59, 75, 88, 96__

5. −65, 34, 7.6, −13, 55, 62.5, −7.6

__−65, −13, −7.6, 7.6, 34, 55, 62.5__

6. Write two inequalities to compare −17 and −22. __−17 > −22; −22 < −17__

7. Write two inequalities to compare 16 and −2. __16 > −2; −2 < 16__

Compare. Write < or >.

8. 9 $<$ 2   **9.** 0 $<$ 6   **10.** 3 $>$ −7   **11.** 5 $>$ −10

12. −1 $>$ −3   **13.** −8 $<$ −4   **14.** −4.5 $<$ 1   **15.** −2 $>$ −2.5

16. Which costs more, a fruit cup or veggies and dip? Use the given prices to write an inequality that shows your answer.

__veggies and dip; 2.86 > 2.49 or 2.49 < 2.86__

Fruit cup	$2.49
Veggies and dip	$2.86
Yogurt	$1.97
Fruit smoothie	$3.83
Pretzels	$1.71

17. Which costs less, pretzels or yogurt? Use the given prices to write an inequality that shows your answer.

__pretzels; 1.71 < 1.97 or 1.97 > 1.71__

18. **Error Analysis** At 9:00 P.M., the outside temperature was −3 °F. The newscaster says that the temperature will be −12 °F by midnight. Bethany says, "It will be warmer outside by midnight." Why is Bethany incorrect?

__−12 < −3, so it will be colder.__

Unit 2   42   Lesson 2

Absolute Value

Essential question: *How do you find and use absolute value?*

© Houghton Mifflin Harcourt Publishing Company

COMMON CORE **Standards for Mathematical Content**

CC.6.NS.7c Understand absolute value of a rational number as its distance from 0 on the number line; interpret absolute value as the magnitude for a positive or negative quantity in a real-world situation.

CC.6.NS.7d Distinguish comparisons of absolute value from statements about order.

Vocabulary

absolute value

Prerequisites

Opposites

Graphing positive and negative numbers

Math Background

The absolute value of a number is its distance from zero on the number line. Absolute value is always expressed as a nonnegative number. The absolute value of 7 is 7. The absolute value of −7 is also 7. Zero is the only number whose absolute value is zero. Absolute value is sometimes known as *magnitude*. Magnitude is useful when you need to express the amount of change rather than the direction of change.

INTRODUCE

Ask students to estimate how far a car travels when it backs out of a driveway. Explain to students that they are describing a distance. Absolute value is a distance; it does not express direction, such as positive or negative. Tell students they will practice finding and using absolute value in this lesson.

TEACH

1 EXPLORE

Questioning Strategies

• How can you find the absolute value of a number plotted on a number line? **Find or count the number of units it is from zero.**

• Can two different numbers have the same absolute value? **Yes, opposites have the same absolute value.**

2 EXPLORE

Questioning Strategies

• Does a negative balance indicate money gained or money owed? **money owed**

• How can you tell which person owes the most money? **The number will be negative and have the greatest absolute value.**

> **MATHEMATICAL PRACTICE** **Highlighting the Standards**
>
> This Explore is an opportunity to address Standard 2 (Reason abstractly and quantitatively). This Explore requires mathematical reasoning. Comparing positive and negative numbers requires thinking in terms of the numbers' magnitudes, or absolute values, and the signs together.

CLOSE

Essential Question

How do you find and use absolute value?
Find its distance from zero on the number line. Absolute value is always expressed as a nonnegative number.

Summarize

Have students write in their journals a definition of absolute value in their own words. Have students include an example of using absolute value in a real-world situation.

Name_____ Class_____ Date_____

Absolute Value

COMMON CORE
CC.6.NS.7c
CC.6.NS.7d

Essential question: *How do you find and use absolute value?*

The **absolute value** of a number is the number's distance from 0 on the number line. For example, the absolute value of −3 is 3 because −3 is 3 units from 0. The absolute value of −3 is written |−3|.

3 units

-5 -4 -3 -2 -1 0 1 2 3

|−3| = 3

Because absolute value represents a distance, it is always nonnegative.

1 EXPLORE Finding Absolute Value

Graph the following numbers on the number line. Then use your number line to find each absolute value.

−7   5   7   −2   4   −4

-10 -9 -8 -7 -6 -5 -4 -3 -2 -1 0 1 2 3 4 5 6 7 8 9 10

A |−7| = __7__   B |5| = __5__   C |7| = __7__

D |−2| = __2__   E |4| = __4__   F |−4| = __4__

REFLECT

1a. Which pairs of numbers have the same absolute value? How are these numbers related?

__−7 and 7; 4 and −4; they are opposites.__

1b. Do you think a number's absolute value can be 0? If so, which number(s) have an absolute value of 0? If not, explain.

__Yes; |0| = 0 because the distance between 0 and 0 is 0.__

1c. If a number is __nonnegative__, then the number is equal to its absolute value. If a number is __negative__, then the number is less than its absolute value.

© Houghton Mifflin Harcourt Publishing Company

1d. Negative numbers are less than positive numbers. Does this mean that the absolute value of a negative number must be less than the absolute value of a positive number? Explain.

__No; sample answer: −7 < 3 but |−7| > |3|. This is because the distance__

__from −7 to 0 is greater than the distance from 3 to 0.__

In real-world situations, absolute values are often used instead of negative numbers. For example, if Susan charges a total of $25 on her credit card, we can say that Susan has a balance of −$25. However, we usually say that Susan owes $25.

2 EXPLORE Comparing Absolute Values

Maria, Susan, George, and Antonio received their credit card statements. The amounts owed are shown.

| You owe: $20 | You owe: $25 | You owe: $30 | You owe: $45 |
| Susan | George | Antonio | Maria |

Answer the following questions. When you have finished, you will have enough clues to match each statement with the correct person.

Remember: When someone owes a positive amount of money, this means that he or she has a *negative* balance.

A Maria's credit card balance is less than −$30. Does Maria owe more than $30 or less than $30? __more than $30__

B Susan's credit card balance is greater than −$25. Does Susan owe more than $25 or less than $25? __less than $25__

C George's credit card balance is $5 less than Susan's balance. Does George owe more than Susan or less than Susan? __more than Susan__

D Antonio owes $15 less than Maria owes. This means that Antonio's balance is __greater__ than Maria's balance.

E Write each person's name underneath his or her credit card statement.

REFLECT

2. Use absolute value to describe the relationship between a negative credit card balance and the amount owed.

__The amount owed is the absolute value of the balance.__

© Houghton Mifflin Harcourt Publishing Company

The Coordinate Plane

Essential question: *How do you locate and name points in the coordinate plane?*

© Houghton Mifflin Harcourt Publishing Company

COMMON CORE Standards for Mathematical Content

CC.6.NS.6b Understand signs of numbers in ordered pairs as indicating locations in quadrants of the coordinate plane; recognize that when two ordered pairs differ only by signs, the locations of the points are related by reflections across one or both axes.

CC.6.NS.6c Find and position pairs of integers and other rational numbers on a coordinate plane.

CC.6.NS.8 Solve real-world and mathematical problems by graphing points in all four quadrants of the coordinate plane.

Vocabulary

coordinate plane

axis

x-axis

y-axis

origin

quadrant

ordered pair

coordinates

x-coordinate

y-coordinate

Prerequisites

Plotting points in the first quadrant

Math Background

Coordinates are pairs of numbers used to locate a point on the coordinate plane. The coordinate plane is a numbered two-dimensional grid. A horizontal line called the *x*-axis runs across the grid intersecting with a vertical line called the *y*-axis. The axes divide the coordinate plane into quadrants. The axes meet at a point called the origin, which is the zero point on both axes. The *x*-axis is numbered with negative numbers on the left and positive numbers on the right of the origin. The *y*-axis is numbered with negative numbers below and positive numbers above the origin.

INTRODUCE

Begin with a display of a coordinate plane with a few points located in the first quadrant only. Discuss with students how to describe the locations of these points. Tell students that in this lesson they will learn how to describe the location of any point in the coordinate plane.

TEACH

1 EXAMPLE

Questioning Strategies

- Which quadrant in the coordinate plane contains points with only positve-number coordinates? **Quadrant I**

- Which quadrant in the coordinate plane contains points with only negative-number coordinates? **Quadrant III**

- What does the first number in a coordinate pair indicate? **position along the *x*-axis**

Differentiated Learning

Students often have success when working in cooperative groups. Allow students to practice getting familiar with negative numbers in the coordinate plane by playing a game. Have teams race to categorize a list of coordinate pairs by the quadrants in which they lie in the coordinate plane.

Name_____ Class_____ Date_____

2-4

The Coordinate Plane

COMMON CORE
CC.6.NS.6b
CC.6.NS.6c
CC.6.NS.8

Essential question: *How do you locate and name points in the coordinate plane?*

A **coordinate plane** is formed by two number lines that intersect at right angles. The point of intersection is the 0 on each number line.

- The two number lines are called the **axes**.
- The horizontal axis is called the **x-axis**.
- The vertical axis is called the **y-axis**.
- The point where the axes intersect is called the **origin**.
- The two axes divide the coordinate plane into four **quadrants**.

An **ordered pair** is a pair of numbers that gives the location of a point on a coordinate plane. The first number tells how far to the right (positive) or left (negative) the point is located from the origin. The second number tells how far up (positive) or down (negative) the point is located from the origin.

The numbers in an ordered pair are called **coordinates**. The first number is the **x-coordinate** and the second number is the **y-coordinate**.

1 EXAMPLE   Identifying Coordinates and Quadrants

Identify the coordinates of point *D* and name the quadrant where the point is located.

Step 1 Start at the origin. Count horizontally along the *x*-axis until you are directly above point *D*.

How many units did you count? _____1_____

Did you move left (negative) or right (positive) from the origin? _____left_____

The *x*-coordinate of *D* is _____−1_____

Step 2 Now count vertically until you reach point *D*.

How many units did you count? _____3_____

Did you move up (positive) or down (negative)? _____down_____

The *y*-coordinate of *D* is _____−3_____

The coordinates of *D* are (−1 , −3).

D is in Quadrant III .

© Houghton Mifflin Harcourt Publishing Company

Unit 2   45   Lesson 4

TRY THIS!

Identify the coordinates of each point in the coordinate plane and name the quadrant where each point is located.

1a. *A* (4, −4); IV   **1b.** *B* (2, 3); I

REFLECT

1c. If both coordinates of a point are negative, in which quadrant is the point located? _____III_____

1d. Describe the coordinates of all points in Quadrant I.

_____Both coordinates are positive._____

Points that are located on the axes are not located in any quadrant. Points on the *x*-axis have a *y*-coordinate of 0, and points on the *y*-axis have an *x*-coordinate of 0.

2 EXAMPLE   Graphing Points on the Coordinate Plane

Leonardo and Christie walk to school each morning. They pass a post office, a coffee shop, and a church on the way. After school, they often study at the library or meet friends at an arcade before walking home.

The coordinate plane represents a map of Leonardo and Christie's town. The post office is located at (0, 3). Graph and label this location on the coordinate plane.

Start at the origin.

The first coordinate of the ordered pair tells how many units to move left or right. How many units will you move?

_____0_____

The second coordinate of the ordered pair tells how many units to move up or down. How many units will you move? _____3_____

Will you move up or down? How do you know? _____Up; the second coordinate is positive._____

The point that represents the post office is located on the _____y-axis_____

TRY THIS!

Graph and label each location on the coordinate plane.

2a. Home: (−4, 2)   **2b.** Coffee shop: (3, 2)   **2c.** Church: (5, −2)

2d. School: (4, −5)   **2e.** Library: (−4, −5)   **2f.** Arcade: (−2, 0)

REFLECT

2g. What are the coordinates of the origin? _____(0, 0)_____

© Houghton Mifflin Harcourt Publishing Company

Unit 2   46   Lesson 4

Questioning Strategies

- What is the ordered pair for the library? How does it describe the path from the origin to the library? **(−4, −5); move along the *x*-axis in a negative direction (left) for 4 units. Then, move vertically in the negative direction (down) 5 units.**

- What is the ordered pair for the school? How does it describe the path from the origin to the school? **(4, −5); move along the *x*-axis in a positive direction (right) for 4 units. Then, move vertically in the negative direction (down) 5 units.**

- How are the locations of the library and the school alike? How are they different? **Both are 4 horizontal units and 5 vertical units away from the origin. The library is located in the negative horizontal direction from the origin, but the school is located in the positive horizontal direction from the origin.**

> ⟋⟋⟋⟋ **MATHEMATICAL** **Highlighting**
> **PRACTICE** **the Standards**
>
> This Example is an opportunity to address Standard 7 (Look for and make use of structure). The coordinate plane provides a structure upon which students can explore the integration of positive and negative numbers. Students must learn to follow the conventional naming system when naming and locating ordered pairs.

3 EXPLORE

Questioning Strategies

- How can you find the coordinates of a point after a reflection across the *x*-axis? **Use the *x*-coordinate of the original point and the opposite of the *y*-coordinate of the original point.**

- How can you find the coordinates of a point after a reflection across the *y*-axis? **Use the opposite of the *x*-coordinate of the original point and the *y*-coordinate of the original point.**

CLOSE

Essential Question

How do you locate and name points in the coordinate plane?
Points in the coordinate plane are located and named by their locations from the origin along the *x*-axis first, followed by the *y*-axis. The order of the coordinates is important; hence, the name "ordered pair."

Summarize

Have students work together to make and label a coordinate plane. Students then take turns writing ordered pairs and plotting them on the coordinate plane.

PRACTICE

Where skills are taught	Where skills are practiced
1 EXAMPLE	EXS. 1–6, 11–13b
2 EXAMPLE	EXS. 7–10, 13a

3 EXPLORE Reflections in the Coordinate Plane

Draw a coordinate plane on graph paper. Label both axes from −10 to 10.

A Graph (3, −2). Then fold your coordinate plane along the y-axis and find the reflection of (3, −2). (Hold the paper up to the light if necessary.)

When (3, −2) is reflected across the y-axis, the coordinates of the new

point are (−3 , −2).

B Unfold your coordinate plane. Then fold it along the x-axis and find the reflection of (3, −2).

When (3, −2) is reflected across the x-axis, the coordinates of the new

point are (3 , 2).

C Choose four additional points and repeat the steps in **A** and **B**. Sample answers given.

Point	Reflected across y-axis	Reflected across x-axis
(3, 5)	(−3, 5)	(3, −5)
(−2, 6)	(2, 6)	(−2, −6)
(−3, 8)	(3, 8)	(−3, −8)
(7, −3)	(−7, −3)	(7, 3)

REFLECT

3a. What is the relationship between the coordinates of a point and the coordinates of its reflection across each axis?

across y-axis: opposite x-coord. and same y-coord. as the orig. point;

across x-axis: same x-coord. and opposite y-coord. as the orig. point

3b. A point in Quadrant II is reflected across the x-axis. The new point is located in Quadrant ___III___.

3c. A point in Quadrant ___I___ is reflected across the y-axis. The new point is located in Quadrant II.

3d. **Conjecture** A point is reflected across the y-axis. Then the reflected point is reflected across the x-axis. How will the coordinates of the final point be related to the coordinates of the original point?

Both coordinates will be the opposites of the coordinates of the original point.

Unit 2   47   Lesson 4

© Houghton Mifflin Harcourt Publishing Company

PRACTICE

Use the coordinate plane for 1–10.

Identify the coordinates of each point and name the quadrant in which it is located.

1. A (3, 3); I   **2.** B (2, 5); I

3. C (2, −2); IV   **4.** D (−4, −2); III

5. E (0, 1); none   **6.** F (−3, 0); none

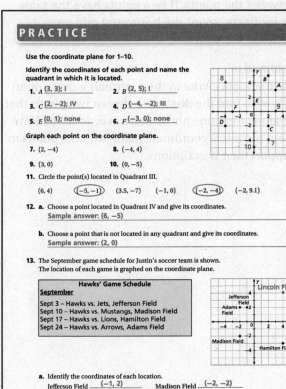

Graph each point on the coordinate plane.

7. (2, −4)   **8.** (−4, 4)

9. (3, 0)   **10.** (0, −5)

11. Circle the point(s) located in Quadrant III.

(6, 4)   (−5, −1)   (3.5, −7)   (−1, 0)   (−2, −4)   (−2, 9.1)

12. a. Choose a point located in Quadrant IV and give its coordinates.
Sample answer: (6, −5)

b. Choose a point that is not located in any quadrant and give its coordinates.
Sample answer: (2, 0)

13. The September game schedule for Justin's soccer team is shown. The location of each game is graphed on the coordinate plane.

Hawks' Game Schedule
September
Sept 3 – Hawks vs. Jets, Jefferson Field
Sept 10 – Hawks vs. Mustangs, Madison Field
Sept 17 – Hawks vs. Lions, Hamilton Field
Sept 24 – Hawks vs. Arrows, Adams Field

a. Identify the coordinates of each location.
Jefferson Field ___(−1, 2)___   Madison Field ___(−2, −2)___
Hamilton Field ___(4, −3)___   Adams Field ___(−2, 2)___

b. On October 1, the team has a game scheduled at Lincoln Field. The coordinates for Lincoln Field are (4, 4). Graph and label this point on the coordinate plane. What quadrant is Lincoln Field located in? ___I___

Unit 2   48   Lesson 4

© Houghton Mifflin Harcourt Publishing Company

Distance in the Coordinate Plane

Essential question: How do you find the distance between two points in the coordinate plane?

COMMON CORE **Standards for Mathematical Content**

CC.6.NS.8 Include use of coordinates and absolute value to find distances between points with the same first coordinate or the same second coordinate.

Prerequisites

Graphing points in the coordinate plane

Math Background

Most students have not learned integer operations yet, so in this lesson, students will use grid units to count horizontal and vertical distances. In future grades, when students are familiar with integer operations, they will be able to calculate distances without counting grid units.

INTRODUCE

Display a number line for the students and ask them to count to find distances between two points on opposite sides of zero. After students find a few distances tell them they will learn how to find distances in the coordinate plane.

TEACH

1 EXPLORE

Questioning Strategies

- What do points *C* and *D* have in common? **Both are located 2 units below the *x*-axis.**

- What do points *B* and *C* have in common? **Both are located on 4 units left of the *y*-axis.**

- What relationship must two points share in order to find their distance apart by counting units? **Points must have one of the coordinates in common so that it is a either a vertical or horizontal distance that is counted.**

2 EXPLORE

Questioning Strategies

- What coordinate do points *M* and *N* have in common? **They both have a *y*-coordinate of 1.**

Teaching Strategies

If students get confused working in the coordinate plane, show them the same distance problem on a number line. Then, have them complete the problem in the coordinate plane.

CLOSE

Essential Question

How do you find the distance between two points in the coordinate plane?
Possible answer: If two points have the same *x*-coordinate, count the vertical grid units between the points. If two points have the same *y*-coordinate, count the horizontal grid units between the points.

Summarize

Have students write in their journals a description of how to find the distance between two points that lie along the same horizontal or vertical line. Have them include a coordinate plane with the points to support their descriptions.

© Houghton Mifflin Harcourt Publishing Company

Name_____ Class_____ Date_____

2-5

Distance in the Coordinate Plane

COMMON CORE
CC.6.NS.8

Essential question: *How do you find the distance between two points in the coordinate plane?*

1 EXPLORE   Distance in the Coordinate Plane

A Graph and label the following points on the coordinate plane.

$A(4, 3)$ $B(-4, 4)$ $C(-4, -2)$ $D(1, -2)$

B Count the number of units between B and C.

The distance between B and C is ___6___ units.

C Count the number of units between C and D.

The distance between C and D is ___5___ units.

TRY THIS!

Use the coordinate plane to answer the following questions.

1a. What are the coordinates of point P? ___(2, 7)___

1b. What are the coordinates of point Q? ___(2, −7)___

1c. What is the distance between P and Q? ___14___ units

1d. What is the distance between $(-4, -4)$ and $(-4, 7)$?
___11___ units

2 EXPLORE   Solving Distance Problems

The coordinate plane represents a map. Each grid unit represents one mile. A retail company has warehouses at $M(-7, 1)$ and $N(5, 1)$. The company also has two stores along the straight road between the two warehouses.

A What is the distance between the warehouses?

12 miles

Each store is the same distance from a warehouse. Also, the distance between the stores is half the distance between the warehouses. The nearest warehouse to store 1 is warehouse M, and the nearest warehouse to store 2 is warehouse N.

B What is the distance between the two stores?

6 miles

C What are the coordinates of store 1's location? Graph and label this point on the map. What is the distance from store 1 to the nearest warehouse?

(−4, 1); 3 miles

D What are the coordinates of store 2's location? Graph and label this point on the map. What is the distance from store 2 to the nearest warehouse?

(2, 1); 3 miles

REFLECT

2. Check that your answers match the information given in the problem.

Is each store the same distance from a warehouse? (Yes) No

Is the distance between the stores half the distance
between the warehouses? (Yes) No

Is warehouse M the nearest warehouse to store 1? (Yes) No

Is warehouse N the nearest warehouse to store 2? (Yes) No

Problem Solving Connections
Treasure Hunt

**Standards for
Mathematical Content**

CC.6.NS.6b Understand signs of numbers in ordered pairs as indicating locations in quadrants in the coordinate plane; recognize that when two ordered pairs differ only by signs, the locations of the points are related by reflections across one or both axes.

CC.6.NS.6c Find and position pairs of integers and other rational numbers on a coordinate plane.

CC.6.NS.7a Interpret statements of inequality as statements about the relative position of two numbers on a number line diagram.

CC.6.NS.7b Write, interpret, and explain statements of order for rational numbers in real-world contexts.

CC.6.NS.8 Solve real-world and mathematical problems by graphing points in all four quadrants of the coordinate plane.

INTRODUCE

Ask students to give examples of when people use maps. Some examples may include maps to specific places, highway maps, maps of the zoo, maps of a mall, and maps of a theme park. Tell students that this project involves treasure hunters who use maps to help them locate a hidden treasure.

TEACH

1 Locations in a Coordinate Plane

Questioning Strategies
- Why do you think Carlos copies the old map onto a coordinate plane? **Possible answer: He uses the grid units to represent steps.**
- How do the positive and negative signs represent north, east, south, and west on Carlos's map? **Positive numbers represent a north or east direction. Negative numbers represent a south or west direction.**

MATHEMATICAL PRACTICE **Highlighting the Standards**

This project provides an opportunity to address Standard 1 (Make sense of problems and persevere in solving them). Students must first understand the problem, and then persist in following clues that lead to the treasure. They may consider using several different strategies to find the treasure. They may need to persevere by trying different approaches with each clue. They must apply their knowledge of positive and negative numbers in the coordinate plane.

2 Distance in a Coordinate Plane

Questioning Strategies
- As Carlos moves from clue to clue on the old map, how does his coordinate plane map help him? **He is able to keep track of the direction he is going in and how far he has traveled so far.**
- How does Carlos calculate the distance in feet that he has traveled? **He estimates the length of his stride to be 3 feet, so he multiplies the number of steps by 3 to find the distance in feet.**

Teaching Strategies
Students may find it helpful to label the coordinate plane axes with North, South, East, and West. If they need help remembering which directions are positive and which are negative, you may suggest that they add positive signs to the labels East and North and add negative signs to the labels West and South.

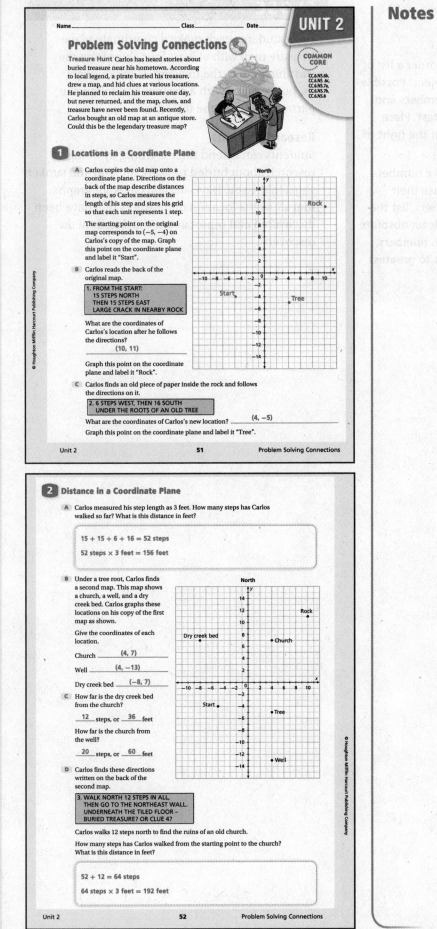

Name_____ Class_____ Date_____

UNIT 2

Problem Solving Connections 🌐

Treasure Hunt Carlos has heard stories about buried treasure near his hometown. According to local legend, a pirate buried his treasure, drew a map, and hid clues at various locations. He planned to reclaim his treasure one day, but never returned, and the map, clues, and treasure have never been found. Recently, Carlos bought an old map at an antique store. Could this be the legendary treasure map?

COMMON CORE
CC.6.NS.6b,
CC.6.NS.6c,
CC.6.NS.7a,
CC.6.NS.7b,
CC.6.NS.8

1 Locations in a Coordinate Plane

A Carlos copies the old map onto a coordinate plane. Directions on the back of the map describe distances in steps, so Carlos measures the length of his step and sizes his grid so that each unit represents 1 step.

The starting point on the original map corresponds to (−5, −4) on Carlos's copy of the map. Graph this point on the coordinate plane and label it "Start".

B Carlos reads the back of the original map.

> 1. FROM THE START:
>   15 STEPS NORTH
>   THEN 15 STEPS EAST
>   LARGE CRACK IN NEARBY ROCK

What are the coordinates of Carlos's location after he follows the directions?

(10, 11)

Graph this point on the coordinate plane and label it "Rock".

C Carlos finds an old piece of paper inside the rock and follows the directions on it.

> 2. 6 STEPS WEST, THEN 16 SOUTH
>   UNDER THE ROOTS OF AN OLD TREE

What are the coordinates of Carlos's new location? _____ (4, −5)

Graph this point on the coordinate plane and label it "Tree".

Unit 2   51   Problem Solving Connections

© Houghton Mifflin Harcourt Publishing Company

2 Distance in a Coordinate Plane

A Carlos measured his step length as 3 feet. How many steps has Carlos walked so far? What is this distance in feet?

> 15 + 15 + 6 + 16 = 52 steps
>
> 52 steps × 3 feet = 156 feet

B Under a tree root, Carlos finds a second map. This map shows a church, a well, and a dry creek bed. Carlos graphs these locations on his copy of the first map as shown.

Give the coordinates of each location.

Church _____ (4, 7)

Well _____ (4, −13)

Dry creek bed _____ (−8, 7)

C How far is the dry creek bed from the church?

_12_ steps, or _36_ feet

How far is the church from the well?

_20_ steps, or _60_ feet

D Carlos finds these directions written on the back of the second map.

> 3. WALK NORTH 12 STEPS IN ALL,
>   THEN GO TO THE NORTHEAST WALL.
>   UNDERNEATH THE TILED FLOOR –
>   BURIED TREASURE? OR CLUE 4?

Carlos walks 12 steps north to find the ruins of an old church.

How many steps has Carlos walked from the starting point to the church? What is this distance in feet?

> 52 + 12 = 64 steps
>
> 64 steps × 3 feet = 192 feet

Unit 2   52   Problem Solving Connections

© Houghton Mifflin Harcourt Publishing Company

3 Comparing and Ordering

Questioning Strategies

- What are the first steps you take to order a list of numbers like those given in the project? **Possible answer: Write only the negative numbers and order those first from least to greatest. Place zero. Write the positive numbers on the right of zero in order from least to greatest.**

- When ordering positive and negative numbers from least to greatest, how do you use their absolute values? **For negative numbers, list the numbers in order from greatest to least absolute value from left to right. For positive numbers, list the numbers in order from least to greatest absolute value from left to right.**

CLOSE

Have students each make a coordinate plane treasure map with at least four clues from the starting point to the treasure. Have students exchange maps with a partner and follow the partner's clues to the treasure.

Research Options

Students can extend their learning by doing research about buried treasure on land and sunken ships in the sea. Have students look for graphs that show the location of treasures that have been discovered and report about the details of the discovery.

E The crafty old pirate has sent Carlos on a long winding route to the old church. Find a shorter path from Carlos's starting point to the church, assuming that Carlos can walk only north, south, east, or west. Draw your path on the coordinate plane.

Describe how to follow your path from the starting point, and find the distance in steps and in feet.

Sample answer: From (−5, −4), walk 9 steps east to (4, −4). Then walk 11 steps north to the church; 20 steps; 60 feet

3 Comparing and Ordering

A The church's roof has collapsed and the tile floor is cracked. Carlos locates the northeast wall and begins to dig. Soon he uncovers an old wooden chest. Has he found the treasure?

Carlos opens the chest and finds... several rocks and another piece of paper.

> 4. CASTLE ISLAND'S *EGHHIST INOPT*
> AT THE TOP, USE YER SCOPE.
> LOOK TO THE SOUTH.
> GO TO THE PLACE YOU SEE
> AND FIND ITS MOUTH.

Carlos knows that Castle Island is nearby, but he does not fully understand the clue. Two of the words are scrambled. Carlos turns the paper over and finds a table:

T	O	N	P	T	H	S	I	G	H	E	I
0	5	10	3	12	−9	−1	8	−6	−4	−2	−7

To unscramble the words, first write the numbers in the table in order from least to greatest.

−9, −7, −6, −4, −2, −1, 0, 3, 5, 8, 10, 12

Now replace each number in your list with the corresponding letter from the table.

The scrambled words are ___HIGHEST POINT___

B When Carlos arrives at Castle Island, he sees this sign.

> WELCOME TO CASTLE ISLAND!
> Bilge Basin, Elev. −6 ft
> ← Buccaneer Beach, Elev. 0 ft
> Galley Ridge, Elev. 509 ft →
> ↖ Pirate's Peak, Elev. 628 ft
> ↙ Polly's Park, Elev. 128 ft

List the locations on the sign in order from the least elevation to the greatest elevation.

Bilge Basin, Buccaneer Beach, Polly's Park, Galley Ridge, Pirate's Peak

The highest point on Castle Island is ___Pirate's Peak___

Its elevation is ___628___ feet.

C From the island's highest point, Carlos looks south through his binoculars and sees a small remote beach.

Write an integer to describe Carlos's descent to this beach. (Assume that the beach is at sea level.) ___−628___

D On the beach, there is an old wooden sign with faded letters. Carlos can barely read *Captain's Cave, Elev. −3 ft.* He sees the opening of a cave nearby. Could this be the beach's "mouth" described in Clue 4?

Is Captain's Cave above or below sea level? ___below___

Write an inequality using the elevations to justify your answer.
___0 > −3 or −3 < 0___

Is Captain's Cave higher or lower than Bilge Basin? ___higher___

Write an inequality using their elevations to justify your answer.
___−3 > −6 or −6 < −3___

E At the back of the cave, Carlos moves several large loose rocks to reveal a small recess in the cave wall. He reaches in and pries out another old wooden chest, similar to the one he found at the church. Is this the treasure at last?

Carlos slowly opens the lid and...

IT'S THE TREASURE!!!!

To find the treasure's value, first rearrange the numbers in the table in order from least to greatest. Then replace each number with its corresponding letter.

The treasure has ___ABSOLUTE___ value!

2	−9	5	−6	−1	9	0	−4
U	A	T	B	O	E	L	S

Standard	Items
CC.6.NS.5	8, 10, 12, 18–20
CC.6.NS.6a	2, 14
CC.6.NS.6b	4, 5, 9, 11, 20
CC.6.NS.6c	8, 13, 15
CC.6.NS.7a	1, 6, 7, 10, 16
CC.6.NS.7c	3, 14, 17–20
CC.6.NS.8	12, 18–20

TEST PREP DOCTOR ⊕

Multiple Choice: Item 2

- Students who answered **F** transposed the digits of the number and added a negative sign.

- Students who answered **G** repeated the original number instead of finding the opposite.

- Students who answered **J** transposed the digits of the number instead of finding the opposite.

Multiple Choice: Item 9

- Students who answered **A** chose the only point that is to the left of the origin instead of to the right.

- Students who answered **B** may have confused the x- and y-axes; they chose the point directly above the origin instead of to the right of the origin.

- Students who answered **C** may have confused the x- and y-axes; they chose the point farthest above the origin instead of farthest to the right of the origin.

Free Response: Item 16

- Students who did not graph six points may have forgotten to include the opposites.

Free Response: Item 19

- Students who answered with a number less than 26 probably did not include all legs of Mark's route.

- Students who answered with a number greater than 26 probably miscounted one leg of Mark's trip.

Name _____ Class _____ Date _____

MULTIPLE CHOICE

1. Which list of numbers is in order from least to greatest?

A. −0.8, 1.2, −19, 13, 16, −4, 25

B. −1, −4, −8, 1.1, 1.6, −19, 23

(C) −19, −8, −4, −1, 1.1, 1.6, 2.5

D. −1, −4, 1.1, 1.3, 16, −19, 25

2. Which of the following numbers is the opposite of −37?

F. −73   (H) 37

G. −37   J. 73

3. What is the absolute value of 45?

A. −45   C. 0.45

B. 0   (D) 45

4. Both coordinates of a point in the coordinate plane are negative. In which quadrant is this point located?

F. Quadrant I   (H) Quadrant III

G. Quadrant II   J. Quadrant IV

5. Which of the points on the coordinate plane has coordinates (−7, 4)?

(A) A   C. C

B. B   D. D

6. Which of the following inequalities is a true statement?

F. 37 > 73   H. 73 < 37

(G) 48 > 24   J. 24 > 48

7. Which of the following numbers is located to the right of −47 on the number line?

(A) −14   C. −49

B. −94   D. −57

8. The elevation of the Dead Sea is about 1,310 feet below sea level. Which integer represents this elevation?

(F) −1,310   H. 131

G. −131   J. 1,310

9. Which of the following coordinates is farthest to the right of the origin on a coordinate plane?

A. (−19, 7)   C. (4, 15)

B. (0, 12)   (D) (7, 0)

10. The table shows the low temperature for several days. Which day was the coldest?

Day	Temperature (°F)
Monday	−4
Tuesday	0
Wednesday	−2
Thursday	5
Friday	3

(F) Monday

G. Tuesday

H. Wednesday

J. Thursday

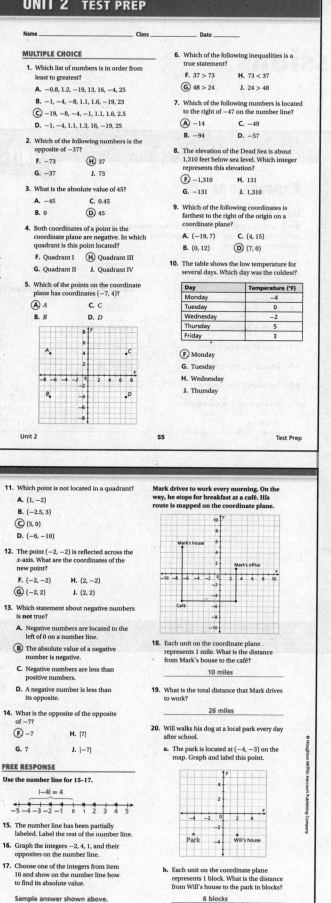

11. Which point is not located in a quadrant?

A. (1, −2)

B. (−2.5, 3)

(C) (5, 0)

D. (−6, −10)

12. The point (−2, −2) is reflected across the x-axis. What are the coordinates of the new point?

F. (−2, −2)   H. (2, −2)

(G) (−2, 2)   J. (2, 2)

13. Which statement about negative numbers is **not** true?

A. Negative numbers are located to the left of 0 on a number line.

(B) The absolute value of a negative number is negative.

C. Negative numbers are less than positive numbers.

D. A negative number is less than its opposite.

14. What is the opposite of the opposite of −7?

(F) −7   H. |7|

G. 7   J. |−7|

FREE RESPONSE

Use the number line for 15–17.

|−4| = 4

−5 −4 −3 −2 −1 0 1 2 3 4 5

15. The number line has been partially labeled. Label the rest of the number line.

16. Graph the integers −2, 4, 1, and their opposites on the number line.

17. Choose one of the integers from item 16 and show on the number line how to find its absolute value.

Sample answer shown above.

Mark drives to work every morning. On the way, he stops for breakfast at a café. His route is mapped on the coordinate plane.

18. Each unit on the coordinate plane represents 1 mile. What is the distance from Mark's house to the café?

_____ 10 miles _____

19. What is the total distance that Mark drives to work?

_____ 26 miles _____

20. Will walks his dog at a local park every day after school.

a. The park is located at (−4, −3) on the map. Graph and label this point.

b. Each unit on the coordinate plane represents 1 block. What is the distance from Will's house to the park in blocks?

_____ 6 blocks _____

© Houghton Mifflin Harcourt Publishing Company

Expressions

Unit Vocabulary

algebraic expression	(3-2)
base	(3-1)
coefficient	(3-3)
constant	(3-2)
equivalent expressions	(3-5)
evaluating	(3-4)
exponent	(3-1)
like terms	(3-5)
power	(3-1)
term	(3-3)
variable	(3-2)

UNIT 3

Expressions

Unit Focus

In this unit, you will write algebraic expressions that contain variables and constants. You will evaluate expressions and work with equivalent expressions.

Unit at a Glance

COMMON CORE

Lesson		Standards for Mathematical Content
3-1	Exponents	CC.6.EE.1
3-2	Writing Expressions	CC.6.EE.2a, CC.6.EE.6
3-3	Parts of an Expression	CC.6.EE.2b
3-4	Evaluating Expressions	CC.6.EE.2c
3-5	Equivalent Expressions	CC.6.EE.3, CC.6.EE.4
	Problem Solving Connections	
	Test Prep	

UNIT 3

Unpacking the Common Core State Standards

Use the table to help you understand the Standards for Mathematical Content that are taught in this unit. Refer to the lessons listed after each standard for exploration and practice.

COMMON CORE Standards for Mathematical Content	What It Means For You
CC.6.EE.1 Write and evaluate numerical expressions involving whole-number exponents. Lesson 3-1	You will use exponents to show repeated multiplication.
CC.6.EE.2a Write expressions that record operations with numbers and with letters standing for numbers. Lesson 3-2	You will write algebraic expressions containing variables to stand for numbers that are not yet known.
CC.6.EE.2b Identify parts of an expression using mathematical terms (sum, term, product, factor, quotient, coefficient); view one or more parts of an expression as a single entity. Lesson 3-3	You will describe expressions and their parts using words such as sum, term, product, factor, quotient, and coefficient.
CC.6.EE.2c Evaluate expressions at specific values of their variables. Include expressions that arise from formulas used in real-world problems. Perform arithmetic operations, including those involving whole-number exponents, in the conventional order when there are no parentheses to specify a particular order. (Order of Operations) Lesson 3-4	You will identify variables in expressions, including expressions that represent real-world problems. You will learn the order in which to perform arithmetic operations.
CC.6.EE.3 Apply the properties of operations to generate equivalent expressions. Lesson 3-5	Given an algebraic expression, you will write equivalent expressions.
CC.6.EE.4 Identify when two expressions are equivalent (i.e., when the two expressions name the same number regardless of which value is substituted into them). Lesson 3-5	You will identify equivalent expressions.
CC.6.EE.6 Use variables to represent numbers and write expressions when solving a real-world or mathematical problem; understand that a variable can represent an unknown number, or, depending on the purpose at hand, any number in a specified set. Lesson 3-2	You will learn to write algebraic expressions to represent real-world and mathematical problems.

This page lists and explains the Standards for Mathematical Content that are addressed in this unit. For information about the Standards for Mathematical Practice, which are integrated throughout the text, see Teacher Edition pages vii–xiii.

UNIT 3

Notes

Exponents

Essential question: *How do you use exponents to represent numbers?*

Standards for Mathematical Content

CC.6.EE.1 Write and evaluate numerical expressions involving exponents.

Vocabulary

power

base

exponent

Prerequisites

Multiplication of whole numbers and fractions

Math Background

Exponents represent repeated multiplication. The power 3^4 indicates $3 \times 3 \times 3 \times 3$, or the base 3 times itself 4 times. The expression 3^4 is read "the fourth power of 3." The second power of a number like 4^2 is commonly called "the square of 4" or "4 squared," although it is also correct to say "the second power of 4."

The use of *square* for the second power comes from the fact that the area of a square is given by the formula $A = s^2$, where s is the length of a side of the square. The third power of a number is commonly called the *cube* of the number because the volume of a cube is given by the formula $V = s^3$. Therefore, 4^3 is usually read "4 cubed," although it is also correct to say "the third power of 4."

INTRODUCE

Write a long product on the board, such as $7 \times 7 \times 7 \times 7 \times 7 \times 7$, and have students read the product aloud. Tell students that a shorter way to write this product is 7^6. Discuss the relationship between 7^6 and $7 \times 7 \times 7 \times 7 \times 7 \times 7$. Tell students that 7^6 is called a power, and in this power, 7 is the base and 6 is the exponent.

TEACH

1 EXPLORE

Questioning Strategies

- How does the number of total bacteria increase from row to row in the table? **Each row after 1 bacterium is the amount in the previous row times 2; so each row doubles the row before it.**

- What does an exponent represent? **the number of times the same number appears in a product**

2 EXAMPLE

Questioning Strategies

- How do you find the exponent? **Count the number of times the base appears in the product.**

Teaching Strategies

Read several products aloud, such as $3 \times 4 \times 5$, $5 \times 5 \times 5$, and $6 \times 7 \times 8$, and have students listen for repeated multiplication. Lead them to see that, of these examples, only $5 \times 5 \times 5$ is repeated multiplication, and it can be written as 5^3.

3 EXAMPLE

Questioning Strategies

- How do you find the value of a power? **Multiply the base the number of times given by the exponent. For example, $6^4 = (6 \times 6) \times 6 \times 6 = (36 \times 6) \times 6 = 216 \times 6 = 1,296$.**

- In part B, what do the parentheses around the fraction mean? **The exponent should be applied to the entire fraction, not just to the numerator or denominator.**

Avoid Common Errors

Students sometimes multiply the exponent by its base; for example, they may write $2^3 = 6$. Encourage them always to write out the repeated multiplication: $2^3 = 2 \times 2 \times 2 = 8$.

Name_____ Class_____ Date_____

Exponents

Essential question: *How do you use exponents to represent numbers?*

1 EXPLORE Exponents

Ricardo observed the hourly growth of bacteria in a test tube and recorded his observations in a table.

Time (h)	Total Bacteria
0	1
1	2
2	$2 \times 2 =$ **4**
3	$2 \times 2 \times 2 =$ **8**
4	$2 \times 2 \times 2 \times 2 =$ **16**

A Complete the table. What pattern(s) do you see in the Total Bacteria column?

Sample answer: Each number is 2 times the previous number.

B At 2 hours, the total is equal to the product of two 2's.

At 3 hours, the total is equal to the product of ___three___ 2's.

At 4 hours, the total is equal to the product of ___four___ 2's.

To show a number multiplied by itself, you can write a *power*. A **power** is an expression with an *exponent* and a *base*. For example, 7^3 means the product of three 7's:

$$7^3 = 7 \times 7 \times 7 = 343$$

The **base** is the number that is multiplied.

The **exponent** tells how many times the base appears in the product.

TRY THIS!

Circle the base.

1a. $④^7$ **1b.** $③^6$ **1c.** $②^5$ **1d.** $\left(\frac{1}{5}\right)^3$ (base circled)

Circle the exponent.

1e. $6^②$ **1f.** $10^⑧$ **1g.** $\left(\frac{7}{10}\right)^②$ **1h.** $9^④$

REFLECT

1i. Conjecture What do you think it means to have an exponent of 1? For example, what is the value of 8^1?

The base appears in the product only once; $8^1 = 8$.

Reading Powers

7^2 "the 2nd power of 7" 7^3 "the 3rd power of 7"

7^4 "the 4th power of 7" 7^5 "the 5th power of 7" and so on…

2 EXAMPLE Using Exponents to Write Expressions

Use exponents to write each expression.

A $6 \times 6 \times 6 \times 6 \times 6 \times 6 \times 6$

What number is being multiplied? __6__ This number is the base.

How many times does the base appear in the product? __7__ This number is the exponent.

$6 \times 6 \times 6 \times 6 \times 6 \times 6 \times 6 =$ __6^7__

B $\frac{2}{3} \times \frac{2}{3} \times \frac{2}{3}$

What number is being multiplied? __$\frac{2}{3}$__ This number is the base.

How many times does the base appear in the product? __3__ This number is the exponent.

$\frac{2}{3} \times \frac{2}{3} \times \frac{2}{3} = \left(\frac{2}{3}\right)^3$

TRY THIS!

Use exponents to write each expression.

2a. $3 \times 3 \times 3 \times 3 \times 3 \times 3 \times 3 \times 3$ __3^8__   **2b.** $4 \times 4 \times 4$ __4^3__

2c. 6 __6^1__   **2d.** $\frac{1}{8} \times \frac{1}{8}$ __$\left(\frac{1}{8}\right)^2$__   **2e.** $5 \times 5 \times 5 \times 5 \times 5 \times 5$ __5^6__

3 EXAMPLE Finding the Value of a Power

Find the value of each power.

A 9^3

What is the base? __9__

The exponent is 3, so the base will appear in the product 3 times.

$9^3 =$ __9__ $\times$ __9__ $\times$ __9__ $=$ __729__

Questioning Strategies

- How does the diagram help you solve this problem? **The diagram allows you to see a pattern.**

- How do exponents help you solve this problem? **It would be difficult to extend the diagram to the seventh generation; the exponent allows you to find the final answer more easily.**

MATHEMATICAL PRACTICE Highlighting the Standards

This Explore is an opportunity to address Standard 7 (Look for and make use of structure). Students look for the most efficient way to represent or solve a problem; in this case, the use of exponents is a more efficient strategy than continuing the diagram. For students to understand that they can solve this problem using exponents, they must first recognize a pattern and then realize that this pattern can be described as repeated multiplication.

CLOSE

Essential Question
How do you use exponents to represent numbers?
Exponents express repeated multiplication. The base is the value that is multiplied by itself repeatedly, and the exponent is the raised number that indicates how many times the base is multiplied.

Summarize
Have students write a journal entry that explains to someone who has never heard of exponents exactly what they are and when and where to use them.

PRACTICE

Where skills are taught	Where skills are practiced
1 EXPLORE	EXS. 1–4
2 EXAMPLE	EXS. 5–8, 17–32
3 EXAMPLE	EXS. 9–16, 34
4 EXPLORE	EX. 33

© Houghton Mifflin Harcourt Publishing Company

B $\left(\frac{1}{2}\right)^2$

What is the base? $\frac{1}{2}$ What is the exponent? 2

$\left(\frac{1}{2}\right)^2 = $ $\frac{1}{2} \times \frac{1}{2} = \frac{1}{4}$

TRY THIS!

Find the value of each power.

3a. 3^4 81 **3b.** 1^9 1 **3c.** $\left(\frac{2}{5}\right)^3$ $\frac{8}{125}$ **3d.** 12^2 144

---

4 EXPLORE   Solving Problems Using Exponents

Judah had two children. When those children grew up, each one also had two children, who later each had two children as well. If this pattern continues, how many children are there in the 7th generation?

You can use a diagram to model this situation. The first point at the top represents Judah. The other points represent children. Complete the diagram to show the 3rd generation.

Judah

1st generation →

2nd generation →

3rd generation →

A How many children are in each generation?

1st __2__   2nd __4__   3rd __8__

B Do you see a pattern in the numbers above? Try to find a pattern using exponents.

increasing powers of 2: $2^1, 2^2, 2^3$

C How is the number of children in a generation related to the generation number?

It is 2 raised to the power of the generation number.

D How many children will be in the 7th generation?

$2^7 = 128$

TRY THIS!

4. A female guinea pig has about 4 litters per year, and a typical litter consists of 4 baby guinea pigs. How many baby guinea pigs would a typical female have in 4 years?

$4^3 = 64$

PRACTICE

Write each power.

1. the 10th power of 8 8^{10}

2. the 8th power of 10 10^8

3. the 11th power of $\frac{1}{2}$ $\left(\frac{1}{2}\right)^{11}$

4. the 6th power of $\frac{2}{3}$ $\left(\frac{2}{3}\right)^6$

Use exponents to write each expression.

5. $6 \times 6 \times 6$ 6^3

6. $10 \times 10 \times 10 \times 10 \times 10 \times 10 \times 10$ 10^7

7. $\frac{3}{4} \times \frac{3}{4} \times \frac{3}{4} \times \frac{3}{4} \times \frac{3}{4}$ $\left(\frac{3}{4}\right)^5$

8. $\frac{7}{9} \times \frac{7}{9} \times \frac{7}{9} \times \frac{7}{9} \times \frac{7}{9} \times \frac{7}{9} \times \frac{7}{9} \times \frac{7}{9}$ $\left(\frac{7}{9}\right)^8$

Find the value of each power.

9. 8^3 512 **10.** 7^4 $2,401$ **11.** 5^3 125 **12.** 4^2 16

13. $\left(\frac{1}{4}\right)^2$ $\frac{1}{16}$ **14.** $\left(\frac{1}{3}\right)^3$ $\frac{1}{27}$ **15.** $\left(\frac{6}{7}\right)^2$ $\frac{36}{49}$ **16.** $\left(\frac{9}{10}\right)^1$ $\frac{9}{10}$

Write the missing exponent.

17. $100 = 10^2$ **18.** $8 = 2^3$ **19.** $25 = 5^2$ **20.** $27 = 3^3$

21. $\frac{1}{169} = \left(\frac{1}{13}\right)^2$ **22.** $14 = 14^1$ **23.** $32 = 2^5$ **24.** $\frac{64}{81} = \left(\frac{8}{9}\right)^2$

Write the missing base.

25. $1,000 = 10^3$ **26.** $256 = 4^4$ **27.** $16 = 2^4$ **28.** $9 = 3^2$

29. $\frac{1}{9} = \left(\frac{1}{3}\right)^2$ **30.** $64 = 8^2$ **31.** $\frac{9}{16} = \left(\frac{3}{4}\right)^2$ **32.** $729 = 9^3$

33. Hadley's softball team has a phone tree in case a game is cancelled. The coach calls 3 players. Then each of those players calls 3 players, and so on. How many players will be notified during the 3rd round of calls? 27 players

34. Reasoning What is the value of all powers of 1? Explain.

1; No matter how many 1's are multiplied, the product is always 1.

Notes

Writing Expressions

Essential question: *How can you use variables and constants to write algebraic expressions?*

COMMON CORE **Standards for Mathematical Content**

CC.6.EE.2a Write expressions that record operations with numbers and with letters standing for numbers.

CC.6.EE.6 Use variables to represent numbers and write expressions when solving a real-world or mathematical problem; understand that a variable can represent... any number in a specified set.

Vocabulary

variable

constant

algebraic expression

Prerequisites

Numeric expressions

Math Background

Algebraic expressions show operations with numbers and one or more variables. They are used in nearly every branch of mathematics, and they are the transition from spoken language to mathematical language.

INTRODUCE

Ask students what the words *variable* and *constant* mean to them. Have them consider their meanings in context, such as in the following:

- The temperature *varies* throughout the day.
- The baby's crying was *constant*.

Explain to students that they will learn new mathematical meanings for these words, meanings that are quite similar to their real-world contextual meanings.

TEACH

1 EXPLORE

Questioning Strategies

- Why was it useful to use n to represent a stage number? **The stage number changes so it cannot be represented with a single number.**
- How does the number of squares change from stage to stage? **Each stage has 3 more squares than the previous stage.**

Differentiated Instruction

Have each student think of a "secret" expression that contains a variable, such as $x + 3$ or $5 \times n$. Students use their expressions to create a table similar to the one in this Explore, omitting the expression and some of the table entries. Then have students exchange tables and complete one another's tables, identify the pattern revealed by the table, and use that pattern to write the corresponding algebraic expression.

2 EXAMPLE

Questioning Strategies

- Why do you think the multiplication symbol $\times$ is not typically used in algebraic expressions? **It might be confused with the variable x.**
- How are the expressions $9 - x$ and $x - 9$ different? **In the first expression, x is subtracted from 9; in the second expression, 9 is subtracted from x.**

© Houghton Mifflin Harcourt Publishing Company

3-2

Writing Expressions

Essential question: *How can you use variables and constants to write algebraic expressions?*

COMMON CORE
CC.6.EE.2a
CC.6.EE.6

1 EXPLORE Using Variables to Describe Patterns

Look at the pattern of squares below.

| Stage 1 | Stage 2 | Stage 3 |

A What is the pattern? At each stage, add 3 more squares.

How many squares will be in stage 4? 12

B What is the relationship between the stage number and the number of squares?

The number of squares is 3 times the stage number.

Use this relationship to complete the table below.

Stage	1	2	3	4	5	6	7	8	n
Squares	3	6	9	12	15	18	21	24	$3 \times n$

C Let *n* represent any stage number. How many squares are in stage *n*?

$$3 \times n$$

Add a column to the end of the table in **B** for stage *n*.

REFLECT

1. When might it be useful to know how many squares are in stage *n*?

Sample answer: When you want to know the number of squares in a large

stage number; for example, it is quick to calculate that the number of squares

in stage 54 is $3 \times 54 = 162$.

A **variable** is a letter or symbol used to represent an unknown or unspecified number. The value of a variable may change. In **1**, the variable *n* was used to represent any stage number.

A **constant** is a number that does not change. For example, the numbers 3, 8.6, and −21 are all constants because their values do not change.

An **algebraic expression** is an expression that contains one or more variables and may also contain operation symbols, such as + or −.

Algebraic Expressions	$150 + y$	$w + n$	x
Not Algebraic Expressions	15	$12 - 7$	$\frac{9}{16}$

In algebraic expressions, multiplication and division are usually written without the symbols × and ÷.

- Instead of $3 \times n$, write $3n$, $3 \cdot n$, or $n \cdot 3$.
- Instead of 3×5, write $3(5)$, $(3)5$, $(3)(5)$, or $3 \cdot 5$.
- Instead of $3 \div n$, write $\frac{3}{n}$.

Expressions can be written with constants and variables, or they may be described in words. When given an expression in words, it is important to be able to translate the words into algebra.

There are several different ways to describe expressions with words.

Operation	Addition	Subtraction	Multiplication	Division
Words	• added to • plus • sum • more than	• subtracted from • minus • difference • less than • take away • taken from	• times • multiplied by • product • groups of	• divided by • divided into • quotient

2 EXAMPLE Writing Algebraic Expressions

Write each phrase as an algebraic expression.

A 5 subtracted from *y*

The operation is _____ subtraction _____.

The algebraic expression is $y - 5$.

B The product of 9 and *p*

The operation is _____ multiplication _____.

The algebraic expression is $9p$.

TRY THIS!

Write each phrase as an algebraic expression.

2a. *n* times 7 $7n$ **2b.** 4 minus *y* $4 - y$ **2c.** 13 added to *x* $x + 13$

2d. *x* divided by 9 $\frac{x}{9}$ **2e.** 9 divided by *x* $\frac{9}{x}$ **2f.** *c* plus 3 $c + 3$

© Houghton Mifflin Harcourt Publishing Company

Notes

Questioning Strategies

- What quantities are unknown? the distance from Sam's house to Center City and the distance from Sam's house to Westonville

- What quantity is known? how much farther Center City is from Sam's house than Westonville is

Teaching Strategies

Students may wonder why variables are used in these problems; after all, the distance from Sam's house to Westonville does not change, so why use a variable to represent it? Make sure that students understand that a variable can represent a value that changes, or it can represent a missing value. Explain that an unknown quantity can be represented by a variable (w) or a combination of variables and constants ($w + 10$).

MATHEMATICAL PRACTICE Highlighting the Standards

This Example is an opportunity to address Standard 4 (Model with mathematics). Students use math to model real-world situations and move easily between a mathematical expression and the real-world context it represents. This example gives students the opportunity to read a real-world situation, identify the essential information, and use that information to write an algebraic expression describing the situation.

CLOSE

Essential Question

How can you use variables and constants to write algebraic expressions? Use variables to represent changing or unknown quantities, and use constants to represent unchanging or known quantities.

Summarize

Have students write a journal entry that summarizes what they have learned about algebraic expressions, including definitions of *algebraic expression, variable,* and *constant.*

PRACTICE

Where skills are taught	Where skills are practiced
1 EXPLORE	EXS. 1–2
2 EXAMPLE	EXS. 3–20
3 EXAMPLE	EXS. 21–24

REFLECT

2g. Error Analysis Erica wrote "5 added to y" as $5 + y$ and "5 subtracted from y" as $5 - y$. Why is the first expression correct but the second incorrect? When is order important in writing an expression?

For addition and multiplication, order is not important because the answer

is the same no matter the order of the addends or factors. This is not true

for subtraction and division, so order is important for these operations.

When solving real-world problems, you may need to identify the action taking place to know which operation to use.

Action	Operation
Put parts together	Addition
Put equal parts together	Multiplication
Find how much more or less	Subtraction
Separate into equal parts	Division

3 EXAMPLE Translating Words into Algebraic Expressions

Center City is 10 miles farther from Sam's house than Westonville is. Write an algebraic expression to represent the distance from Sam's house to Center City.

Let w represent the distance from Sam's house to Westonville.

The distance from Sam's house to Center City is 10 miles (more) / less than w.

So, to find the distance from Sam's house to Center City, put together __w__ and __10__.

Which operation represents this action? __addition__

The distance from Sam's house to Center City can be represented by the expression __$w + 10$, or $10 + w$__.

TRY THIS!

3a. Sonia worked 25 hours last week. She was paid the same amount of money per hour that she worked. Let h represent Sonia's hourly pay. Write an algebraic expression that represents Sonia's total pay last week.

$25h$

3b. Noah is saving to buy a new laptop computer. He has saved $119 so far. Let c represent the cost of the laptop. Write an algebraic expression that represents the amount of money Noah still needs to save.

$c - 119$

PRACTICE

1. Identify the constant(s) and variable(s) in the algebraic expression $t - 4n + 2$.

Constant(s) __4, 2__   Variable(s) __t, n__

2. Circle the algebraic expression(s) in the list below.

$180 + 25$ $(x - 79)$ $7(12)$ $(a + b)$ -220 $(13t)$ $(\frac{n}{15})$ $(24 - 3h)$ $\frac{4}{7}$ (r)

Write each phrase as an algebraic expression.

3. n divided by 8 __$\frac{n}{8}$__

4. p multiplied by 4 __$4p$__

5. b plus 14 __$b + 14$__

6. 90 times x __$90x$__

7. a take away 16 __$a - 16$__

8. k less than 24 __$24 - k$__

9. 3 groups of w __$3w$__

10. the sum of 1 and q __$1 + q$__

11. the quotient of 13 and z __$\frac{13}{z}$__

12. c added to 45 __$45 + c$__

Write a phrase in words for each algebraic expression. Sample answers given.

13. $m + 83$ __83 added to m__

14. $42s$ __42 times s__

15. $\frac{9}{d}$ __9 divided by d__

16. $t - 29$ __t minus 29__

17. $2 + g$ __g more than 2__

18. $11x$ __the product of 11 and x__

19. $\frac{h}{12}$ __the quotient of h and 12__

20. $5 - k$ __k less than 5__

21. Kayla's score on yesterday's math test was 12 points greater than Julianne's score. Let k represent Kayla's score. Write an algebraic expression to represent Julianne's score.

$k - 12$

22. The town of Rayburn received 6 more inches of snow than the town of Greenville. Let g represent the amount of snow in Greenville. Write an algebraic expression to represent the amount of snow in Rayburn.

$g + 6$

23. Abby baked 48 cookies and divided them evenly into bags. Let b represent the number of bags. Write an algebraic expression to represent the number of cookies in each bag.

$\frac{48}{b}$

24. Eli is driving at a speed of 55 miles per hour. Let h represent the number of hours that Eli drives at this speed. Write an algebraic expression to represent the number of miles that Eli travels during this time.

$55h$

Parts of an Expression

Essential question: *How do you identify and describe parts of an expression?*

Standards for Mathematical Content

CC.6.EE.2b Identify parts of an expression using mathematical terms (sum, term, product, factor, quotient, coefficient); view one or more parts of an expression as a single entity.

Vocabulary
coefficient

term

Prerequisites
Numeric expressions

Writing algebraic expressions

Math Background
This lesson reinforces student knowledge of algebraic expressions and terminology specific to expressions. Students reinforce their knowledge of terms like *variable, constant, term,* and *coefficient.*

INTRODUCE

Read aloud definitions and have student volunteers respond with the proper term. For example, say, "A mathematical statement that contains numbers and letters that stand for something unknown." Students should respond with "algebraic expression." You could make this into a game, dividing the class into teams that earn points for correct answers.

TEACH

1 EXPLORE

Questioning Strategies
- What are the key terms in a definition of an algebraic expression? **unknown quantity; variable**
- In part E, what two words from the box involve multiplication? **product and factor**

2 EXPLORE

Materials
Index cards or sticky notes

Questioning Strategies
- How are the meanings of *constant* and *coefficient* alike? How are they different? **Both are numbers that do not vary. A coefficient is a number that appears in a variable term as the multiplier. A constant is a number that appears without a variable.**
- Which two descriptions can be used for two different expressions in Part B? *Sum of two terms* **can be used with both addition expressions and** *product of two factors* **can be used with both multiplication expressions.**

CLOSE

Essential Question
How do you identify and describe parts of an expression? **Possible answer: An expression contains one or more of the following: sum, product, factor, quotient, term, constant, or coefficient. All of those terms can be identified by the way in which they are used in the expression.**

Name_____ Class_____ Date_____

3-3

COMMON
CORE
CC.6.EE.2b

Parts of an Expression

Essential question: *How do you identify and describe parts of an expression?*

1 EXPLORE Definitions

A–C. Sample answers given.

A Write the definitions of these words from Lesson 3-2 in your own words.

variable A symbol used to represent an unknown or unspecified value;
a value that may change

constant A value that does not change
_____

algebraic expression An expression that contains at least one variable
_____

B In the expressions $9a$, $5y$, $6n$, and $12x$, the blue numbers are *coefficients*.
Write a definition of *coefficient* in your own words.

coefficient A number that is multiplied by a variable
_____

C The expression $5y + z - 8$ has three terms. The expression $15 + x$ has two terms.
The expression $5c$ has one term. Write a definition of *term* in your own words.

term The parts of an expression which are added or subtracted
_____

D Compare your definitions in **B** and **C** to those of other students and discuss
any differences in them. If necessary, make changes to your definitions.

E Use words from the box to complete each sentence.

| factor | product | quotient | sum | difference |

$15 + x$ represents a ___sum___ of two terms.

$9a$ represents the ___product___ of 9 and a.

$p \div 3$ represents a ___quotient___.

$12 - x$ is a ___difference___ of two terms.

Unit 3   67   Lesson 3

REFLECT

1. Conjecture What is the coefficient of a term that consists of a single variable?
For example, what is the coefficient of x? _____1_____

2 EXPLORE Describing Expressions

There may be several different ways to describe a given expression.

A Write each description on individual index cards or sticky notes.

| algebraic expression | sum of two terms | product of two factors | sum of a quotient and a constant | product of a coefficient and a variable |

B Write each of the following expressions at the top of its own sheet of paper. Then
place the index card(s) or sticky note(s) that describe an expression onto its paper.
Write the descriptions you placed on each paper next to the expression.

$\frac{9a}{5} + 32$ algebraic expression; sum of a quotient and a constant
_____

$3(m + 1)$ algebraic expression; product of two factors
_____

$7c$ algebraic expression; product of a coefficient and a variable
_____

$5 + 9$ sum of two terms
_____

C Compare your answers in **B** with those of other students and make changes
to them, if necessary.

TRY THIS!

Write an algebraic expression that matches each description. Sample answers given.

2a. A product of two variables _____xy_____

2b. A sum of a product and a constant _____$3x + 2$_____

2c. An expression with 3 terms _____$7a + b - 9$_____

2d. A product of two factors, where one factor is a difference of two terms
_____$6(5 - x)$_____

Unit 3   68   Lesson 3

Evaluating Expressions

Essential question: *How do you evaluate expressions?*

© Houghton Mifflin Harcourt Publishing Company

COMMON CORE Standards for Mathematical Content

CC.6.EE.2c Evaluate expressions at specific values of their variables. Include expressions that arise from formulas used in real-world problems. Perform arithmetic operations, including those involving whole-number exponents, in the conventional order when there are no parentheses to specify a particular order (Order of Operations).

Vocabulary

evaluating

Prerequisites

Order of operations

Rational number operations

Math Background

Evaluating an algebraic expression involves substituting a given value for a variable in the expression and performing the operations to find the resulting value. Operations inside parentheses are performed first; then, exponents are simplified; next, perform multiplication and division from left to right; and finally, perform addition and subtraction from left to right.

INTRODUCE

Connect to previous learning by giving students numeric expressions, such as those shown below, to review the order of operations.

$\frac{40}{5}$ **8**   (4)(5) **20**

$67 - 29$ **38** $15 + 50$ **65**

Remind students of the correct order of operations, shown below, and the mnemonic device *PEMDAS*, which can help them remember.

- **P**arentheses
- **E**xponents
- **M**ultiplication/**D**ivision
- **A**ddition/**S**ubtraction

TEACH

1 EXAMPLE

Questioning Strategies

- What is the first step in evaluating an expression for a given variable? **Substitute the given value for the variable in the expression.**

- What is the second step in evaluating an expression for a given variable? **Perform the operations to find the value of the expression.**

Avoid Common Errors

In parts C and D, students may forget that a coefficient and variable that are written next to each other indicate multiplication. Guide students to insert a multiplication symbol when they substitute the given value for the variable.

2 EXAMPLE

Questioning Strategies

- Which operation do you do after substituting 7 for x in part A? **Subtract 4 from 7.**

- Which operation do you do after substituting 7 for x in part B? **Multiply 4 by 7.**

Teaching Strategies

Encourage students to perform one step at a time. Students often try to perform the substitution and operations in their heads. Require students to show each step. Showing all steps of their work will allow students to check their own work and identify any errors.

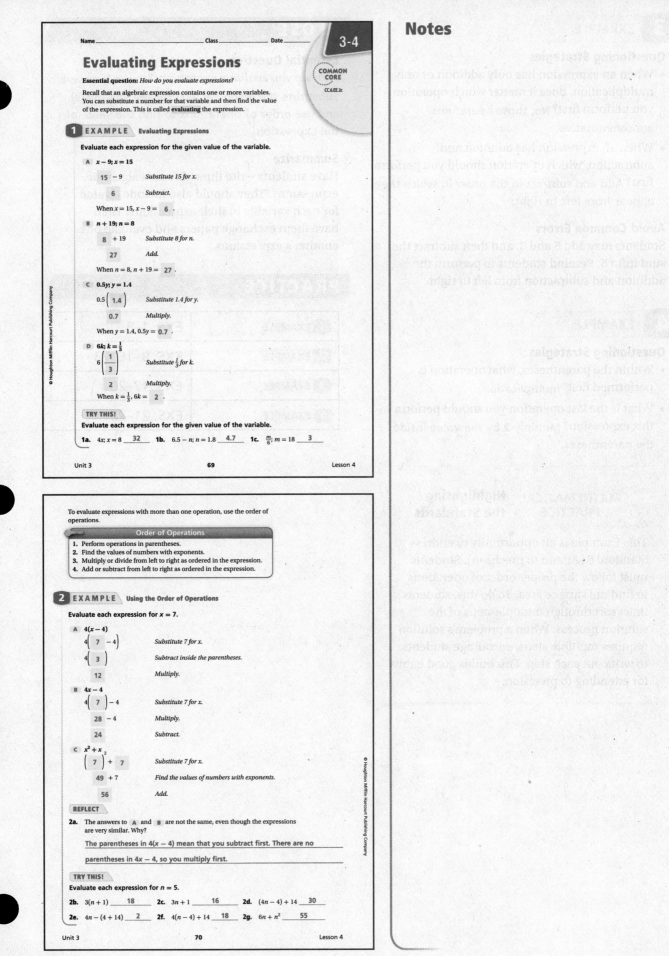

Name_____ Class_____ Date_____

3-4

COMMON CORE

CC.6.EE.2c

Evaluating Expressions

Essential question: *How do you evaluate expressions?*

Recall that an algebraic expression contains one or more variables. You can substitute a number for that variable and then find the value of the expression. This is called **evaluating** the expression.

1 EXAMPLE   Evaluating Expressions

Evaluate each expression for the given value of the variable.

A $x - 9; x = 15$

   15 − 9   *Substitute 15 for x.*

   6   *Subtract.*

   When $x = 15$, $x - 9 =$ 6 .

B $n + 19; n = 8$

   8 + 19   *Substitute 8 for n.*

   27   *Add.*

   When $n = 8$, $n + 19 =$ 27 .

C $0.5y; y = 1.4$

   0.5(1.4)   *Substitute 1.4 for y.*

   0.7   *Multiply.*

   When $y = 1.4$, $0.5y =$ 0.7 .

D $6k; k = \frac{1}{3}$

   $6\left(\dfrac{1}{3} \right)$ *Substitute $\frac{1}{3}$ for k.*

   2   *Multiply.*

   When $k = \frac{1}{3}$, $6k =$ 2 .

TRY THIS!

Evaluate each expression for the given value of the variable.

1a. $4x; x = 8$ __32__   **1b.** $6.5 - n; n = 1.8$ __4.7__   **1c.** $\frac{m}{6}; m = 18$ __3__

Unit 3   69   Lesson 4

To evaluate expressions with more than one operation, use the order of operations.

Order of Operations

1. Perform operations in parentheses.
2. Find the values of numbers with exponents.
3. Multiply or divide from left to right as ordered in the expression.
4. Add or subtract from left to right as ordered in the expression.

2 EXAMPLE   Using the Order of Operations

Evaluate each expression for $x = 7$.

A $4(x - 4)$

   4(7 − 4)   *Substitute 7 for x.*

   4(3)   *Subtract inside the parentheses.*

   12   *Multiply.*

B $4x - 4$

   4(7) − 4   *Substitute 7 for x.*

   28 − 4   *Multiply.*

   24   *Subtract.*

C $x^2 + x$

   (7)^2 + 7   *Substitute 7 for x.*

   49 + 7   *Find the values of numbers with exponents.*

   56   *Add.*

REFLECT

2a. The answers to A and B are not the same, even though the expressions are very similar. Why?

The parentheses in $4(x - 4)$ mean that you subtract first. There are no

parentheses in $4x - 4$, so you multiply first.

TRY THIS!

Evaluate each expression for $n = 5$.

2b. $3(n + 1)$ __18__   **2c.** $3n + 1$ __16__   **2d.** $(4n - 4) + 14$ __30__

2e. $4n - (4 + 14)$ __2__   **2f.** $4(n - 4) + 14$ __18__   **2g.** $6n + n^2$ __55__

Unit 3   70   Lesson 4

© Houghton Mifflin Harcourt Publishing Company

3 EXAMPLE

Questioning Strategies

- When an expression has only addition or only multiplication, does it matter which operation you perform first? **No, those operations are commutative.**

- When an expression has addition and subtraction, which operation should you perform first? **Add and subtract in the order in which they appear from left to right.**

Avoid Common Errors

Students may add 5 and 3, and then subtract the sum from 6. Remind students to perform the addition and subtraction from left to right.

4 EXAMPLE

Questioning Strategies

- Within the parentheses, what operation is performed first? **multiplication**

- What is the last operation you should perform in this expression? **Multiply 2 by the value inside the parentheses.**

MATHEMATICAL PRACTICE **Highlighting the Standards**

This Example is an opportunity to address Standard 6 (Attend to precision). Students must follow the proper order of operations to find the surface area. To do this, students must sort through multiple steps of the solution process. When a problem's solution requires multiple steps, encourage students to write out each step. This builds good habits for attending to precision.

Essential Question

How do you evaluate expressions? **Possible answer: Substitute the given value(s) for the variable(s), and use order of operations to find the value of the expression.**

Summarize

Have students write three different algebraic expressions. They should also include a value for each variable in their expressions. Then have them exchange papers and evaluate one another's expressions.

PRACTICE

1 EXAMPLE	EXS. 1–8
2 EXAMPLE	EXS. 9–16, 23
3 EXAMPLE	EXS. 17–20
4 EXAMPLE	EXS. 21–22

3 EXAMPLE   Expressions with More than One Variable

Evaluate $w - x + y$ for $w = 6$, $x = 5$, and $y = 3$.

$6 - 5 + 3$ Substitute 6 for w, 5 for x, and 3 for y.

$1 + 3$ Subtract.

4 Add.

REFLECT

3a. In this example, why do you subtract before adding?

According to the order of operations, you perform addition and subtraction

from left to right in the order they appear in the expression.

TRY THIS!

Evaluate each expression for $a = 3$, $b = 4$, and $c = 5$.

3b. $ab - c$ ___7___   **3c.** $bc + 5a$ ___35___

4 EXAMPLE   Using Formulas

The expression $2(\ell w + \ell h + hw)$ gives the surface
area of a rectangular prism with length ℓ, width w,
and height h. Find the surface area of the
rectangular prism shown.

$h = 3$ m
$w = 2$ m
$\ell = 6$ m

Use the diagram to find the values of ℓ, w, and h.

$\ell = $ 6 $w = $ 2 $h = $ 3

Substitute these values into the expression $2(\ell w + \ell h + hw)$.

$2\left[\left(\,6\,\right)\left(\,2\,\right) + \left(\,6\,\right)\left(\,3\,\right) + \left(\,3\,\right)\left(\,2\,\right)\right]$

$= 2\left(\,12 + 18 + 6\,\right)$ Multiply inside the parentheses.

$= 2\left(\,36\,\right)$ Add inside the parentheses.

$= 72$ Multiply.

The surface area of the rectangular prism is 72 m^2.

TRY THIS!

4a. The expression $6x^2$ gives the surface area of a cube, and the expression x^3
gives the volume of a cube, where x is the length of one side of the cube.
Find the surface area and the volume of a cube with a side length of 2 m.
$S = $ ___24___ m^2; $V = $ ___8___ m^3

4b. The expression $60m$ gives the number of seconds in m minutes.
How many seconds are there in 7 minutes? ___420___ seconds

PRACTICE

Evaluate each expression for the given value(s) of the variable(s).

1. $x - 7$; $x = 23$ ___16___   **2.** $3r$; $r = 6$ ___18___

3. $\frac{8}{t}$; $t = 4$ ___2___   **4.** $9 + m$; $m = 1.5$ ___10.5___

5. $p - 2$; $p = 19$ ___17___   **6.** $3h$; $h = \frac{1}{6}$ ___$\frac{1}{2}$___

7. $2.5 - n$; $n = 1.8$ ___0.7___   **8.** k^2; $k = 4$ ___16___

9. $4(b - 4)$; $b = 5$ ___4___   **10.** $38 - \frac{x}{2}$; $x = 12$ ___32___

11. $\frac{30}{d} - 2$; $d = 6$ ___3___   **12.** $x^2 - 34$; $x = 10$ ___66___

13. $\frac{1}{2}w + 2$; $w = \frac{1}{9}$ ___$2\frac{1}{18}$___   **14.** $5(6.2 + z)$; $z = 3.8$ ___50___

15. $2a^2 + a$; $a = 8$ ___136___   **16.** $7y + 32$; $y = 9$ ___95___

17. xy; $x = 8$ and $y = 6$ ___48___   **18.** $x + y - 1$; $x = 12$ and $y = 4$ ___15___

19. $3x + 4y$; $x = 4$ and $y = 5$ ___32___   **20.** $4x + 1 + 3y$; $x = 6$ and $y = 8$ ___49___

21. The expression ℓwh gives the volume of a rectangular prism
with length ℓ, width w, and height h. Find the volume of
the rectangular prism.   ___160___ in^3

$h = 4$ in.
$w = 5$ in.
$\ell = 8$ in.

22. The expression $1.8c + 32$ gives the temperature in
degrees Fahrenheit for a given temperature
in degrees Celsius c. Find the temperature in
degrees Fahrenheit that is equivalent to 30 °C.   ___86___ °F

23. Error Analysis Marjorie evaluated the expression $3x + 2$ for $x = 5$ as shown:

$3x + 2 = 35 + 2 = 37$

What was Marjorie's mistake? What is the correct value of $3x + 2$ for $x = 5$?

$3x$ means that 3 should be multiplied by the value of x; 17

Equivalent Expressions

Essential question: *How can you identify and write equivalent expressions?*

COMMON CORE **Standards for Mathematical Content**

CC.6.EE.3 Apply the properties of operations to generate equivalent expressions.

CC.6.EE.4 Identify when two expressions are equivalent (i.e., when the two expressions name the same number regardless of which value is substituted into them).

Vocabulary
equivalent expressions
like terms

Prerequisites
Order of operations
Evaluating expressions

Math Background
Equivalent expressions are expressions that have the same value. Algebraic expressions are equivalent if they simplify to the same value for any number(s) substituted for the variable(s). The Commutative, Associative, and Distributive Properties give you rules about how to rewrite an expression without changing its value. You can use these properties to combine like terms and generate equivalent expressions.

INTRODUCE

Explain to students that they will learn some properties of operations that allow them to write an expression in different ways without changing its value.

TEACH

1 EXPLORE

Questioning Strategies
- If two different expressions have the same value when you substitute a given value of the variable, does that mean they are equivalent? Explain. **Not necessarily; they are equivalent only if they simplify to the same value when any value for the variable is substituted in the expression.**

Teaching Strategies
You can sometimes determine whether two expressions are equivalent by substituting specific values for the variable. However, you cannot test every possible value, so this method is not always reliable. Explain to students that the Commutative, Associative, and Distributive Properties help you identify and generate equivalent expressions without substituting values for variables.

2 EXAMPLE

Questioning Strategies
- How does the Commutative Property of Addition or Multiplication allow you to rewrite an expression without changing the value? **You can change the order of the terms in an addition or multiplication expression.**
- How does the Associative Property of Addition or Multiplication allow you to rewrite an expression without changing the value? **You can group the numbers differently in an addition or multiplication expression.**
- How does the Distributive Property allow you to rewrite an expression without changing the value? **The product of a number and a sum or difference can be written as a sum or difference of two products, or vice versa.**

3-5

Equivalent Expressions

COMMON
CORE

CC.6.EE.3
CC.6.EE.4

Essential question: *How can you identify and write equivalent expressions?*

Equivalent expressions are expressions that simplify to the same value for any numbers(s) substituted for the variable(s). For example, the expression $y + y + y$ is equivalent to $3y$ because the two expressions will have the same value for any number that is substituted for y.

1 EXPLORE Identifying Equivalent Expressions

Match the expressions in List A with their equivalent expressions in List B.

List A	List B
$5x + 65$	$5x + 1$
$5(x + 1)$	$5x + 5$
$1 + 5x$	$5(13 + x)$

A One way to test whether two expressions might be equivalent is to evaluate them for the same value of the variable. Evaluate each of the expressions in the lists for $x = 3$.

List A		List B	
$5(3) + 65 =$	80	$5(3) + 1 =$	16
$5(3 + 1) =$	20	$5(3) + 5 =$	20
$1 + 5(3) =$	16	$5(13 + 3) =$	80

B Which pair(s) of expressions have the same value for $x = 3$?

$5(x + 1)$ and $5x + 5$; $1 + 5x$ and $5x + 1$; $5x + 65$ and $5(13 + x)$

C How could you further test whether the expressions in each pair are equivalent?

Sample answer: Evaluate for several other values of x.

D Do you think the expressions in each pair are equivalent? Why or why not?

Sample answer: Yes; it appears that they will always have the same value.

REFLECT

1a. Lisa evaluated the expressions $2x$ and x^2 for $x = 2$ and found that both expressions were equal to 4. Lisa concluded that $2x$ and x^2 are equivalent expressions. How could you show Lisa that she is incorrect?

Evaluate the expressions for a different value of x; for example, when $x = 1$,

$2x = 2$ and $x^2 = 1$.

1b. What does **1a** demonstrate about expressions?

Two nonequivalent expressions may sometimes have the same value.

Properties of operations can be used to identify equivalent expressions.

Properties of Operations	Examples
Commutative Property of Addition: When adding, changing the order of the numbers does not change the sum.	$3 + 4 = 4 + 3$
Commutative Property of Multiplication: When multiplying, changing the order of the numbers does not change the product.	$2 \times 4 = 4 \times 2$
Associative Property of Addition: When adding more than two numbers, the grouping of the numbers does not change the sum.	$(3 + 4) + 5 = 3 + (4 + 5)$
Associative Property of Multiplication: When multiplying more than two numbers, the grouping of the numbers does not change the product.	$(2 \times 4) \times 3 = 2 \times (4 \times 3)$
Distributive Property: Multiplying a number by a sum or difference is the same as multiplying by each number in the sum or difference and then adding or subtracting.	$6(2 + 4) = 6(2) + 6(4)$ $8(5 - 3) = 8(5) - 8(3)$

2 EXAMPLE Writing Equivalent Expressions

Use one of the properties in the table above to write an expression that is equivalent to $x + 3$.

The operation in the expression is _____addition_____.

Which property of this operation can be applied to $x + 3$?

Commutative Property of Addition

Use this property to write an equivalent expression:

$x + 3 =$ _____$3 + x$_____

Notes

Questioning Strategies

- Are terms that have the same variable with different exponents like terms? No; for example, x and x^2 are not like terms.

- What two parts of a term should be the same for like terms with variables? the variable and the exponent

MATHEMATICAL PRACTICE   Highlighting the Standards

This Example is an opportunity to address Standard 3 (Construct viable arguments and critique the reasoning of others.). Students provide a justification for their selection of like terms. They also have to identify non-examples of like terms and explain why they are not like terms.

4 EXAMPLE

Questioning Strategies

- What are the like terms in part A? $6x^2$ and $4x^2$

- In part A, what property is used to write the difference of products as a product of a difference? Distributive Property

Teaching Strategies

A fun way to help students remember how to combine like terms is to have students name the variable part of like terms. For example, to add $6x^2$ and $4x^2$, students can name the variable part *monkeys* and think of the expression as 6 monkeys plus 4 monkeys, which totals 10 monkeys, or $10x^2$.

CLOSE

Essential Question

How can you identify and write equivalent expressions? You can use the Commutative, Associative, and Distributive Properties to identify equivalent expressions, simplify expressions by combining like terms, and rewrite equivalent expressions.

Summarize

Have students write their own explanations of equivalent expressions and how to identify them. Have them include each property in this lesson and give an example of how each property can be used to identify equivalent expressions.

PRACTICE

1 EXPLORE	EX. 1
2 EXAMPLE	EXS. 2–5
3 EXPLORE	EXS. 6–11
4 EXAMPLE	EXS. 12–17

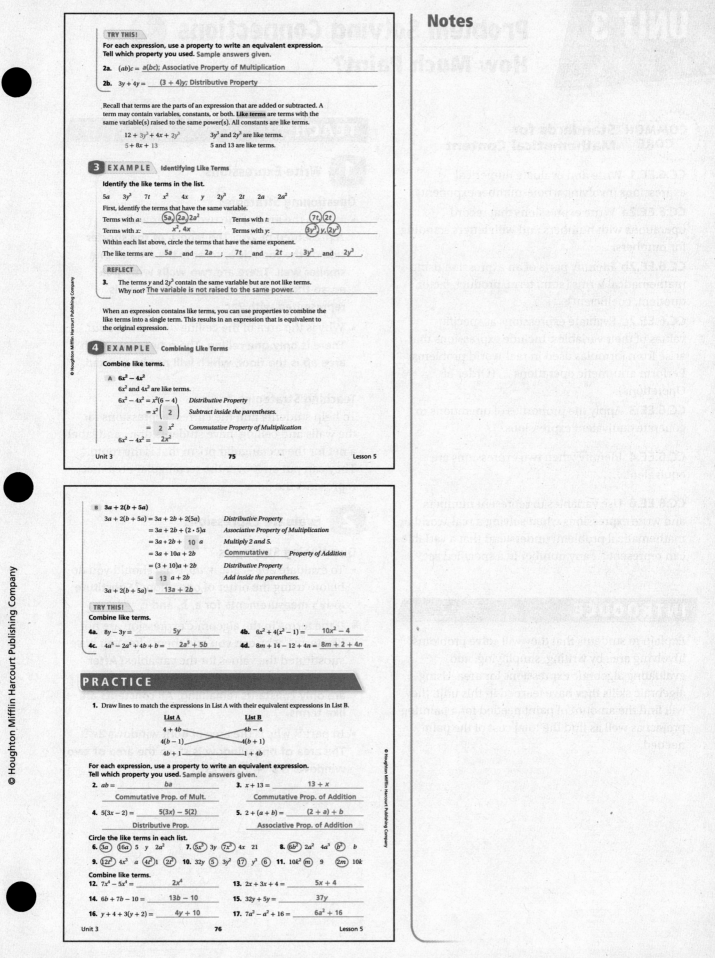

TRY THIS!

For each expression, use a property to write an equivalent expression. Tell which property you used. Sample answers given.

2a. $(ab)c = $ ____ $a(bc)$; Associative Property of Multiplication

2b. $3y + 4y = $ ____ $(3 + 4)y$; Distributive Property

Recall that terms are the parts of an expression that are added or subtracted. A term may contain variables, constants, or both. **Like terms** are terms with the same variable(s) raised to the same power(s). All constants are like terms.

$12 + 3y^3 + 4x + 2y^3$ $3y^3$ and $2y^3$ are like terms.
$5 + 8x + 13$ 5 and 13 are like terms.

3 EXAMPLE   Identifying Like Terms

Identify the like terms in the list.

$5a$ $3y^3$ $7t$ x^2 $4x$ y $2y^3$ $2t$ $2a$ $2a^2$

First, identify the terms that have the same variable.

Terms with a: (5a) (2a) $2a^2$ Terms with t: ____ (7t) (2t)

Terms with x: ____ x^2, $4x$ Terms with y: ____ (3y³) y, (2y³)

Within each list above, circle the terms that have the same exponent.

The like terms are ____ $5a$ and ____ $2a$; $7t$ and ____ $2t$; $3y^3$ and ____ $2y^3$.

REFLECT

3. The terms y and $2y^3$ contain the same variable but are not like terms. Why not? The variable is not raised to the same power.

When an expression contains like terms, you can use properties to combine the like terms into a single term. This results in an expression that is equivalent to the original expression.

4 EXAMPLE   Combining Like Terms

Combine like terms.

A $6x^2 - 4x^2$

$6x^2$ and $4x^2$ are like terms.

$6x^2 - 4x^2 = x^2(6 - 4)$ *Distributive Property*
       $= x^2 \left(\boxed{2} \right)$ *Subtract inside the parentheses.*
       $= \boxed{2} \ x^2$ *Commutative Property of Multiplication*

$6x^2 - 4x^2 = $ ____ $2x^2$

Unit 3   75   Lesson 5

B $3a + 2(b + 5a)$

$3a + 2(b + 5a) = 3a + 2b + 2(5a)$ *Distributive Property*
       $= 3a + 2b + (2 \cdot 5)a$ *Associative Property of Multiplication*
       $= 3a + 2b + \boxed{10} \ a$ *Multiply 2 and 5.*
       $= 3a + 10a + 2b$ Commutative ____ *Property of Addition*
       $= (3 + 10)a + 2b$ *Distributive Property*
       $= \boxed{13} \ a + 2b$ *Add inside the parentheses.*

$3a + 2(b + 5a) = $ ____ $13a + 2b$

TRY THIS!

Combine like terms.

4a. $8y - 3y = $ ____ $5y$ **4b.** $6x^2 + 4(x^2 - 1) = $ ____ $10x^2 - 4$

4c. $4a^5 - 2a^5 + 4b + b = $ ____ $2a^5 + 5b$ **4d.** $8m + 14 - 12 + 4n = $ ____ $8m + 2 + 4n$

PRACTICE

1. Draw lines to match the expressions in List A with their equivalent expressions in List B.

List A	List B
$4 + 4b$	$4b - 4$
$4(b - 1)$	$4(b + 1)$
$4b + 1$	$1 + 4b$

For each expression, use a property to write an equivalent expression. Tell which property you used. Sample answers given.

2. $ab = $ ____ ba
Commutative Prop. of Mult.

3. $x + 13 = $ ____ $13 + x$
Commutative Prop. of Addition

4. $5(3x - 2) = $ ____ $5(3x) - 5(2)$
Distributive Prop.

5. $2 + (a + b) = $ ____ $(2 + a) + b$
Associative Prop. of Addition

Circle the like terms in each list.

6. (3a) (16a) 5 y $2a^2$ **7.** (5x³) $3y$ (7x³) $4x$ 21   **8.** (6b²) $2a^2$ $4a^3$ (b²) b

9. (12r²) $4x^3$ a (4r²) 1 (2r²)   **10.** $32y$ (5) $3y^2$ (17) y^3 (6)   **11.** $10k^2$ (m) 9 (2m) $10k$

Combine like terms.

12. $7x^4 - 5x^4 = $ ____ $2x^4$ **13.** $2x + 3x + 4 = $ ____ $5x + 4$

14. $6b + 7b - 10 = $ ____ $13b - 10$ **15.** $32y + 5y = $ ____ $37y$

16. $y + 4 + 3(y + 2) = $ ____ $4y + 10$ **17.** $7a^2 - a^2 + 16 = $ ____ $6a^2 + 16$

Unit 3   76   Lesson 5

© Houghton Mifflin Harcourt Publishing Company

COMMON CORE Standards for Mathematical Content

CC.6.EE.1 Write and evaluate numerical expressions involving whole-number exponents.

CC.6.EE.2a Write expressions that record operations with numbers and with letters standing for numbers.

CC.6.EE.2b Identify parts of an expression using mathematical terms (sum, term, product, factor, quotient, coefficient); …

CC.6.EE.2c Evaluate expressions at specific values of their variables. Include expressions that arise from formulas used in real-world problems. Perform arithmetic operations … (Order of Operations).

CC.6.EE.3 Apply the properties of operations to generate equivalent expressions.

CC.6.EE.4 Identify when two expressions are equivalent.…

CC.6.EE.6 Use variables to represent numbers and write expressions when solving a real-world or mathematical problem; understand that a variable can represent … any number in a specified set.

INTRODUCE

Explain to students that they will solve problems involving area by writing, simplifying, and evaluating algebraic expressions for area. Using algebraic skills they have learned in this unit, they will find the amount of paint needed for a painting project as well as find the total cost of the paint needed.

TEACH

1 Write Expressions

Questioning Strategies

- Why is the area of the two smaller walls represented by $2ac$? **The length of the shorter side of the room is a, so ac is the area of one smaller wall. There are two walls with area ac, so the area of the two smaller walls is represented with $2ac$.**

- Why is the area of the ceiling ab and not $2ab$? **There is only one ceiling. The other space with area ab is the floor, which will not be painted.**

Teaching Strategies

To help students find the correct expressions for the walls and ceiling, have students draw and label a net for the rectangular prism that is the room. They can put an X over the rectangular area that represents the floor.

2 Evaluate Expressions

Questioning Strategies

- To evaluate $2bc + 2ac + ab$, what should you do before using the order of operations? **Substitute Jody's measurements for a, b, and c.**

- If the terms in the algebraic expression are not like terms, why can you add them after you have substituted the values for the variables? **After substituting and simplifying each term, there are only constants remaining. All constants are like terms.**

- In part F, why is the area of both windows $2s^2$? **The area of one window is s^2, so the area of two windows is $s^2 + s^2$, or $2s^2$.**

Name _____ Class _____ Date _____

UNIT 3

Problem Solving Connections 🌎

How Much Paint? Jody's family has moved into a new house, and Jody is going to repaint her new bedroom. Jody's dad says that she first has to calculate how much paint to buy. How can Jody use algebraic expressions to find the amount of paint she will need?

COMMON CORE
CC.6.EE.1
CC.6.EE.2a, b, c
CC.6.EE.3
CC.6.EE.4
CC.6.EE.6

1 Write Expressions

A Jody's bedroom is rectangular. Let a represent the width (shorter side) of the room, and let b represent the length (longer side). Let c represent the height of each wall.

The rectangular prism below can be used to model Jody's bedroom. Label a, b, and c on the prism.

B Write an algebraic expression to represent the combined area of the two larger walls of the room. Explain your thinking.

The area of one of the larger walls is bc, so the area of both walls is $2bc$.

C Write an algebraic expression to represent the combined area of the two smaller walls. Explain your thinking.

The area of one of the smaller walls is ac, so the area of both walls is $2ac$.

D Write an algebraic expression to represent the area of the ceiling.

ab

E Use your answers above to write an algebraic expression to represent the total area of all four walls and the ceiling.

$2bc + 2ac + ab$

2 Evaluate Expressions

A Now Jody must measure her bedroom so she can substitute the measurements into the algebraic expressions. First Jody measures the height c of the walls and the length b of the longer wall. She finds that $c = 12$ feet and $b = 20$ feet.

Rewrite the expression that represents the combined area of the two larger walls. Then evaluate this expression using the values of b and c that Jody found. What is the total area of these two walls?

$2bc = 2(20)(12) = 480;\ 480\ \text{ft}^2$

B Jody cannot reach high enough to measure the ceiling, so she measures the floor instead. She already knows that the longer side of the floor b measures 20 feet. She finds that the shorter side a measures 8 feet.

Rewrite the expression that represents the area of the ceiling. Then evaluate this expression using the values of a and b that Jody found. What is the area of the ceiling?

$ab = 8(20) = 160;\ 160\ \text{ft}^2$

C Does Jody need to measure anything else to find the area of the two smaller walls? Why or why not?

No; the area of the two smaller walls is represented by $2ac$, and Jody has

already found the values of a and c.

D Rewrite the expression that represents the combined area of the two smaller walls. Then evaluate this expression using the appropriate values. What is the total area of these two walls?

$2ac = 2(8)(12) = 192;\ 192\ \text{ft}^2$

Questioning Strategies

- Can you find the area of the walls without the ceiling by just adding the areas of the two pairs of walls? No, the area of the windows must still be subtracted.

- In part B, do you agree with Jody's estimate of 600 square feet for the area of the four walls? Explain. Possible answer: Jody's estimate is an underestimate. I would overestimate by rounding the area of the large walls up to 500 square feet and the area of the small walls to 200 square feet. I would estimate 700 square feet for the area of the four walls.

- In part D, how can you estimate the number of cans needed for two coats of blue paint? Jody wants to cover about 700 square feet with blue paint. For two coats, she will need enough blue paint for about 1400 square feet. $1400 \div 300 = 4.666\ldots$, so Jody will need 5 cans of blue paint.

Teaching Strategy

Remind students to use answers that they already have calculated. Explain that recalculating the area of the four walls is not necessary when they have the area of the room and only need to subtract the area of the ceiling.

CLOSE

Journal

Have students describe in their journals how to write, simplify, and evaluate algebraic expressions to solve area problems. Have students include anything they may have learned about finding areas in real-world situations, such as omitting windows or adjusting for two coats of paint.

Research Options

Students can extend their learning by doing online research to find the cost of covering an area in their home with various materials such as flooring, wallpaper, paint, and so on.

E Find the total area of the four walls and the ceiling. Explain how you found your answer.

> Add the areas of the two larger walls, the two smaller walls, and the ceiling.
> $480 + 160 + 192 = 832 \text{ ft}^2$

F "Now we can go to the paint store and buy the paint," Jody says. "Wait!" says Dad. "Some of the walls are not really rectangles. Your room has a door and two square windows. You can paint the door if you want, but you are definitely not going to paint the windows!" After thinking about it, Jody decides that she will paint her door.

Both windows are the same size. Let s represent the side length of one of the windows. Write an algebraic expression with an exponent to represent the combined area of both windows. Explain your thinking.

The area of one window is $s \cdot s = s^2$, so the area of both windows is $2s^2$.

_____

G Jody returns to her room to measure one of the windows. She measures the window's length as 4 feet.

Rewrite the expression that represents the combined area of the two windows. Then evaluate that expression using Jody's measurement. What is the total area of the two windows?

> $2(4^2) = 2(16) = 32 \text{ ft}^2$

H Explain how you used the order of operations to evaluate the expression for the windows' area.

I followed the order of operations by finding the value of the power

first and then multiplying.

I What operation should Jody use to find the total area of the surfaces she is going to paint?

subtraction

_____

Find the total area that Jody will paint.

> $832 - 32 = 800 \text{ ft}^2$

---

3 Answer the Question

A Jody and her dad arrive at the paint store, where Jody chooses two paint colors—light blue for the walls and white for the ceiling.

Look back to find the area of the ceiling and write it here: _____160_____ ft^2

How can Jody find the total area of just the four walls (not including the ceiling)?
Subtract 160 from the total area previously calculated.

Find the area of only the four walls.

> $800 - 160 = 640 \text{ ft}^2$

B The label on each paint can reads "Covers 300 square feet." Jody reasons that the area of the four walls is about 600 ft^2, so she will need $\frac{600}{300} = 2$ cans of blue paint. Do you agree with Jody? Why or why not? If not, how many cans of blue paint do you think Jody should buy?

No; 2 cans of paint will cover 600 ft^2, but the area of the walls is more than

600 ft^2. Jody needs 3 cans of blue paint.

C How many cans of white paint does Jody need? Explain your thinking.

1 can; the total area of the ceiling (160 ft^2) is less than 300 ft^2, the amount

covered by 1 can.

D The paint store associate recommends that Jody put two coats on each surface to completely cover the existing color. Does one can of white paint contain enough paint for two coats on the ceiling? Explain.

No; 2(160) = 320, which is more than 300. Jody will need 2 cans of

white paint.

Jody and her dad agree with the paint store associate and decide to apply two coats. Jody says, "Then we need twice as much paint, two cans of white paint and six cans of blue paint." Is Jody correct? Explain.

Jody is correct about the amount of white paint needed. However, for 2 coats

on the walls, the square footage is 640 × 2 = 1,280. Each can covers 300 ft^2

and 300 × 5 = 1,500, which is greater than 1,280, so 5 cans of blue paint will

be enough.

COMMON CORE CORRELATION

Standard	Items
CC.6.EE.1	1–3
CC.6.EE.2a	4, 6, 7, 20
CC.6.EE.2b	18–19
CC.6.EE.2c	9, 16, 20–21
CC.6.EE.3	8, 13, 14, 21
CC.6.EE.4	5, 10–11, 15
CC.6.EE.6	4, 7, 12, 17

TEST PREP DOCTOR

Multiple Choice: Item 9

- Students who answered **A** may have found the difference of $24 - 13$ without making any substitutions for x and y.
- Students who answered **B** may have substituted the values for variables in the expression correctly but miscalculated.
- Students who answered **C** may have found the sum of $24 + 13$ without making any substitutions for x and y.

Multiple Choice: Item 17

- Students who answered **A** may have read the question incorrectly and chosen the first correct answer.
- Students who answered **B** may have thought a correct expression of "per serving" would involve division.
- Students who answered **C** may have thought a correct expression of area would have a squared variable.

Free Response: Item 20a

- Students who answered **3.5c** may not have understood how to translate the distance from Ray's house to the shopping center into a mathematical expression.
- Students who answered **3.5 − c** may not have understood how to translate the distance from Ray's house to the shopping center into a mathematical expression.
- Students who answered **c − 3.5** may not have understood how to translate the distance from Ray's house to the shopping center into a mathematical expression.

Free Response: Item 20c

- Students who answered **7** may have evaluated the expression $3.5c$ for $c = 2$.
- Students who answered **1.5** may have evaluated the expression $3.5 - c$ for $c = 2$.
- Students who answered **−1.5** may have evaluated the expression $c - 3.5$ for $c = 2$.

UNIT 3 TEST PREP

Name _____ Class _____ Date _____

MULTIPLE CHOICE

1. Which is a shorthand way to write $5 \times 5 \times 5 \times 5$?

   A. $5 \times 5 + 5 \times 5$ C. 5^4

   B. 5^3 D. 4^5

2. Which word describes a number that tells you how many times to multiply a number by itself?

   F. Variable   H. Expression

   G. Exponent   J. Constant

3. Andre made the table below to show the results of his experiments on the reproduction of flies.

Day	Number of Flies	Total
1	3	3
2	3×3	9
3	$3 \times 3 \times 3$	27
4	$3 \times 3 \times 3 \times 3$	81

   How could Andre write his results for day 4 using exponents?

   A. 4^2 C. 3^2

   B. 3^3 D. 3^4

4. Erik made a model train that was 25 feet shorter in length than an actual train. Let m represent the length of Erik's model. Which expression represents the length of the actual train?

   F. $25 - m$ H. $m + 25$

   G. $25m$ J. $m - 25$

5. Which of the following expressions is equivalent to $7x + 12$?

   A. $12 + 7x$ C. $19x$

   B. $7 + 12x$ D. $7(x + 12)$

6. Mark has been asked to find the value of $4(9 + 24) + 7$. What should he do first?

   F. Add 4 and 7.

   G. Multiply 4 and 9.

   H. Multiply 4 and 24.

   J. Add 9 and 24.

7. The new county park has an area that is 3.5 times the area of the old park. Let p represent the area of the old park. Which expression represents the area of the new park?

   A. $3.5p$ C. $p + 3.5$

   B. $p - 3.5$ D. $\frac{p}{3.5}$

8. Which of the following is an example of the Commutative Property of Multiplication?

   F. $(15 \times 5) \times 5 = 15 \times (5 \times 5)$

   G. $15 \times 5 = 5 \times 15$

   H. $5 + 15 = 15 + 5$

   J. $5(15 + 5) = 5(5 + 15)$

9. Evaluate the expression $24x - 13y$ for $x = 3$ and $y = 2$.

   A. 11   C. 37

   B. 33   D. 46

10. Which expression does **not** equal 15?

    F. $3k$ for $k = 5$

    G. $3 + k$ for $k = 12$

    H. $\frac{k}{3}$ for $k = 60$

    J. $k - 10$ for $k = 25$

11. Combine like terms in $5m^2 + 16k^2 + 13m^2$.

    A. $34m^2$ C. $18m^2 + 16k^2$

    B. $34k^2$ D. $18m^4 + 16k^2$

12. The new building in City Center is 345 feet taller than the Jefferson Building. Let h represent the height of the Jefferson Building. Which expression represents the height of the new building?

    F. $h + 345$ H. $h - 345$

    G. $345 - h$ J. $345h$

13. $5(20 + x) = 5(20) + 5x$ is an example of which property?

    A. Associative Property of Addition

    B. Associative Property of Multiplication

    C. Commutative Property of Addition

    D. Distributive Property

14. Which expression contains like terms?

    F. $x + y + xy$ H. $7y^2 - 7y - 7$

    G. $17x^2 + x^3 + x$ J. $x^4 + 15 + 4x^4$

15. Which expression is equivalent to $9n + 3$ after combining like terms?

    A. $10n^2 - n^2 - 3$

    B. $3n + 7 - 4 + 3n$

    C. $18 - 15 + 4n + 5n$

    D. $7n^2 + 2n + 6 - 3$

16. Which expression has a value of 74 when $a = 10$, $b = 8$, and $c = 12$?

    F. $4abc$ H. $2ac - 3b$

    G. $a + 5b + 2c$ J. $6abc + 8$

17. Which quantity **cannot** be represented by the expression $0.20x$?

    A. The total cost of x text messages, where each text message costs $0.20

    B. The total amount of calcium in x servings of a cereal that contains 0.2 gram of calcium per serving

    C. The area of a rectangle with length x and width 0.2

    D. The amount of change due when an item that costs $0.20 is paid for with x dollars

FREE RESPONSE

18. Write two different phrases in words that describe the expression $7z$.

    Sample answers: 7 times z; the
    _____
    product of 7 and z.
    _____

19. Write an algebraic expression...
    Sample answers given.

    a. that has three terms. $3xy + 14y - 7$

    b. in which one term is the product of two variables. $ab - 12$

    c. that is the sum of a product and a constant. $3y + 1$

20. The distance from Ray's house to the shopping center is 3.5 miles more then the distance from Ray's house to the city park.

    a. Let c equal the distance from Ray's house to the city park. Write an expression to represent the distance from Ray's house to the shopping center.

    $c + 3.5$

    b. The distance from Ray's house to the city park is 2 miles. How can you use this information and your answer to part **a** to find the distance from Ray's house to the shopping center?

    Evaluate $c + 3.5$ for $c = 2$.

    c. What is the distance from Ray's house to the shopping center?

    5.5 miles

21. a. What is the first step in finding the value of $12 + (6 + 4)$?

    Add 6 and 4.

    b. $12 + (6 + 4) = $ ___22___

    c. What is the first step in finding the value of $(12 + 6) + 4$?

    Add 12 and 6.

    d. $(12 + 6) + 4 = $ ___22___

    e. What property is demonstrated by your answers to parts **b** and **d**?

    Associative Property of Addition

UNIT 4

Equations

Unit Vocabulary

dependent variable	(4-4)
equation	(4-1)
independent variable	(4-4)
input	(4-4)
output	(4-4)
solution	(4-1)

UNIT 4

Equations

Unit Focus

You have already learned how to write and evaluate expressions and to identify parts of an expression. In this unit, you will learn to solve equations and use substitution to check solutions. You will analyze relationships between variables using equations, tables, and graphs. You will also learn about inequalities.

Unit at a Glance

COMMON CORE

Lesson	Standards for Mathematical Content
4-1 Equations and Solutions	CC.6.EE.5, CC.6.EE.6
4-2 Addition and Subtraction Equations	CC.6.EE.7
4-3 Multiplication and Division Equations	CC.6.EE.7
4-4 Equations, Tables, and Graphs	CC.6.EE.9
4-5 Solutions of Inequalities	CC.6.EE.5, CC.6.EE.6, CC.6.EE.8
Problem Solving Connections	
Test Prep	

Unit 4   83   Equations

Unpacking the Common Core Standards

Use the table to help you understand the Standards for Mathematical Content that are taught in this unit. Refer to the lessons listed after each standard for exploration and practice.

COMMON CORE Standards for Mathematical Content	What It Means For You
CC.6.EE.5 Understand solving an equation or inequality as a process of answering a question: which values from a specified set, if any, make the equation or inequality true? Use substitution to determine whether a given number in a specified set makes an equation or inequality true. Lessons 4-1, 4-5	You will learn how to use substitution to determine whether a number is a solution of an equation or inequality.
CC.6.EE.6 Use variables to represent numbers and write expressions when solving a real-world or mathematical problem; understand that a variable can represent an unknown number, or, depending on the purpose at hand, any number in a specified set. Lessons 4-1, 4-5	You will write expressions to represent real-world or mathematical problems.
CC.6.EE.7 Solve real-world and mathematical problems by writing and solving equations of the form $x + p = q$ and $px = q$ for cases in which p, q and x are all nonnegative rational numbers. Lessons 4-2, 4-3	You will use your knowledge of operations to solve equations.
CC.6.EE.8 Write an inequality of the form $x > c$ or $x < c$ to represent a constraint or condition in a real-world or mathematical problem. Recognize that inequalities of the form $x > c$ or $x < c$ have infinitely many solutions; represent solutions of such inequalities on number line diagrams. Lesson 4-5	You will understand that an inequality has many solutions and you will graph these solutions on a number line. You will write inequalities to represent real-world situations.
CC.6.EE.9 Use variables to represent two quantities in a real-world problem that change in relationship to one another; write an equation to express one quantity, thought of as the dependent variable, in terms of the other quantity, thought of as the independent variable. Analyze the relationship between the dependent and independent variables using graphs and tables, and relate these to the equation. Lesson 4-4	You will analyze relationships between two variables and write equations in two variables to represent real-world problems.

Unpacking the Common Core State Standards

This page lists and explains the Standards for Mathematical Content that are addressed in this unit. For information about the Standards for Mathematical Practice, which are integrated throughout the text, see Teacher Edition pages vii–xiii.

Notes

UNIT 4

Solutions of Equations

Essential question: *How can you determine whether a number is a solution of an equation?*

Standards for Mathematical Content

CC.6.EE.5 Understand solving an equation or inequality as a process of answering a question: which values from a specified set, if any, make the equation or inequality true? Use substitution to determine whether a given number in a specified set makes an equation or inequality true.

CC.6.EE.6 Use variables to represent numbers and write expressions when solving a real-world or mathematical problem; understand that a variable can represent an unknown number, or, depending on the purpose at hand, any number in a specified set.

Vocabulary
equation

solution

Prerequisites
Numeric expressions

Math Background
An equation is a statement that two expressions are equal. An expression does not have an equal sign, but an equation does. The solution of an equation is the value of the variable that makes the equation true. Real-world situations can be modeled by equations by translating words such as *more than*, *less than*, *combined*, or *total* into operations such as addition and subtraction.

INTRODUCE

Connect to prior learning by writing the following numeric expressions on the board, and have students identify some corresponding word phrases for each expression.

$7 + 3$ **seven plus three, three more than seven**

$6 - 2$ **six minus two; two less than six**

9×5 **nine times five; the product of nine and five**

$12 \div 4$ **twelve divided by four; the quotient of twelve and four**

TEACH

1 EXPLORE

Questioning Strategies

- What is one difference between an expression and an equation? **Possible answer: An equation contains an equals sign.**

- How do you know if a given value is the solution of an equation? **When you substitute it for the variable and simplify both sides of the equation, both sides will be the same value (equal).**

Avoid Common Errors

Students may think the last line of their work when substituting a given value is the solution. For example, when students are asked to identify whether 6 is a solution of $x + 9 = 15$, they may think 15 is the solution because $15 = 15$ is the last line. Students have grown accustomed to the last line having the answer, or "solution." Make sure that students really understand that the solution of an equation is the *value of the variable* that makes the equation true.

2 EXAMPLE

Questioning Strategies

- What is another equation that could represent this situation? $46 - p = 17$

- What does the variable represent? **the number of points scored by Mark's teammates**

TRY THIS

In Try This items **2c** and **2e**, students write multiplication or division equations. Point out to students that the key word *each* indicates the operation of multiplication or division.

Name_____ Class_____ Date_____

Equations and Solutions

4-1

COMMON CORE

CC.6.EE.5
CC.6.EE.6

Essential question: *How do you determine whether a number is a solution of an equation?*

An **equation** is a mathematical statement that two expressions are equal. An equation may or may not contain variables. For an equation that has a variable, a **solution** of the equation is a value of the variable that makes the equation true.

1 EXAMPLE Checking Solutions

Determine whether the given value is a solution of the equation.

A $x + 9 = 15; x = 6$

| 6 | $+ 9 \overset{?}{=} 15$ | Substitute 6 for x. |
| $15 \overset{?}{=} 15$ | | Add. |

6 is /is not a solution of $x + 9 = 15$.

B $5 = t - 4; t = 11$

| $5 \overset{?}{=} 11 - 4$ | Substitute 11 for t. |
| $5 \overset{?}{=} 7$ | Subtract. |

11 is / is not a solution of $5 = t - 4$.

C $8x = 72; x = 9$

| $8\left(9 \right) \overset{?}{=} 72$ | Substitute 9 for x. |
| $72 \overset{?}{=} 72$ | Multiply. |

9 is /is not a solution of $8x = 72$.

D $\dfrac{y}{4} = 32; y = 8$

| $\dfrac{8}{4} \overset{?}{=} 32$ | Substitute 8 for y. |
| $2 \overset{?}{=} 32$ | Divide. |

8 is / is not a solution of $\dfrac{y}{4} = 32$.

© Houghton Mifflin Harcourt Publishing Company

TRY THIS!

Determine whether the given value is a solution of the equation.

1a. $11 = n + 6; n = 5$ **1b.** $y - 6 = 24; y = 18$ **1c.** $\dfrac{36}{x} = 9; x = 4$

    yes   no   yes

REFLECT

1d. Write an equation containing a variable that has a solution of 16.

Sample answer: $x + 4 = 20$

2 EXAMPLE Writing an Equation

Mark scored 17 points in a basketball game. His teammates scored a total of *p* points, and the team as a whole scored 46 points. Write an equation to represent this situation.

Mark's points	+	Teammates' points	=	Total points
17	+	P	=	46

REFLECT

2a. Write an equation containing an operation other than addition that also represents the situation.

Sample answer: $46 - p = 17$

TRY THIS!

Write an equation to represent each situation.

2b. Marilyn has a fish tank that contains 38 fish. There are 9 goldfish and *f* other fish.

Sample answer: $f + 9 = 38$

2c. Juanita has 102 beads to make *n* necklaces. Each necklace will have 17 beads.

Sample answer: $17n = 102$

2d. Craig is *c* years old. His 12-year-old sister Caitlin is 3 years younger than Craig.

Sample answer: $c - 3 = 12$

2e. Sonia rented ice skates for *h* hours. The rental fee was $2 per hour and she paid a total of $8.

Sample answer: $2h = 8$

© Houghton Mifflin Harcourt Publishing Company

Questioning Strategies

- What is another equation you could use to represent this situation? $47 + 18 = x$ or $x - 18 = 47$

- What two numbers are you given as possible solutions? **65 and 59**

Avoid Common Errors

Students may choose the incorrect operation when trying to write and solve an equation. Have students underline or circle key words in the problem that signal addition, subtraction, multiplication or division. Then have students write the equations.

MATHEMATICAL PRACTICE | **Highlighting the Standards**

Example 3 is an opportunity to address Standard 2 (Reason abstractly and quantitatively). Students are asked to write an equation based on a real-world situation. They must analyze the situation to determine which operation to use. Then students must check the two given solutions to figure out which is the correct answer.

CLOSE

Essential Question

How can you determine whether a number is a solution of an equation?

Possible answer: Substitute the given number for the variable into the equation. If both sides of the equation are still equal, then the given number is a solution.

Summarize

Have students create their own word problems and write them in their journal. Have students include one problem using each operation.

PRACTICE

Where skills are taught	Where skills are practiced
1 EXAMPLE	EXS. 1–16
2 EXAMPLE	EXS. 17–22
3 EXAMPLE	EXS. 17–22

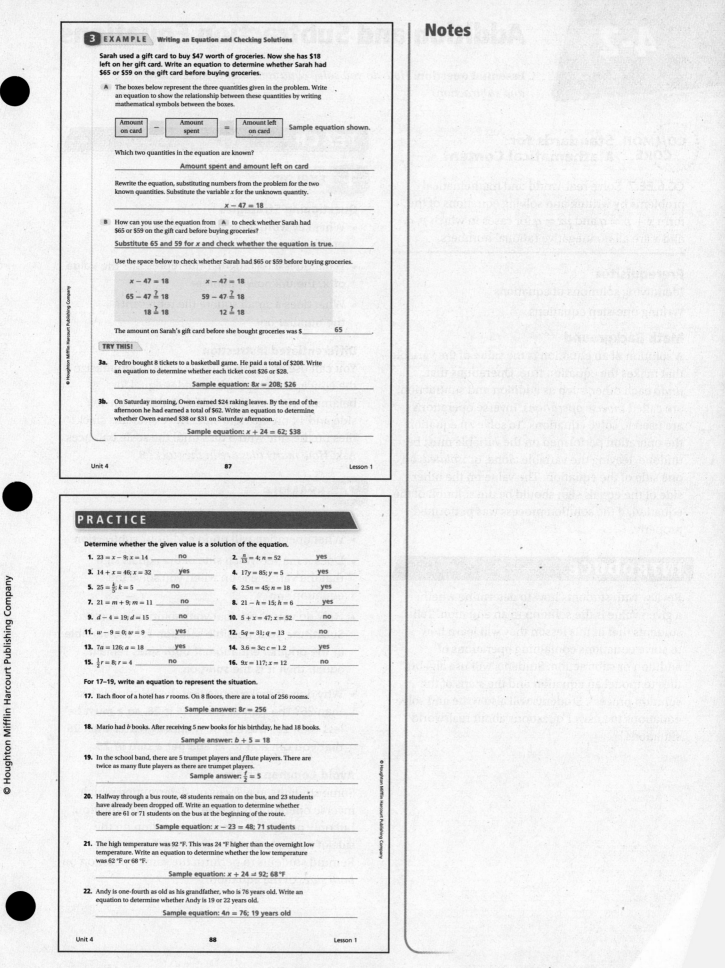

3 EXAMPLE Writing an Equation and Checking Solutions

Sarah used a gift card to buy $47 worth of groceries. Now she has $18 left on her gift card. Write an equation to determine whether Sarah had $65 or $59 on the gift card before buying groceries.

A The boxes below represent the three quantities given in the problem. Write an equation to show the relationship between these quantities by writing mathematical symbols between the boxes.

| Amount on card | − | Amount spent | = | Amount left on card |

Sample equation shown.

Which two quantities in the equation are known?

_____Amount spent and amount left on card_____

Rewrite the equation, substituting numbers from the problem for the two known quantities. Substitute the variable x for the unknown quantity.

$$x - 47 = 18$$

B How can you use the equation from **A** to check whether Sarah had $65 or $59 on the gift card before buying groceries?

_____Substitute 65 and 59 for x and check whether the equation is true._____

Use the space below to check whether Sarah had $65 or $59 before buying groceries.

$$x - 47 = 18 \qquad\qquad x - 47 = 18$$
$$65 - 47 \overset{?}{=} 18 \qquad\qquad 59 - 47 \overset{?}{=} 18$$
$$18 \overset{?}{=} 18 \qquad\qquad 12 \overset{?}{=} 18$$

The amount on Sarah's gift card before she bought groceries was $ _____65_____ .

TRY THIS!

3a. Pedro bought 8 tickets to a basketball game. He paid a total of $208. Write an equation to determine whether each ticket cost $26 or $28.

_____Sample equation: $8x = 208$; $26_____

3b. On Saturday morning, Owen earned $24 raking leaves. By the end of the afternoon he had earned a total of $62. Write an equation to determine whether Owen earned $38 or $31 on Saturday afternoon.

_____Sample equation: $x + 24 = 62$; $38_____

PRACTICE

Determine whether the given value is a solution of the equation.

1. $23 = x - 9$; $x = 14$ _____no_____
2. $\frac{n}{13} = 4$; $n = 52$ _____yes_____
3. $14 + x = 46$; $x = 32$ _____yes_____
4. $17y = 85$; $y = 5$ _____yes_____
5. $25 = \frac{k}{5}$; $k = 5$ _____no_____
6. $2.5n = 45$; $n = 18$ _____yes_____
7. $21 = m + 9$; $m = 11$ _____no_____
8. $21 - h = 15$; $h = 6$ _____yes_____
9. $d - 4 = 19$; $d = 15$ _____no_____
10. $5 + x = 47$; $x = 52$ _____no_____
11. $w - 9 = 0$; $w = 9$ _____yes_____
12. $5q = 31$; $q = 13$ _____no_____
13. $7a = 126$; $a = 18$ _____yes_____
14. $3.6 = 3c$; $c = 1.2$ _____yes_____
15. $\frac{1}{2}r = 8$; $r = 4$ _____no_____
16. $9x = 117$; $x = 12$ _____no_____

For 17–19, write an equation to represent the situation.

17. Each floor of a hotel has r rooms. On 8 floors, there are a total of 256 rooms.

_____Sample answer: $8r = 256$_____

18. Mario had b books. After receiving 5 new books for his birthday, he had 18 books.

_____Sample answer: $b + 5 = 18$_____

19. In the school band, there are 5 trumpet players and f flute players. There are twice as many flute players as there are trumpet players.

_____Sample answer: $\frac{f}{2} = 5$_____

20. Halfway through a bus route, 48 students remain on the bus, and 23 students have already been dropped off. Write an equation to determine whether there are 61 or 71 students on the bus at the beginning of the route.

_____Sample equation: $x - 23 = 48$; 71 students_____

21. The high temperature was 92 °F. This was 24 °F higher than the overnight low temperature. Write an equation to determine whether the low temperature was 62 °F or 68 °F.

_____Sample equation: $x + 24 = 92$; 68 °F_____

22. Andy is one-fourth as old as his grandfather, who is 76 years old. Write an equation to determine whether Andy is 19 or 22 years old.

_____Sample equation: $4n = 76$; 19 years old_____

Notes

Addition and Subtraction Equations

Essential question: *How do you solve equations that involve addition and subtraction?*

COMMON CORE **Standards for Mathematical Content**

CC.6.EE.7 Solve real-world and mathematical problems by writing and solving equations of the form $x + p = q$ and $px = q$ for cases in which p, q, and x are all nonnegative rational numbers.

Prerequisites

Identifying solutions of equations

Writing one-step equations

Math Background

A solution of an equation is the value of the variable that makes the equation true. Operations that *undo* each other, such as addition and subtraction, are called *inverse operations*. Inverse operations are used to solve equations. To solve an equation, the operation performed on the variable must be undone, leaving the variable alone, or *isolated*, on one side of the equation. The value on the other side of the equals sign should be the solution of the equation, if the solution process was performed properly.

INTRODUCE

Review with students how to determine whether a given value is the solution to an equation. Tell students that in this lesson they will learn how to solve equations containing operations of addition or subtraction. Students will use algebra tiles to model an equation and the steps of the solution process. Students will also write and solve equations to answer questions about real-world situations.

TEACH

1 EXPLORE

Questioning Strategies

- What key word indicates addition in this problem? **gain**
- What does a rectangular tile represent? **the value of x, the unknown number**
- What does a small square tile represent? **the number one**

Differentiated Instruction

You can use an actual balance scale to emphasize the concept of keeping both sides equal, or balanced. Have students place 6 tiles on the left side and 14 on the right side. Have students stack tiles on the side with 6 tiles until the scale balances. Ask: *How many tiles are in the stack?* **8**

2 EXAMPLE

Questioning Strategies

- What operation will undo addition? **subtraction**
- Does it matter which side of the equals sign that the variable is on when you solve the equation? **no**
- How do you check that your solution is correct? **Substitute your possible solution for the variable in the original equation. If both sides remain equal, then it is the solution.**
- Why does it make sense that the solution is less than 26? **The sum of a and 15 is 26, so a must be less than 26. There is no number greater than 26 that you can add to 15 and get a sum of 26.**

Avoid Common Errors

Some students may focus on determining which inverse operation is needed to solve the equation, but only perform the inverse operation on the side of the equation that contains the variable. Remind students to perform the same operation on *both sides* of the equation.

© Houghton Mifflin Harcourt Publishing Company

Lesson 2

Name_____ Class_____ Date_____

4-2

Addition and Subtraction Equations

COMMON
CORE
CC.6.EE.7

Essential question: *How do you solve equations that contain addition or subtraction?*

1 EXPLORE Addition Equations

A puppy weighed 6 ounces at birth. After two weeks, the puppy weighed 14 ounces. How much weight did the puppy gain?

Let x represent the number of ounces gained.

Weight at birth	+	Weight gained	=	Weight after 2 weeks
6	+	x	=	14

To answer this question, you can solve the equation $6 + x = 14$.

Algebra tiles can model some equations. An equation mat represents the two sides of an equation. To solve the equation, remove the same number of tiles from both sides of the mat until the x-tile is by itself on one side.

A Model $6 + x = 14$.

$6 + x$ 14

B How many unit tiles must you remove on the left side so that the x-tile is by itself? __6__ Cross out these tiles on the equation mat.

C Whenever you remove tiles from one side of the mat, you must remove the same number of tiles from the other side of the mat. Cross out the tiles that should be removed on the right side of the mat.

D How many tiles remain on the right side of the mat? __8__ This is the solution of the equation.

The puppy gained __8__ ounces.

TRY THIS!

Solve each equation.

1a. $x + 2 = 7$ **1b.** $x + 9 = 12$ **1c.** $6 + x = 11$

$x =$ __5__ $x =$ __3__ $x =$ __5__

Unit 4   89   Lesson 2

Removing the same number of tiles from each side of an equation mat models subtracting the same number from both sides of an equation.

Subtraction Property of Equality

You can subtract the same number from both sides of an equation, and the two sides will remain equal.

When an equation contains addition, solve by subtracting the same number from both sides.

2 EXAMPLE Using the Subtraction Property of Equality

Solve each equation.

A $a + 15 = 26$

What number is added to a? __15__

Subtract this number from both sides of the equation.

$$
\begin{array}{rcl}
a + 15 &=& 26 \\
-15 && -15 \\
\hline
a &=& 11
\end{array}
$$
                    Subtract.

Check: $a + 15 = 26$

$11 + 15 \overset{?}{=} 26$ *Substitute 11 for a.*

$26 \overset{?}{=} 26$ *Add on the left side.*

B $23 = d + 17$

What number is added to d? __17__

Subtract this number from both sides of the equation.

$$
\begin{array}{rcl}
23 &=& d + 17 \\
-17 && -17 \\
\hline
6 &=& d
\end{array}
$$
                    Subtract.

TRY THIS!

Solve each equation.

2a. $n + 34 = 56$ **2b.** $w + 31 = 72$ **2c.** $z - 7.12 = 0.54$

$n =$ __22__ $w =$ __41__ $z =$ __7.66__

Unit 4   90   Lesson 2

Questioning Strategies

• What operation will undo subtraction? **addition**

• What happens to both sides of an equation when you add or subtract the same number from both sides? **They remain equal.**

Differentiated Instruction

Have students work together to write and solve addition and two subtraction equations. Students can write equations, exchange papers to solve them, and exchange them again to check the solutions. If a student finds an error, the group can discuss the correction until all are agreed.

MATHEMATICAL PRACTICE   Highlighting the Standards

This example is an opportunity to address Standard 7 (Look for and make use of structure). Students solve one-step equations by using properties of equality. The properties of equality describe mathematical structure that exists in algebra. Students discover that when the correct inverse operation is identified and performed on both sides of the equation, the resulting statement gives the solution of the equation.

CLOSE

Essential Question

How do you solve equations that involve addition and subtraction?

Possible answer: Identify the operation performed on the variable, and perform the inverse operation on both sides of the equation to get the variable by itself.

Summarize

Have students write in their journal their own explanation of how to solve one-step equations involving addition or subtraction. Have students include an equation and its solution to support their explanations.

PRACTICE

Where skills are taught	Where skills are practiced
1 EXPLORE	EXS. 1–2, 5–10, 12, 14, 16–17
2 EXAMPLE	EXS. 1–2, 5–10, 12, 14, 16–17
3 EXAMPLE	EXS. 3–4, 11, 13, 15, 18

© Houghton Mifflin Harcourt Publishing Company

When an equation contains subtraction, solve by adding the same number to both sides.

Addition Property of Equality

You can add the same number to both sides of an equation, and the two sides will remain equal.

3 EXAMPLE Using the Addition Property of Equality

Solve each equation.

A $y - 21 = 18$

What number is subtracted from y? _____ 21 _____

Add this number to both sides of the equation.

$$y - 21 = 18$$
$$+ 21 = + 21$$
$$y = 39 \quad \textit{Add.}$$

B $31 = g - 16$

What number is subtracted from g? _____ 16 _____

Add this number to both sides of the equation.

$$31 = g - 16$$
$$+ 16 \quad + 16$$
$$47 = g \quad \textit{Subtract.}$$

Check: $31 = g - 16$

$$31 \overset{?}{=} 47 - 16 \quad \textit{Substitute 47 for g.}$$

$$31 \overset{?}{=} 31 \quad \textit{Subtract on the right side.}$$

TRY THIS!

Solve each equation.

3a. $x - 16 = 72$

$x =$ _____ 88 _____

3b. $h - \frac{1}{2} = \frac{3}{4}$

$h = \frac{5}{4}$, or $1\frac{1}{4}$

3c. $t - 17 = 84$

$t =$ _____ 101 _____

© Houghton Mifflin Harcourt Publishing Company

REFLECT

3d. How do you know whether to add or subtract on both sides when solving an equation?

If the equation contains addition, subtract on both sides. If the equation

contains subtraction, add on both sides.

PRACTICE

Solve each equation.

1. $t + 6 = 10$

$t =$ _____ 4 _____

2. $a + 7 = 15$

$a =$ _____ 8 _____

3. $x - 16 = 72$

$x =$ _____ 88 _____

4. $d - 125 = 55$

$d =$ _____ 180 _____

5. $w + 87 = 102$

$w =$ _____ 15 _____

6. $k + 13 = 61$

$k =$ _____ 48 _____

7. $h + 6.9 = 11.4$

$h =$ _____ 4.5 _____

8. $y + 2.3 = 10.5$

$y =$ _____ 8.2 _____

9. $82 + p = 122$

$p =$ _____ 40 _____

10. $n + \frac{1}{2} = \frac{7}{4}$

$n =$ _____ $\frac{5}{4}$ _____

11. $z - \frac{2}{3} = \frac{3}{5}$

$z = \frac{19}{15}$, or $1\frac{4}{15}$

12. $19 + m = 29$

$m =$ _____ 10 _____

13. $16 = q - 125$

$q =$ _____ 141 _____

14. $9.6 = 5.6 + g$

$g =$ _____ 4 _____

15. $r - 8 = 56$

$r =$ _____ 64 _____

For 16–18, write and solve an equation to answer each question.

16. Kim bought a poster that cost $8.95 and some colored pencils. The total cost was $21.35. How much did the colored pencils cost?

Sample equation: $x + 8.95 = 21.35$; $12.40

17. The Acme Car Company sold 37 vehicles in June. How many compact cars were sold in June?

Sample equation: $x + 8 = 37$;

29 compact cars

Acme Car Company – June Sales	
Type of Car	Number Sold
SUV	8
Compact	?

18. Lindsey finished a race in 58.4 seconds. This was 2.6 seconds faster than her practice time. What was Lindsey's practice time?

Sample equation: $x - 2.6 = 58.4$; 61 s

© Houghton Mifflin Harcourt Publishing Company

Multiplication and Division Equations

Essential question: *How do you solve equations that contain multiplication or division?*

COMMON CORE **Standards for Mathematical Content**

CC.6.EE.7 Solve real-world and mathematical problems by writing and solving equations of the form $x + p = q$ and $px = q$ for cases in which $p, q,$ and x are all nonnegative rational numbers.

Prerequisites

Identifying solutions of equations

Writing one-step equations

Math Background

Students will learn to solve one-step equations that contain multiplication and division in this lesson. Multiplication and division are inverse operations, so they are used to undo each other. Multiplication can be indicated in an equation by a multiplication cross, multiplication dot, parentheses, or by proximity with no space, such as with a number and a variable: $2x$. Division can be indicated in an equation by a division symbol or a fraction bar.

INTRODUCE

To connect with previous learning, review some related multiplication and division operations, such as $(3)(15) = 45$ and $\frac{45}{15} = 3$. Discuss with students the steps used for solving addition and subtraction equations: (1) identify the operation performed on the variable; (2) perform the inverse of that operation on both sides of the equation; and (3) check the result to make sure it is the solution. Tell students that the same steps are used to solve equations with multiplication and division.

TEACH

1 EXPLORE

Questioning Strategies

- What key word indicates multiplication or division? **per**

- Why do you need to divide by 3? **to undo the operation on the variable**

- Why do you need to divide on both sides? **to maintain the balance of the equation**

> MATHEMATICAL PRACTICE **Highlighting the Standards**
>
> This Example is an opportunity to address Standard 4 (Model with mathematics). Students solve an application problem by writing an equation to represent the situation and using algebra tiles to model the equation and solve it.

2 EXAMPLE

Questioning Strategies

- What operation will undo multiplication? **division**

- By what number can you never divide? Why? **Zero, because division by zero is undefined.**

- Can dividing both sides of the equation by the variable help you solve this equation? **No, the variable might be zero, and it does not lead to the solution.**

- How do you solve a one-step equation that contains multiplication? **Divide both sides of the equation by the constant, not the variable.**

© Houghton Mifflin Harcourt Publishing Company

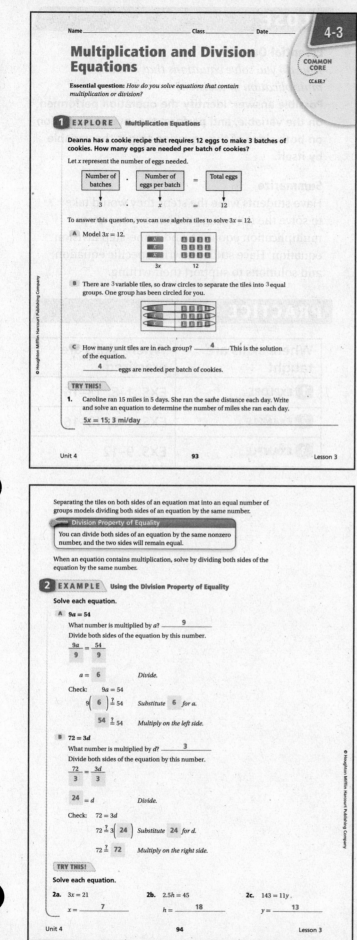

4-3

COMMON
CORE
CC.6.EE.7

Name_____ Class_____ Date_____

Multiplication and Division Equations

Essential question: *How do you solve equations that contain multiplication or division?*

1 EXPLORE Multiplication Equations

Deanna has a cookie recipe that requires 12 eggs to make 3 batches of cookies. How many eggs are needed per batch of cookies?

Let *x* represent the number of eggs needed.

Number of batches	·	Number of eggs per batch	=	Total eggs
3		*x*		12

To answer this question, you can use algebra tiles to solve $3x = 12$.

A Model $3x = 12$.

$3x$ 12

B There are 3 variable tiles, so draw circles to separate the tiles into 3 equal groups. One group has been circled for you.

C How many unit tiles are in each group? ____4____ This is the solution of the equation.

____4____ eggs are needed per batch of cookies.

TRY THIS!

1. Caroline ran 15 miles in 5 days. She ran the same distance each day. Write and solve an equation to determine the number of miles she ran each day.

   $5x = 15$; 3 mi/day

Unit 4   93   Lesson 3

Separating the tiles on both sides of an equation mat into an equal number of groups models dividing both sides of an equation by the same number.

Division Property of Equality

You can divide both sides of an equation by the same nonzero number, and the two sides will remain equal.

When an equation contains multiplication, solve by dividing both sides of the equation by the same number.

2 EXAMPLE Using the Division Property of Equality

Solve each equation.

A $9a = 54$

What number is multiplied by *a*? ____9____

Divide both sides of the equation by this number.

$$\frac{9a}{9} = \frac{54}{9}$$

$a = $ 6   *Divide.*

Check: $9a = 54$

$9\left(6 \right) \stackrel{?}{=} 54$ *Substitute* 6 *for a.*

$54 \stackrel{?}{=} 54$ *Multiply on the left side.*

B $72 = 3d$

What number is multiplied by *d*? ____3____

Divide both sides of the equation by this number.

$$\frac{72}{3} = \frac{3d}{3}$$

24 $= d$ *Divide.*

Check: $72 = 3d$

$72 \stackrel{?}{=} 3\left(24 \right)$ *Substitute* 24 *for d.*

$72 \stackrel{?}{=} 72$ *Multiply on the right side.*

TRY THIS!

Solve each equation.

2a. $3x = 21$ **2b.** $2.5h = 45$ **2c.** $143 = 11y$

$x = $ ____7____ $h = $ ____18____ $y = $ ____13____

Unit 4   94   Lesson 3

Questioning Strategies

- How can you translate the expression $\frac{x}{5}$ into words? **x divided by 5**

- How can you undo division by 5? **Multiply by 5.**

- Can multiplying both sides of the equation by the variable help you solve this equation? **No, it does not lead to the solution.**

- How do you solve a one-step equation that contains division? **Multiply both sides of the equation by the constant, not the variable.**

Avoid Common Errors

Student may try to *divide* both sides by the denominator when they should multiply. For example, to solve $\frac{x}{5} = 20$ students may try to divide both sides by 5 instead of multiply. Remind students that multiplication will undo the division indicated by a fraction.

Essential Question

How do you solve equations that contain multiplication or division?
Possible answer: Identify the operation performed on the variable, and perform the inverse operation on both sides of the equation to get the variable by itself.

Summarize

Have students write the steps they would take to solve the following problems: a one-step multiplication equation and a one-step division equation. Have students write specific equation, and solutions to support their writing.

PRACTICE

Where skills are taught	Where skills are practiced
1 EXPLORE	EXS. 1–8, 13–16
2 EXAMPLE	EXS. 1–8, 13–16
3 EXAMPLE	EXS. 9–12

When an equation contains division, solve by multiplying both sides of the equation by the same number.

Multiplication Property of Equality

You can multiply both sides of an equation by the same number, and the two sides will remain equal.

3 EXAMPLE Using the Multiplication Property of Equality

Solve each equation.

A $\frac{x}{5} = 20$

What number is x divided by? _____5_____

Multiply both sides of the equation by this number.

$$5 \cdot \frac{x}{5} = 5 \cdot 20$$

$$x = 100 \qquad \text{Multiply.}$$

Check: $\frac{x}{5} = 20$

$$\frac{100}{5} \stackrel{?}{=} 20 \qquad \text{Substitute } 100 \text{ for } x.$$

$$20 \stackrel{?}{=} 20 \qquad \text{Divide on the left side.}$$

B $15 = \frac{r}{2}$

What number is r divided by? _____2_____

Multiply both sides of the equation by this number.

$$2 \cdot 15 = 2 \cdot \frac{r}{2}$$

$$30 = r \qquad \text{Multiply.}$$

Check: $15 = \frac{r}{2}$

$$15 \stackrel{?}{=} \frac{30}{2} \qquad \text{Substitute } 30 \text{ for } r.$$

$$15 \stackrel{?}{=} 15 \qquad \text{Divide on the right side.}$$

Unit 4   95   Lesson 3

TRY THIS!

Solve each equation.

3a. $\frac{y}{9} = 12$

$y = $ _____108_____

3b. $\frac{x}{4} = 24$

$x = $ _____96_____

3c. $9 = \frac{w}{9}$

$w = $ _____81_____

REFLECT

3d. One way to solve the equation $4x = 32$ is to divide both sides by 4. $\frac{1}{4}$
Another way to solve this equation is to multiply both sides by _____
(*Hint:* Remember that dividing is the same as multiplying by the reciprocal.)

PRACTICE

Solve each equation.

1. $6c = 18$

$c = $ _____3_____

2. $2a = 14$

$a = $ _____7_____

3. $75 = 15x$

$x = $ _____5_____

4. $25d = 350$

$d = $ _____14_____

5. $9.5w = 76$

$w = $ _____8_____

6. $2.5k = 17.5$

$k = $ _____7_____

7. $805 = 7h$

$h = $ _____115_____

8. $9y = 81$

$y = $ _____9_____

9. $\frac{n}{4} = 68$

$n = $ _____272_____

10. $12 = \frac{m}{9}$

$m = $ _____108_____

11. $\frac{n}{2.4} = 15$

$n = $ _____36_____

12. $\frac{z}{64} = 8$

$z = $ _____512_____

For 13–16, write and solve an equation to answer each question.

13. Carmen participated in a read-a-thon. Mr. Cole pledged $4.00 per book and gave Carmen $44. How many books did Carmen read?

Sample equation: $4k = 44$; 11 books

14. Lee drove 420 miles and used 15 gallons of gasoline. How many miles did Lee's car travel per gallon of gasoline?

Sample equation: $15m = 420$; 28 mi/gal

15. Last week Tina worked 38 hours in 5 days. How many hours did she work each day?

Sample equation: $5h = 38$; 7.6 h

16. On some days, Melvin commutes 3.5 hours per day to the city for business meetings. Last week he commuted for a total of 14 hours. How many days did he commute to the city?

Sample equation: $3.5d = 14$; 4 days

Unit 4   96   Lesson 3

Equations, Tables, and Graphs

Essential question: *How can you use equations, tables, and graphs to represent relationships between two variables?*

© Houghton Mifflin Harcourt Publishing Company

COMMON CORE Standards for Mathematical Content

CC.6.EE.9 Use variables to represent two quantities in a real-world problem that change in relationship to one another; write an equation to express one quantity, thought of as the dependent variable, in terms of the other quantity, thought of as the independent variable. Analyze the relationship between the dependent and independent variables using graphs and tables, and relate these to the equation.

Vocabulary

dependent variable

independent variable

input

output

Prerequisites

Writing one-step equations

Evaluating variable expressions

Graphing in the coordinate plane

Math Background

Although the word *function* is not used, students are actually working with functions in this lesson. A function is a rule that assigns one input value to exactly one output value. The output depends on the input, so the output variable is called the dependent variable. The input value is the independent value. Two-variable equations use a *rule* to describe a *relationship* between two variables, often between an input- and an output-value. Solutions of two-variable equations are pairs of values that satisfy the rule described in the equation.

INTRODUCE

Connect to prior learning by discussing the meanings of the words *dependent* and *independent*. Lead students to understand that when something is dependent, it reacts to the behavior of something else. In this lesson, relationships between numerical values are described in terms of dependence. These numerical relationships can also be described in terms of an *input* resulting in an *output*.

TEACH

1 EXPLORE

Questioning Strategies

- What information is given about the shipping fee? **Flat fee of $6; it does not change as the number of DVDs changes.**

- What information is given about the cost of DVDs? **DVDs cost $8 each; the total cost of the purchase will change as the number of DVDs changes.**

- How can you find the total cost of DVDs and shipping? **Multiply 8 by the number of DVDs purchased; then add $6 for shipping.**

Technology Connection

After students write the equation, they can use a spreadsheet to generate a table. Show students how to set up the columns as shown in the student book by entering formulas instead of calculating values in each cell.

2 EXPLORE

Questioning Strategies

- What does it mean for the train to move at a *constant* speed? **The train goes the same speed the whole time.**

- How can you tell which variable is dependent on the other? **The phrase "*distance… traveled after x hours*" indicates that distance depends on hours.**

- How can you find the distance traveled in a given number of hours? **Substitute the given number of hours, or the input, for x and multiply to find the output y, or the distance traveled.**

Differentiated Instruction

The notes you hear played by a musical instrument are an example of a dependent relationship. For example, a clarinet's pitch depends on the number of holes covered while playing the instrument. A harp's pitch depends on the length of the string being plucked.

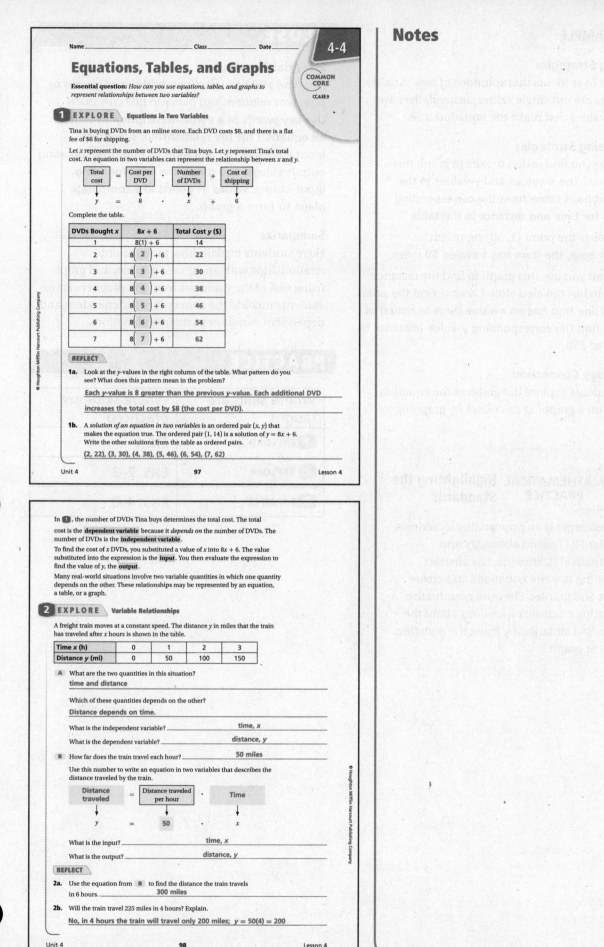

Name_____ Class_____ Date_____

Equations, Tables, and Graphs

COMMON CORE
CC.6.EE.9

Essential question: *How can you use equations, tables, and graphs to represent relationships between two variables?*

1 EXPLORE   Equations in Two Variables

Tina is buying DVDs from an online store. Each DVD costs $8, and there is a flat fee of $6 for shipping.

Let x represent the number of DVDs that Tina buys. Let y represent Tina's total cost. An equation in two variables can represent the relationship between x and y.

Total cost	=	Cost per DVD	·	Number of DVDs	+	Cost of shipping
y	=	8	·	x	+	6

Complete the table.

DVDs Bought x	$8x + 6$	Total Cost y ($)
1	8(1) + 6	14
2	8(2) + 6	22
3	8(3) + 6	30
4	8(4) + 6	38
5	8(5) + 6	46
6	8(6) + 6	54
7	8(7) + 6	62

REFLECT

1a. Look at the y-values in the right column of the table. What pattern do you see? What does this pattern mean in the problem?

Each y-value is 8 greater than the previous y-value. Each additional DVD

increases the total cost by $8 (the cost per DVD).

1b. A *solution of an equation in two variables* is an ordered pair (x, y) that makes the equation true. The ordered pair $(1, 14)$ is a solution of $y = 8x + 6$. Write the other solutions from the table as ordered pairs.

(2, 22), (3, 30), (4, 38), (5, 46), (6, 54), (7, 62)

Unit 4   97   Lesson 4

In 1 , the number of DVDs Tina buys determines the total cost. The total cost is the **dependent variable** because it *depends on* the number of DVDs. The number of DVDs is the **independent variable**.

To find the cost of x DVDs, you substituted a value of x into $8x + 6$. The value substituted into the expression is the **input**. You then evaluate the expression to find the value of y, the **output**.

Many real-world situations involve two variable quantities in which one quantity depends on the other. These relationships may be represented by an equation, a table, or a graph.

2 EXPLORE   Variable Relationships

A freight train moves at a constant speed. The distance y in miles that the train has traveled after x hours is shown in the table.

Time x (h)	0	1	2	3
Distance y (mi)	0	50	100	150

A What are the two quantities in this situation?

time and distance

Which of these quantities depends on the other?

Distance depends on time.

What is the independent variable? _____ time, x

What is the dependent variable? _____ distance, y

B How far does the train travel each hour? _____ 50 miles

Use this number to write an equation in two variables that describes the distance traveled by the train.

Distance traveled	=	Distance traveled per hour	·	Time
y	=	50	·	x

What is the input? _____ time, x

What is the output? _____ distance, y

REFLECT

2a. Use the equation from B to find the distance the train travels in 6 hours. _____ 300 miles

2b. Will the train travel 225 miles in 4 hours? Explain.

No, in 4 hours the train will travel only 200 miles; $y = 50(4) = 200$

Unit 4   98   Lesson 4

© Houghton Mifflin Harcourt Publishing Company

Teaching Strategies

Point out to students that solutions of two-variable equations are not single values; instead, they are pairs of values that make the equation true.

Questioning Strategies

- How do you find ordered pairs to graph this equation? **The *x*-values and *y*-values in the ordered pairs come from the corresponding values for time and distance in the table.**

- What does the point (1, 50) represent? **After 1 hour, the train has traveled 50 miles.**

- How can you use this graph to find the distance the train has traveled after 7 hours? **Find the point on the line that has an *x*-value (time in hours) of 7, and find the corresponding *y*-value (distance in miles) of 350.**

Technology Connection

Have students explore the graph of the equation $d = 50h$ on a graphing calculator by graphing $y = 50x$.

MATHEMATICAL PRACTICE **Highlighting the Standards**

This example is an opportunity to address Standard 2 (Reason abstractly and quantitatively). Students use abstract reasoning to write equations and create tables and graphs. They use quantitative reasoning to answer questions about the real-world situation by using the equation, table, or graph.

CLOSE

Essential Question

How can you use equations, tables, and graphs to represent relationships between two variables?
Use key words in a verbal description to write an equation for the relationship; substitute input values in the equation to find corresponding output values; and graph the corresponding input-output values as points in a coordinate plane to form a graph.

Summarize

Have students explain how to represent relationships with an equation, table, and graph using one of the exercises from the practice. Have students include the concepts of independent and dependent variables in their explanations.

PRACTICE

Where skills are taught	Where skills are practiced
1 EXPLORE	EX. 1
2 EXPLORE	EXS. 2–3
3 EXAMPLE	EXS. 4–8

3 EXAMPLE Graphing Solutions

In **2**, you wrote the equation $y = 50x$ to describe the distance traveled by a train. Graph the solutions to this equation.

Write ordered pairs to represent the solutions to this equation that are given in the table in **2**.

(0, 0) (1, **50**) (2, **100**) (**3**, 150)

Graph these ordered pairs on the coordinate plane.

Connect the ordered pairs with a line. Extend the line to the right beyond your ordered pairs. Every point on this line is a solution to $y = 50x$. In other words, this line represents all solutions to $y = 50x$.

REFLECT

3a. Are there any other ordered pair solutions to the equation? If so, how can you find them? Where will the points be located in the coordinate plane?

Yes; substitute other values for x into the equation and find the corresponding

values of y. The points will be located on the line.

3b. Find three more ordered pair solutions and graph them on the coordinate plane.

Sample answer: (4, 200), (5, 250), (6, 300)

3c. What do the points between (0, 0) and (1, 50) represent?

The distances traveled for times between 0 and 1 hour; for example,

the point (0.5, 25) represents the distance traveled after half an hour.

3d. Why is the graph not extended past (0, 0) on the left?

Points with x-values less than 0 would correspond to negative times,

which doesn't make sense in this situation.

TRY THIS!

3e. Use the table to record solutions to the equation $y = x + 2$. Write the solutions as ordered pairs and graph the ordered pairs. Then graph all of the solutions to this equation.

x	−2	−1	0	1	2	3
y = x + 2	0	1	2	3	4	5

Ordered pairs: (−2, 0), (−1, 1),

(0, 2), (1, 3), (2, 4), (3, 5)

PRACTICE

Ship to Shore rents paddleboats for a fee of $10 plus an additional $5 per hour that the boat is rented.

1a. Let x represent the number of hours a paddleboat is rented, and let y represent the total cost of the rental. Complete the equation to show the relationship between x and y.

$$\boxed{\text{Total cost}} = \boxed{\text{Cost per hour}} \cdot \boxed{\text{Number of hours}} + \boxed{\text{Fee}}$$

$$y = 5 \cdot x + 10$$

b. What is the input? _____ time, x

c. What is the output? _____ cost, y

2a. What are the two quantities in this situation? _____ time and cost

b. Which of these quantities depends on the other? _____ Cost depends on time.

c. What is the independent variable? _____ time, x

d. What is the dependent variable? _____ cost, y

3. Complete the table.

Time Rented x (h)	1	2	3	4	5	6
Total Cost y ($)	15	20	25	30	35	40

4. Write the ordered pairs from the table.

(1, 15), (2, 20), (3, 25), (4, 30), (5, 35), (6, 40)

5. Graph the ordered pairs on the coordinate plane. Connect the points and extend the line to the right.

6a. What is the cost to rent a paddleboat for 8 hours? _____ $50

b. The cost to rent a paddleboat for 8 hours is represented on the graph by the point _____ (8, 50)

7. The cost to rent a paddleboat for _____ 10 hours is $60. This is represented on the graph by the point _____ (10, 60)

8. Describe two ways to find the cost to rent a paddleboat for 9 hours.

1. Substitute 9 for x in the equation $y = 10 + 5x$.

2. Find the y-coord. of the point on the graph whose x-coord. is 9.

© Houghton Mifflin Harcourt Publishing Company

Solutions of Inequalities

Essential question: *How do you represent solutions of inequalities?*

COMMON CORE Standards for Mathematical Content

CC.6.EE.5 Understand solving an equation or inequality as a process of answering a question: which values from a specified set, if any, make the equation or inequality true? Use substitution to determine whether a given number in a specified set makes an equation or inequality true.

CC.6.EE.6 Use variables to represent numbers and write expressions when solving a real-world or mathematical problem; understand that a variable can represent an unknown number, or, depending on the purpose at hand, any number in a specified set.

CC.6.EE.8 Write an inequality of the form $x > c$ or $x < c$ to represent a constraint or condition in a real-world or mathematical problem. Recognize that inequalities of the form $x > c$ or $x < c$ have infinitely many solutions; represent solutions of such inequalities on number line diagrams.

Prerequisites

Comparing and ordering rational numbers

Math Background

An equation is a mathematical sentence with an equals sign. An *inequality* is a mathematical sentence with an inequality symbol: $<$ (less than), $>$ (greater than), $\leq$ (less than or equal to), or $\geq$ (greater than or equal to). In this lesson, students will work with one-variable inequalities. The solution of a one-variable inequality consists of all values for the variable that make the inequality a true statement. You can graph the solution of a one-variable inequality on a number line to represent all the values in the solution.

INTRODUCE

Connect to prior learning by reviewing that fact that one-variable equations have one solution. Tell students they will be working with one-variable inequalities that have many solutions. Sometimes the solutions of an inequality are infinite in number.

TEACH

1 EXPLORE

Questioning Strategies

- Where are negative numbers positioned in relation to 0 on the number line? **to the left of 0**
- Where are positive numbers positioned in relation to 0 on the number line? **to the right of 0**
- Would -8 and -10 be included with the graphed solutions on the number line described in part E? **No, those values are less than -2. Solutions of this inequality are values greater than -2.**

Teaching Strategies

In part E, point out to students that a ray shows all of the solutions, including values between integers. For example, 8.5, 8.65, and 8.999 are all solutions of this inequality.

2 EXAMPLE

Questioning Strategies

- Which inequality symbols indicate that the endpoint is a solid circle? **$\geq$ and $\leq$**
- Which inequality symbols indicate that the endpoint is an empty circle? **$>$ and $<$**
- On a number line, on which side of 5 are the solutions of $x < 5$? **left** of $x > 5$? **right**
- On a number line, on which side are the solutions of $5 < x$? **right** of $5 > x$? **left**

Avoid Common Errors

Some students get confused about which direction to shade solutions on the graph, especially when the variable appears on the right side of the inequality symbol. Remind students that the tip of the arrow points to the lesser value. Encourage them to substitute a number for the variable to see if it makes the inequality true. If so, shade the side containing that number. If not, shade the other side.

Name _____ **Class** _____ **Date** _____

4-5

Solutions of Inequalities

COMMON CORE
CC.6.EE.5
CC.6.EE.6
CC.6.EE.8

Essential question: *How can you represent solutions of inequalities?*

You have seen the symbols > and < used in inequalities.

- The symbol > means ___is greater than___
- The symbol < means ___is less than___

Two additional symbols used in inequalities are ≥ and ≤.

- The symbol ≥ means "is greater than or equal to".
- The symbol ≤ means "is less than or equal to".

1 EXPLORE   Inequalities with Variables

A The lowest temperature ever recorded in Florida was −2 °F.
Graph this temperature on the number line.

−10 −9 −8 −7 −6 −5 −4 −3 −2 −1 0 1 2 3 4 5 6 7 8 9 10

B The temperatures 0 °F, 3 °F, 6 °F, 5 °F, and −1 °F have also been recorded in Florida.
Graph these temperatures on the number line.

C How do the temperatures in **B** compare to −2?

___They are all greater than −2.___

How can you see this relationship on the number line?

___All of the temperatures are located to the right of −2.___

D How many other numbers have the same relationship to −2 as the
temperatures in **B**? Give some examples.

___Infinitely many; any number greater than −2; sample answer: 1, 2, 8.5, 10___

E Suppose you could graph all of the possible answers to **D** on a number line.
What would the graph look like?

___A ray extending to the right with its endpoint at −2___

Let the variable *x* represent any of the possible answers to **D** .

Complete this inequality: *x* ___>___ −2

When an inequality contains a variable, a solution of that inequality is any
value of the variable that makes the inequality true. For example, 7 is a solution
of *x* > −2, since 7 > −2 is a true statement. In **1**, the numbers you listed
in **D** are solutions of the inequality *x* > −2.

Unit 4   101   Lesson 5

This number line shows the solutions of *x* > −2:

−10 −9 −8 −7 −6 −5 −4 −3 −2 −1 0 1 2 3 4 5 6 7 8 9 10

An *empty* circle means the
number *is not* included in the
solution. −2 is **not** a solution
of *x* > −2.

Shade the number line to the right of −2
to indicate all numbers greater than −2.
The arrowhead means that the shaded
region extends indefinitely.

This number line shows the solutions of *x* ≥ −2:

−10 −9 −8 −7 −6 −5 −4 −3 −2 −1 0 1 2 3 4 5 6 7 8 9 10

A *solid* circle means the
number *is* included in the
solution. −2 is a solution of
x ≥ −2.

Shade the number line to the right of −2
to indicate all numbers greater than −2.
The arrowhead means that the shaded
region extends indefinitely.

2 EXAMPLE   Graphing Inequalities

Graph the solutions of each inequality.

A *y* ≤ −3

−10 −9 −8 −7 −6 −5 −4 −3 −2 −1 0 1 2 3 4 5 6 7 8 9 10

Step 1 Draw a circle at −3.

Is −3 a solution of *y* ≤ −3? ___yes___

Will you draw an empty circle or a solid circle? ___solid___

Step 2 Shade the number line.

The variable *y* represents numbers less than or equal to −3. Where
are numbers less than −3 located on the number line?

___to the left of −3___

B *w* > 2

−10 −9 −8 −7 −6 −5 −4 −3 −2 −1 0 1 2 3 4 5 6 7 8 9 10

Step 1 Draw a circle at 2.

Is 2 a solution of *w* > 2? ___no___

Will you draw an empty circle or a solid circle? ___empty___

Step 2 Shade the number line.

The variable *w* represents numbers greater than 2. Where are
these numbers located on the number line?

___to the right of 2___

Unit 4   102   Lesson 5

3 EXAMPLE

Questioning Strategies

- What is the meaning of the phrase *at least* 5? no less than 5; 5 is the least value; 5 or more

- Is 5 included in the solution of $g \geq 5$? yes

- How can you determine whether -1 is a solution of $g \geq 5$? Substitute -1 for g in the inequality to see if it makes a true statement. Is $-1 \geq 5$ true? No; -1 is not a solution.

Teaching Strategy

Challenge students to rewrite the inequality with the variable on the other side of the inequality symbol so it has the same solutions. Lead them to see that $g \geq 5$ has the same solutions as $5 \leq g$, and $t < -1$ has the same solutions as $-1 > t$.

CLOSE

Essential Question
How do you represent solutions of inequalities?
Possible answer: On a number line, use a solid circle for inequalities that contain $\geq$ or $\leq$, and use an empty circle for inequalities that contain $<$ or $>$.

Summarize
Have students copy and complete the table below.

Words	Symbol	Solid or Empty Circle
Greater than	$>$	empty
Less than	$<$	empty
Greater than or equal to	$\geq$	solid
Less than or equal to	$\leq$	solid

PRACTICE

Where skills are taught	Where skills are practiced
1 EXPLORE	EXS. 1, 6–10
2 EXAMPLE	EXS. 2–10
3 EXAMPLE	EXS. 5–10

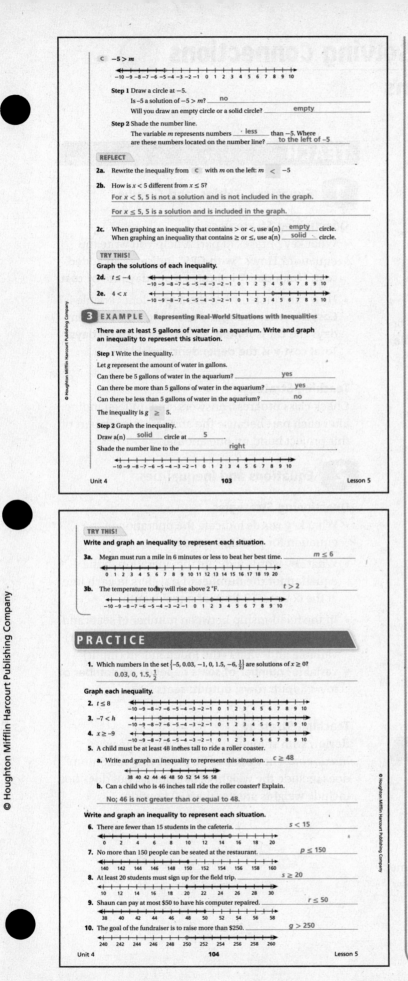

c −5 > m

-10 -9 -8 -7 -6 -5 -4 -3 -2 -1 0 1 2 3 4 5 6 7 8 9 10

Step 1 Draw a circle at −5.

Is −5 a solution of −5 > m? _____no_____

Will you draw an empty circle or a solid circle? _____empty_____

Step 2 Shade the number line.

The variable m represents numbers ____less____ than −5. Where are these numbers located on the number line? __to the left of −5__

REFLECT

2a. Rewrite the inequality from c with m on the left: m __<__ −5

2b. How is x < 5 different from x ≤ 5?

For x < 5, 5 is not a solution and is not included in the graph.

For x ≤ 5, 5 is a solution and is included in the graph.

2c. When graphing an inequality that contains > or <, use a(n) __empty__ circle.
When graphing an inequality that contains ≥ or ≤, use a(n) __solid__ circle.

TRY THIS!

Graph the solutions of each inequality.

2d. t ≤ −4

-10 -9 -8 -7 -6 -5 -4 -3 -2 -1 0 1 2 3 4 5 6 7 8 9 10

2e. 4 < x

-10 -9 -8 -7 -6 -5 -4 -3 -2 -1 0 1 2 3 4 5 6 7 8 9 10

3 EXAMPLE Representing Real-World Situations with Inequalities

There are at least 5 gallons of water in an aquarium. Write and graph an inequality to represent this situation.

Step 1 Write the inequality.

Let g represent the amount of water in gallons.

Can there be 5 gallons of water in the aquarium? ____yes____

Can there be more than 5 gallons of water in the aquarium? ____yes____

Can there be less than 5 gallons of water in the aquarium? ____no____

The inequality is g __≥__ 5.

Step 2 Graph the inequality.

Draw a(n) __solid__ circle at __5__

Shade the number line to the ____right____

-10 -9 -8 -7 -6 -5 -4 -3 -2 -1 0 1 2 3 4 5 6 7 8 9 10

Unit 4   **103**   Lesson 5

TRY THIS!

Write and graph an inequality to represent each situation.

3a. Megan must run a mile in 6 minutes or less to beat her best time. ____m ≤ 6____

0 1 2 3 4 5 6 7 8 9 10 11 12 13 14 15 16 17 18 19 20

3b. The temperature today will rise above 2 °F. ____t > 2____

-10 -9 -8 -7 -6 -5 -4 -3 -2 -1 0 1 2 3 4 5 6 7 8 9 10

PRACTICE

1. Which numbers in the set $\{-5, 0.03, -1, 0, 1.5, -6, \frac{1}{2}\}$ are solutions of x ≥ 0?

0.03, 0, 1.5, $\frac{1}{2}$

Graph each inequality.

2. t ≤ 8

-10 -9 -8 -7 -6 -5 -4 -3 -2 -1 0 1 2 3 4 5 6 7 8 9 10

3. −7 < h

-10 -9 -8 -7 -6 -5 -4 -3 -2 -1 0 1 2 3 4 5 6 7 8 9 10

4. x ≥ −9

-10 -9 -8 -7 -6 -5 -4 -3 -2 -1 0 1 2 3 4 5 6 7 8 9 10

5. A child must be at least 48 inches tall to ride a roller coaster.

a. Write and graph an inequality to represent this situation. ____c ≥ 48____

38 40 42 44 46 48 50 52 54 56 58

b. Can a child who is 46 inches tall ride the roller coaster? Explain.

No; 46 is not greater than or equal to 48.

Write and graph an inequality to represent each situation.

6. There are fewer than 15 students in the cafeteria. ____s < 15____

0 2 4 6 8 10 12 14 16 18 20

7. No more than 150 people can be seated at the restaurant. ____p ≤ 150____

140 142 144 146 148 150 152 154 156 158 160

8. At least 20 students must sign up for the field trip. ____s ≥ 20____

10 12 14 16 18 20 22 24 26 28 30

9. Shaun can pay at most $50 to have his computer repaired. ____r ≤ 50____

38 40 42 44 46 48 50 52 54 56 58

10. The goal of the fundraiser is to raise more than $250. ____g > 250____

240 242 244 246 248 250 252 254 256 258 260

Unit 4   **104**   Lesson 5

COMMON CORE Standards for Mathematical Content

CC.6.EE.5 Understand solving an equation or inequality as a process of answering a question: which values from a specified set, if any, make the equation or inequality true? Use substitution to determine whether a given number in a specified set makes an equation or inequality true.

CC.6.EE.6 Use variables to represent numbers and write expressions when solving a real-world or mathematical problem; understand that a variable can represent an unknown number…

CC.6.EE.7 Solve real-world and mathematical problems by writing and solving equations of the form $x + p = q$ and $px = q$ for cases in which p, q, and x are all nonnegative rational numbers.

CC.6.EE.8 Write an inequality of the form $x > c$ or $x < c$ to represent a constraint or condition in a real-world or mathematical problem. Recognize that inequalities of the form $x > c$ or $x < c$ have infinitely many solutions; represent solutions of such inequalities on number line diagrams.

CC.6.EE.9 Use variables to represent two quantities in a real-world problem that change in relationship to one another; write an equation to express one quantity, thought of as the dependent variable, in terms of the other quantity, thought of as the independent variable. Analyze the relationship between the dependent and independent variables using graphs and tables, and relate these to the equation.

INTRODUCE

When taking a trip, whether for business or pleasure, there is a lot of planning to do. Ask students to imagine they are going on a trip. What do they need to plan for? You may want to record students' responses on the board. Explain to students that, in this project, they will explore some of these ideas and use mathematical concepts they have learned in this unit.

TEACH

1 Equations, Tables, and Graphs

Questioning Strategies

- What key phrases in part A help you write the equation? How? **"with GPS" indicates an added cost; "for x days" indicates a per-day rate of cost**

- How can you tell what the dependent variable is? **Cost of rental changes depending on how many days the car is rented, so cost depends on days. Total cost y is the dependent variable.**

Teaching Strategy
Check class progress, answers, and understanding after each part because the answers in each part of this project build on one another.

2 Equations and Inequalities

Questioning Strategies

- What key words indicate the operation in the equation for parking? **per day**

- What key words indicate the operation in the equation for the number of travelers in each line at the counter? **3 lines of equal length**

- In the relationship between number of seats and number of rows, what is the dependent (output) variable and what is the independent (input) variable? **number of seats depends on number of rows; input: rows; output: seats**

Teaching Strategy
Review with students the meaning of the word *maximum*. They need to be aware that maximum does include the weight of 50 pounds, but does not include weights greater than 50 pounds.

UNIT 4

Problem Solving Connections

Travel Plans Mr. Arimoto has won a seven-day trip to Anchorage, Alaska! The prize package will pay for airfare from his home in New Mexico, as well as his hotel, meals, and activities in Anchorage. Mr. Arimoto must pay for any additional travel expenses, including a rental car. Will $400 be enough to cover these expenses?

Greetings From ALASKA

COMMON CORE
CC.6.EE.5
CC.6.EE.6
CC.6.EE.7
CC.6.EE.8
CC.6.EE.9

1 Equations, Tables, and Graphs

A Before leaving for the trip, Mr. Arimoto reserves a rental car that he will pick up when he arrives in Anchorage. Mr. Arimoto wants a mid-size car with GPS. He is unsure how many days he will rent the car.

Rental Car Costs			
	Per Day	Extras	
Compact	$18	GPS	$20
Mid-Size	$30	Car Seat	$12
SUV	$50	XM Radio	$25

Let y represent the cost of renting a mid-size car with GPS for x days. Write an equation to describe the relationship between x and y.

$y =$ _____ $30x + 20$

B Use your equation to complete the table.

Number of Days	1	2	3	4	5
Total Cost ($)	50	80	110	140	170

Write the information in the table as ordered pairs.

(1, 50), (2, 80), (3, 110), (4, 140), (5, 170)

What do these ordered pairs represent?

solutions of the equation $y = 30x + 20$

C Graph the solutions of the equation on the coordinate plane.

2 Equations and Inequalities

A Mr. Arimoto lives 29 miles from the airport. Write and solve an equation to find the remaining distance to the airport when Mr. Arimoto has driven 14 miles.

Sample equation: $x + 14 = 29$; 15 mi

B Parking at the airport will cost Mr. Arimoto $9 per day. Use this information to complete the table.

Days	1	2	3	4	5	6	7
Cost ($)	9	18	27	36	45	54	63

Let y represent the cost to park for x days. Write an equation that describes the relationship between x and y. $y =$ _____ $9x$

What is the independent variable? _____ number of days, x

What is the dependent variable? _____ cost, y

C When Mr. Arimoto arrives at the check-in counter, he sees that there are 3 clerks at the counter and 63 travelers waiting ahead of him. The travelers have formed 3 lines of equal length. Write and solve an equation to find how many travelers are in each line.

Sample equation: $3x = 63$; 21 people

D This sign is posted at the check-in counter.

Baggage		
	Maximum Weight per Bag	Cost per Bag
Domestic Flights (U.S.)	50 lb (23 kg)	$25
International	70 lb (32 kg)	$35

Write an inequality to represent the allowable weight of a bag on a domestic flight. How do you know which inequality symbol to use?

$w \leq 50$; 50 lb is an allowable weight, so you must use $\leq$.

Graph the inequality. 0 10 20 30 40 50 60 70 80 90 100

Notes

CLOSE

Questioning Strategies

- How do you find the cost of Mr. Arimoto's baggage? Use the table from part 2.

- How do you find the cost of the rental car? Use the equation from part 1.

- How do you find the total cost of parking? Use the equation from part 2.

- How do you determine whether Mr. Arimoto has enough money to cover all the travel expenses? Add all the individual costs (car rental, parking, luggage, and snacks) to see if the total is less than $400.

Journal

Have students write a journal entry in which they describe a vacation they would like to take. Have them do research to find information about the costs for various travel expenses, and write and graph equations and inequalities to represent the information they find.

> ⋰ **MATHEMATICAL** **Highlighting the**
> **PRACTICE** **Standards**
>
> Part 3 Answer the Question is an opportunity to address Standard 1 (Make sense of problems and persevere in solving them). Throughout this project, students use information given to them in tables and verbal descriptions to determine relationships and write equations or inequalities. They graph their models based on their interpretation of the information given, and use their graphs to answer more questions. Finally, in this last part of the project, students will use answers and information from previous parts of the project and perform additional calculations to solve problems.

E While waiting in line, Mr. Arimoto uses his phone to check the weather in Anchorage. The weather report says that today's high temperature will be 2 °F. Write and graph an inequality to show the possible temperatures in Anchorage today.

$t \leq 2$

F Mr. Arimoto is traveling on an airplane that has 12 seats in first class and 150 seats in coach. There are 3 rows of seating in first class. Write and solve an equation to find the number of seats in each first-class row.

Sample equation: $3x = 12$; 4 seats

G There are 25 rows of seating in coach. Write and solve an equation to determine the number of seats in each row.

Sample equation: $25x = 150$; 6 seats

H On the flight, Mr. Arimoto purchases a cup of coffee and a blueberry muffin for $8.79. He pays with a $10 bill. Write and solve an equation to determine the amount of change he will receive.

Sample equation: $x + 8.79 = 10$; $1.21

I The airline is showing a movie that is 97 minutes long. Mr. Arimoto falls asleep before the movie starts and misses the first 48 minutes of the movie. Write and solve an equation to determine the amount of time left in the movie when Mr. Arimoto wakes.

Sample equation: $x + 48 = 97$; 49 min

3 Answer the Question

Use some of your answers from previous questions to complete the following. You may also have to perform additional calculations.

A Mr. Arimoto takes two bags on his trip. Find the cost for his baggage.

Each bag costs $25; $2(25) = $50

B Mr. Arimoto returns his rental car after 7 days. Explain how to find the total cost of the rental car. What is the total cost of the rental car?

Substitute 7 for x in the equation $y = 30x + 20$;
$y = 30(7) + 20 = $230

C A snowstorm in Anchorage delays Mr. Arimoto's return home by 2 days. How much will he pay for parking at the airport when he returns to New Mexico?

He will pay for $7 + 2 = 9$ days;
$y = 9x = 9(9) = $81

D Complete the table. Is $400 enough to pay for Mr. Arimoto's travel expenses not covered by his prize package?

Item	Cost ($)
Car rental	230
Parking	81
Luggage	50
In-flight snack	8.79
Total	369.79

yes; $400 > $369.79

© Houghton Mifflin Harcourt Publishing Company

COMMON CORE CORRELATION

Standard	Items
CC.6.EE.5	2, 5, 6, 7
CC.6.EE.6	2, 5, 7
CC.6.EE.7	1, 3, 4, 6–9
CC.6.EE.8	11
CC.6.EE.9	10, 12–18

TEST PREP DOCTOR ⊕

Multiple Choice: Item 5
- Students who answered **B** may have divided 15 by 3 instead of 5.
- Students who answered **C** may have subtracted 5 from 15.
- Students who answered **D** may have just counted the number of single unit tiles.

Multiple Choice: Item 6
- Students who answered **F** may have divided 17 by 4.5.
- Students who answered **G** may have subtracted 4.5 from 17.
- Students who answered **J** may have multiplied 17 by 4.5.

Multiple Choice: Item 11
- Students who answered **A** showed understanding that the direction of the arrow to the right means *greater than*, they incorrectly included the value of −4.
- Students who answered **C** correctly omitted the value of −4, but they did not demonstrate understanding of *greater than*.
- Students who answered **D** did not demonstrate understanding of *greater than* and incorrectly included the value of −4.

Free Response: Item 12
- Students who answered $y = 8x + 0.5$ did not demonstrate understanding of the fixed amount and the variable amount.
- Students who answered **$8.50** or **$8.50x** demonstrated a lack of understanding of the independent and dependent variables.

Free Response: Item 16
- Students who answered $y = 60 + x$ did not properly apply the relationship between distance, rate, and time: $d = rt$.
- Students who answered $4x = 240y$ appear to have understood the relationship between distance, rate, and time, but did not write the equation in terms of an independent variable (input) and dependent variable (output).

© Houghton Mifflin Harcourt Publishing Company

Name _____ Class _____ Date _____

MULTIPLE CHOICE

1. Miguel and his team must answer the following question correctly in order to win a quiz bowl contest.

   A sunflower grows 5 inches every month. How many months will it take for the sunflower to reach a height of 60 inches?

   Which equation can be used to solve this problem?

   A. $m + 5 = 60$ C. $5m = 60$ ⓒ
   B. $m - 5 = 60$ D. $\frac{m}{5} = 60$

2. Look at the model.

   What is the value of x?

   F. 3   H. 10
   ⓖ 7   J. 13

3. Leon had some change in his pocket. Then a friend loaned him $0.25. Now Leon has $1.45 in his pocket. Which equation can be used to find the original amount of money m that Leon had in his pocket?

   Ⓐ $m + 0.25 = 1.45$
   B. $1.45 = m - 0.25$
   C. $m + 1.45 = 0.25$
   D. $m = 1.45(0.25)$

4. Last week Randy worked 42 hours in 5 days. Which equation could Randy use to find the average number of hours he worked each day?

   F. $\frac{h}{5} = 42$ H. $\frac{h}{42} = 5$
   ⓖ $5h = 42$ J. $42h = 5$

5. Look at the model.

   What is the value of x?

   Ⓐ 3   C. 10
   B. 5   D. 15

6. Solve the equation $x - 4.5 = 17$.

   F. $x = 3.8$ Ⓗ $x = 21.5$
   G. $x = 12.5$ J. $x = 76.5$

7. Eight batches of pancakes can be made with 16 eggs. How many eggs are needed for one batch of pancakes?

   Ⓐ 2 eggs   C. 8 eggs
   B. 4 eggs   D. 24 eggs

8. Jenna's basketball team scored 54 points in its last game. Jenna scored 18 of the points. Which equation could be used to determine the number of points p scored by Jenna's teammates?

   F. $18p = 54$ H. $p - 18 = 54$
   G. $\frac{54}{p} = 18$ Ⓙ $p + 18 = 54$

9. Lucinda is arranging 150 patio blocks to build a patio. Let p represent the number of patio blocks Lucinda arranged in one hour. Which equation describes the relationship between p and h, the total number of hours Lucinda needed to arrange all 150 patio blocks?

   A. $h = 150 + p$ C. $h = 150p$
   Ⓑ $h = \frac{150}{p}$ D. $h = 150 - p$

10. Ella builds butterfly houses. The table shows the number of nails n needed to build b butterfly houses.

Butterfly Houses	
Number of Houses b	Number of Nails n
2	24
3	36
4	48
5	60
6	72

Which equation describes the relationship between butterfly houses and nails shown in the table?

   Ⓕ $12b = n$ H. $12 - b = n$
   G. $12 + b = n$ J. $\frac{b}{12} = n$

11. Which graph represents the statement "the temperature will be greater than -4 °F"?

   A.
   B.
   C.
   D.

FREE RESPONSE

12. Maria has a newspaper route. She earns $8 per week plus an additional $0.50 for each newspaper that she delivers.

   a. Write an equation to describe the total amount y that Maria earns for delivering x newspapers in a week.

   $y = 0.50x + 8$

   b. Use your equation to find the amount of money Maria will earn for a week in which she delivers 30 newspapers.

   $y = 0.50(30) + 8 = \$23$

The graph describes the motion of a car. Use the graph for 13–18.

13. What are the two quantities in this situation?

   time and distance

14. Identify the independent and dependent variables.

   Independent: time x; dependent:

   distance y

15. Use the graph to complete the table.

Time x (h)	Distance y (mi)
1	60
2	120
3	180
4	240

16. Write an equation that gives the distance the car travels y in x hours.

   $y = 60x$

17. Use your equation to find the distance the car travels in 3.5 hours.

   $y = 60(3.5) = 210$ miles

18. Suppose you extend the graph so that it passes through the point $(8, a)$. What is the value of a? What does this point represent?

   $a = 8(60) = 480$; the point $(8, 480)$

   represents the distance (480 mi) that

   the car travels in 8 hours.

Ratios and Proportional Relationships

Unit Vocabulary

conversion factor	(5-6)
equivalent ratios	(5-1)
percent	(5-4)
rate	(5-3)
ratio	(5-1)
unit rate	(5-3)

UNIT 5

Ratios and Proportional Relationships

Unit Focus

In this unit you will learn about ratios. You will learn about and use special kinds of ratios, such as rates, percents, and conversion factors.

COMMON CORE

Unit at a Glance

Lesson	Standards for Mathematical Content
5-1 Ratios	CC.6.RP.1
5-2 Ratios, Tables, and Graphs	CC.6.RP.3a
5-3 Unit Rates	CC.6.RP.2, CC.6.RP.3b
5-4 Percents	CC.6.RP.3c
5-5 Percent Problems	CC.6.RP.3c
5-6 Converting Measurements	CC.6.RP.3d
Problem Solving Connections	
Test Prep	

UNIT 5

Unit 5   111   Ratios and Proportional Relationships

© Houghton Mifflin Harcourt Publishing Company

Unpacking the Common Core Standards

Use the table to help you understand the Standards for Mathematical Content that are taught in this unit. Refer to the lessons listed after each standard for exploration and practice.

COMMON CORE Standards for Mathematical Content	What It Means For You
CC.6.RP.1 Understand the concept of a ratio and use ratio language to describe a ratio relationship between two quantities. Lesson 5-1	You will learn how to write ratios to compare two numbers.
CC.6.RP.2 Understand the concept of a unit rate a/b associated with a ratio $a:b$ with $b \neq 0$, and use rate language in the context of a ratio relationship. Lesson 5-3	You will learn how to write and calculate unit rates.
CC.6.RP.3a Make tables of equivalent ratios relating quantities with whole number measurements, find missing values in the tables, and plot the pairs of values on the coordinate plane. Use tables to compare ratios. Lessons 5-1, 5-2	You will make and use tables and graphs that represent ratios.
CC.6.RP.3b Solve unit rate problems including those involving unit pricing and constant speed. Lesson 5-3	You will solve problems involving unit rates and unit prices.
CC.6.RP.3c Find a percent of a quantity as a rate per 100 (e.g., 30% of a quantity means 30/100 times the quantity); solve problems involving finding the whole, given a part and the percent. Lessons 5-4, 5-5	You will solve real-world problems involving percents, and you will find a percent of a number. You will learn the relationship between the percent, the part, and the whole.
CC.6.RP.3d Use ratio reasoning to convert measurement units; manipulate and transform units appropriately when multiplying or dividing quantities. Lesson 5-6	You will convert between customary and metric measurements using a conversion factor.

UNIT 5

Unpacking the Common Core State Standards

This page lists and explains the Standards for Mathematical Content that are addressed in this unit. For information about the Standards for Mathematical Practice, which are integrated throughout the text, see Teacher Edition pages vii–xiii.

UNIT 5

Notes

_____

_____

_____

_____

_____

_____

_____

_____

_____

Ratios

Essential question: *How do you find equivalent ratios?*

© Houghton Mifflin Harcourt Publishing Company

Standards for Mathematical Content

CC.6.RP.1 Understand the concept of a ratio and use ratio language to describe a ratio relationship between two quantities.

CC.6.RP.3a Make tables of equivalent ratios relating quantities with whole-number measurements, find missing values in the tables, and plot pairs of values on the coordinate plane. Use tables to compare ratios.

Vocabulary

ratio

equivalent ratios

Prerequisites

Equivalent fractions

Math Background

A ratio compares two numbers. The comparison can be between parts or between a part and a whole. Ratios are read as "the ratio of a to b." A ratio can be written in the following three forms:

$$a \text{ to } b \qquad a{:}b \qquad \frac{a}{b}$$

INTRODUCE

Write a fraction on the board, and review with students which number is the numerator and which number is the denominator. Remind students that the numerator of a fraction, the number on top, represents the number of parts of the whole; and the denominator of a fraction, the number on bottom, represents the total number of parts that make the whole.

TEACH

1 EXAMPLE

Questioning Strategies

- How does the ratio of pretzels to party mix compare with the ratio of party mix to pretzels? **The ratio of pretzels to party mix is 4:8; the ratio of party mix to pretzels is 8:4. They are inverses. Written as fractions, they would be reciprocals.**

- Which ingredient forms the greatest ratio of ingredient to party mix? **pretzels**

- Which ingredients form the same ratio of ingredient to bagel chips? **cheese crackers and peanuts**

Differentiated Learning

Give students a handful of different colored counters (two or three different colors). Have the students count and record the number of each colored counter. Ask questions such as, "What is the ratio of red to yellow? What is the ratio of red to all the counters?" and so on.

2 EXPLORE

Questioning Strategies

- How many cups of cranberry juice are in the punch? How many cups of apple juice? **3; 2**

- When you increase the amount of punch you make, how does that affect the ratio? **The ratio remains the same.**

Teaching Strategies

Review with students that multiplying any number by 1 will not change the value of that number, and that any fraction with the same numerator and denominator is equal to 1. Write the ratio 3:2 as a fraction on the board, and ask students how to change its appearance, but not its value. Show students some examples:

$$\frac{3}{2}\left(\frac{10}{10}\right) = \frac{30}{20} \qquad \frac{3}{2}\left(\frac{50}{50}\right) = \frac{150}{100}$$

Name_____ Class_____ Date_____

Ratios

Essential question: *How do you write ratios and equivalent ratios?*

COMMON CORE
CC.6.RP.1
CC.6.RP.3a

A **ratio** is a comparison of two numbers by division. The two numbers in a ratio are called *terms*. A ratio can be written in several different ways:

5 dogs to 3 cats   5 to 3   5:3 $\frac{5}{3}$

1 EXAMPLE   Writing Ratios

A The party mix recipe requires __4__ cup(s) of pretzels and __2__ cup(s) of bagel chips. Write the ratio of pretzels to bagel chips in three different ways.

4:2; 4 to 2; $\frac{4}{2}$

> **Party Mix**
> **Makes 8 cups**
> 4 cups pretzels
> 2 cups bagel chips
> 1 cup cheese crackers
> 1 cup peanuts

B The recipe makes a total of __8__ cups of party mix. Write the ratio of pretzels to total party mix in three different ways.

4:8; 4 to 8; $\frac{4}{8}$

TRY THIS!

Write each ratio in three different ways.

1a. bagel chips to peanuts _____   2:1; 2 to 1; $\frac{2}{1}$

1b. total party mix to pretzels _____   8:4; 8 to 4; $\frac{8}{4}$

1c. cheese crackers to peanuts _____   1:1; 1 to 1; $\frac{1}{1}$

REFLECT

1d. What does it mean when the terms in a ratio are equal?

The quantities being compared are equal.

1e. The ratio of floor seats to balcony seats in a theater is 20:1. Does this theater have more floor seats or more balcony seats? How do you know?

Floor; there are 20 floor seats for each balcony seat.

1f. At another theater, the ratio of floor seats to balcony seats is 20:19. How do the number of floor seats and the number of balcony seats compare at this theater?

There are about as many balcony seats as floor seats.

Equivalent ratios are ratios that name the same comparison. Find equivalent ratios by multiplying or dividing both terms of a ratio by the same number.

$$\frac{2}{7} \xrightarrow[\times 2]{\times 2} \frac{4}{14} \qquad \frac{8}{24} \xrightarrow[\div 4]{\div 4} \frac{2}{6}$$

2 EXPLORE   Equivalent Ratios

You are in charge of making punch for an upcoming school dance. The punch recipe makes 5 cups of punch by mixing 3 cups of cranberry juice with 2 cups of apple juice.

A What is the ratio of cranberry juice to apple juice? _____ $\frac{3}{2}$

Do you think the punch will taste more like cranberry juice or more like apple juice? Explain.

Cranberry; there is more cranberry juice than apple juice.

B You must increase the recipe to serve a large number of people. Fill in the boxes to find the ratio of cranberry juice to apple juice when the recipe is doubled and tripled.

$$\frac{3}{2} \xrightarrow[\times 2]{\times 2} \frac{6}{4} \qquad \frac{3}{2} \xrightarrow[\times 3]{\times 3} \frac{9}{6}$$

To double the recipe, you need __6__ cups of cranberry juice and __4__ cups of apple juice. This makes a total of __10__ cups of punch.

To triple the recipe, you need __9__ cups of cranberry juice and __6__ cups of apple juice. This makes a total of __15__ cups of punch.

C The ratios you found in **B** are equivalent to $\frac{3}{2}$. Find three other ratios that are equivalent to $\frac{3}{2}$. _____ Sample answer: $\frac{12}{8}, \frac{15}{10}, \frac{18}{12}$

D How much of each juice would you need to make a total of 40 cups of punch? _____ 24 c cranberry juice, 16 c apple juice

TRY THIS!

Complete each pair of equivalent ratios.

2a. $\frac{5}{6} = \frac{20}{24}$ **2b.** $\frac{1}{4} = \frac{8}{32}$ **2c.** $\frac{30}{6} = \frac{15}{3}$

Find three ratios equivalent to the given ratio. Sample answers given.

2d. $\frac{6}{8}$ $\frac{3}{4}, \frac{12}{16}, \frac{18}{24}$ **2e.** $\frac{24}{18}$ $\frac{4}{3}, \frac{8}{6}, \frac{12}{9}$ **2f.** $\frac{15}{10}$ $\frac{3}{2}, \frac{30}{20}, \frac{45}{30}$

Questioning Strategies

- **How can you use the ratios to determine which recipe makes stronger lemonade?** The recipe with a greater ratio of lemon juice to water (or a greater ratio of lemon juice to lemonade) makes stronger lemonade.

- **How can you compare the two ratios in the problem if they have different denominators?** You can observe the pattern in the table and compare the amounts of lemon juice for the same amount of water.

MATHEMATICAL PRACTICE | Highlighting the Standards

This explore is an opportunity to address Standard 2 (Reason abstractly and quantitatively). Students are asked to compare ratios that have different denominators to determine which is the greater ratio indicating a stronger lemonade. Students may compare corresponding lemon juice amounts for the same amount of water, or they may compare corresponding water amounts for the same amount of lemon juice. Students may use a variety of methods; ask students to share their reasoning.

CLOSE

Essential Question

How do you find equivalent ratios? Possible answer: Multiply or divide the ratio by a fraction form of the number 1.

Summarize

Ask students to think of a ratio of things the students have, such as pencils and pens. Have them use this ratio to explain what a ratio is, how to model the ratio, and how to compare ratios.

PRACTICE

Where skills are taught	Where skills are practiced
1 EXAMPLE	Exs. 1–4
2 EXPLORE	Exs. 5–7
3 EXPLORE	Ex. 8

REFLECT

2g. Why can you multiply or divide both terms of a ratio by the same number without changing the value of the ratio?

Multiplying/dividing both terms by the same number is equivalent

to multiplying/dividing by 1.

3 EXPLORE Comparing Ratios

Anna's recipe for lemonade calls for 2 cups of lemon juice and 3 cups of water. Bailey's recipe calls for 3 cups of lemon juice and 5 cups of water.

A In Anna's recipe, the ratio of lemon juice to water is $\frac{2}{3}$
Complete the table with equivalent ratios.

		2 · 2	2 · 3	2 · 5
Lemon Juice (c)	2	4	6	10
Water (c)	3	6	9	15
		3 · 2	3 · 3	3 · 5

B In Bailey's recipe, the ratio of lemon juice to water is $\frac{3}{5}$
Complete the table with equivalent ratios.

		3 · 3	3 · 4	3 · 5
Lemon Juice (c)	3	9	12	15
Water (c)	5	15	20	25
		5 · 3	5 · 4	5 · 5

C In each table, there is a column in which the amount of water is the same. Circle these columns in the tables.

D Examine these two columns. Whose recipe makes stronger lemonade? How do you know?

Anna's; it contains more lemon juice for the same amount of water, so

the lemon juice is less diluted.

E The ratio of lemon juice to water in the stronger recipe is ___greater___ than the ratio of lemon juice to water in the other recipe.
Write inequality symbols to compare the ratios: $\frac{10}{15}$ > $\frac{9}{15}$

$\frac{2}{3}$ > $\frac{3}{5}$

© Houghton Mifflin Harcourt Publishing Company

REFLECT

3a. Describe another way to determine which recipe makes stronger lemonade.

Sample answer: Extend the tables until you find a column in each table

where the two recipes have the same amount of lemon juice. The recipe

with less water in that column has the stronger flavor.

3b. **Error Analysis** Marisol said, "Bailey's lemonade is stronger because it has more lemon juice. Bailey's lemonade has 3 cups of lemon juice, and Anna's lemonade has only 2 cups of lemon juice." Explain why Marisol is incorrect.

Sample answer: It is not enough to compare the amounts of lemon juice. You

also need to know the amount of water in which the lemon juice is diluted.

PRACTICE

The contents of Dean's pencil box are shown. Write each ratio in three different ways.

1. pencils to pens ___5:3, 5 to 3, $\frac{5}{3}$___

2. total items to crayons ___46:24, 46 to 24, $\frac{46}{24}$___

3. erasers to pencils ___2:5, 2 to 5, $\frac{2}{5}$___

4. markers to total items ___12:46, 12 to 46, $\frac{12}{46}$___

Dean's Pencil Box
5 pencils
2 erasers
3 pens
12 markers
24 crayons

Write three ratios equivalent to the given ratio. Sample answers given.

5. $\frac{12}{28}$ $\frac{3}{7}, \frac{6}{14}, \frac{24}{56}$

6. $\frac{5}{2}$ $\frac{10}{4}, \frac{15}{6}, \frac{20}{8}$

7. $\frac{10}{3}$ $\frac{20}{6}, \frac{30}{9}, \frac{40}{12}$

8. Aaron's math homework includes the following problem: $\frac{15}{25} = \frac{9}{15}$

a. How is this problem different from the problems involving equivalent ratios in this lesson?

There is no whole number that 15 can be multiplied/divided by to get 9.

b. You can use a table to solve this problem. Complete the table to find the answer to Aaron's homework problem.

÷ 5   × 3

15	3	9
25	5	15

÷ 5   × 3

© Houghton Mifflin Harcourt Publishing Company

Ratios, Tables, and Graphs

Essential question: *How can you use tables and graphs to understand ratios?*

© Houghton Mifflin Harcourt Publishing Company

COMMON CORE Standards for Mathematical Content

CC.6.RP.3a Make tables of equivalent ratios relating quantities with whole number measurements, find missing values in the tables, and plot the pairs of values on the coordinate plane. Use tables to compare ratios.

Prerequisites
Equivalent ratios

Math Background
Equivalent ratios can be represented in multiple forms, including proportions, table of values, ordered pairs, and graphs. Equivalent ratios form a linear pattern when graphed as ordered pairs in the coordinate plane.

INTRODUCE

Suppose a train travels at a constant speed of 60 miles per hour. Ask students to write that speed as a ratio, 60 mi : 1 hr. Then ask students to estimate how long it would take the train to travel 320 miles. Guide students to see that the answer is about 4.5 hours. Tell students that in this lesson they will learn ways to quickly answer these types of questions involving ratios.

TEACH

1 EXPLORE

Questioning Strategies
- How can you determine how far the train traveled in 1 hour? **Find a ratio equivalent to 120:2 that has a denominator of 1.** $\frac{120}{2} = \frac{?}{1}$

Teaching Strategies
Remind students that rates are also ratios. For example, 65 mph is $\frac{65\text{ mi}}{1\text{ h}}$ and \$10 per hour is $\frac{\$10}{1\text{ h}}$.

2 EXPLORE

Questioning Strategies
- Why is time represented by the *x*-coordinate and distance represented by the *y*-coordinate? **because the distance traveled depends on the amount of time that passes**
- How can you tell from the graph that the rate of speed is constant? **The points form a line.**

Teaching Strategies
Explain to students that when connecting the points to form a line in this example that all points on the line represent equivalent ratios, and that there are infinitely many points between the points with integer coordinates.

CLOSE

Essential Question
How can you use tables and graphs to understand ratios? **Possible answer: When the points that are represented in a table of equivalent ratios are graphed on a coordinate plane, the points all lie in a line. You can use the line to generate more equivalent ratios.**

Summarize
Tell students that they have been introduced to generating ratios from a table and using these tables to create graphs. Have students work in pairs to create a real-world problem similar to the one in Explore 3, where students must form an equivalent ratio to compare quantities.

Name _____ Class _____ Date _____

5-2

COMMON CORE
CC.6.RP.3a

Ratios, Tables, and Graphs

Essential question: How can you use tables and graphs to understand ratios?

1 EXPLORE   Finding Ratios from Tables

The Webster family is taking a train to Washington, D.C. The train travels at a constant speed. The table shows the distance that the train travels in various amounts of time.

Distance (mi)	120	150	180	240	300
Time (h)	2	2.5	3	4	5

A   Use the numbers in the first column of the table to write a ratio of distance to time. $\frac{120}{2}$

B   How far does the train travel in one hour? __60 mi__
Use your answer to write another ratio of distance to time. $\frac{60}{1}$

C   The ratios in A and B are __equivalent__.

D   How can you use your answer to B to find the distance the train travels in a given number of hours?

Sample answer: Multiply the number of hours by $\frac{60}{1}$, or 60.

E   Complete the table. What are the equivalent ratios shown in the table?

$$\frac{120}{2} = \frac{150}{2.5} = \frac{180}{3} = \frac{240}{4} = \frac{300}{5}$$

REFLECT

1a. What information given in the problem explains why all of the ratios are equivalent? __The train travels at a constant speed.__

1b. What is the train's speed? __60 mi/h__

Write the train's speed as a ratio. $\frac{60 \text{ miles}}{1 \text{ hour}}$

How is this ratio related to the ratios in E ? __They are all equivalent.__

1c. When the time increases by 1 hour, the distance increases by __60__ miles. The distance traveled in 5 hours is __300__ miles, so the distance traveled in 6 hours is __360__ miles.

Unit 5   117   Lesson 2

---

2 EXPLORE   Graphing with Ratios

A   Copy the table from 1 that shows the time and distance information for the train.

Distance (mi)	120	150	180	240	300
Time (h)	2	2.5	3	4	5

B   Write the information in the table as ordered pairs. Use Time as the x-coordinates and Distance as the y-coordinates.

$(2, 120)\ \big(2.5, 150\big)\big(3, 180\big)\big(4, 240\big)\big(5, 300\big)$

Graph the ordered pairs and connect the points.

Describe your graph. _____line_____

C   For each ordered pair that you graphed, write the ratio of the y-coordinate to the x-coordinate. $\frac{120}{2}, \frac{150}{2.5}, \frac{180}{3}, \frac{240}{4}, \frac{300}{5}$

D   The train's speed is $\frac{60 \text{ miles}}{1 \text{ hour}}$. How are the ratios in C related to the train's speed? __They are equivalent.__

E   The point (3.5, 210) is on the graph but not in the table. The ratio of the y-coordinate to the x-coordinate is $\frac{210}{3.5}$. How is this ratio related to the ratios in C and D ? __They are equivalent.__

So, in 3.5 hours, the train travels __210__ miles.

F   **Conjecture** What do you think is true about every point on the graph?

Sample answer: For every point (x, y) on the line, the train travels y miles in x hours.

REFLECT

2a. How can you use the graph to find the distance the train travels in 4.5 hours?

Find the point on the graph whose x-coord. is 4.5. The y-coord. of that point is the distance traveled in 4.5 hours.

2b. If the graph were continued further, would the point (7, 420) be on the graph? How do you know? Yes; Sample answer: $\frac{420}{7}$ is equivalent to $\frac{60}{1}$.

Unit 5   118   Lesson 2

© Houghton Mifflin Harcourt Publishing Company

5-3 Unit Rates

Essential question: *How can you use unit rates to solve problems and make comparisons?*

COMMON CORE **Standards for Mathematical Content**

CC.6.RP.2 Understand the concept of a unit rate a/b associated with a ratio $a:b$ with $b \neq 0$, and use rate language in the context of a ratio relationship.

CC.6.RP.3b Solve unit rate problems including those involving unit pricing and constant speed.

Vocabulary

rate

unit rate

Prerequisites

Equivalent ratios

Math Background

A rate is a special kind of ratio that compares two quantities that have different units. A unit rate is a special kind of rate in which the second quantity is equal to 1. For example, rates such as miles per hour and miles per gallon are unit rates because they are expressed in terms of *per 1 unit*.

INTRODUCE

Have students choose something to do that they can count in one minute, such as hopping on one foot or tapping a pencil eraser on the desk. Have students keep track of the number of times they perform the action in one minute, and write the number they counted as a ratio with 1 minute in the denominator. Explain to students that they have written a *rate* because the ratio has different units. Explain to students the rate is a *unit rate* because the denominator is 1. The unit rate can be expressed in terms of units per minute, such as *hops per minute* or *taps per minute*.

TEACH

1 EXPLORE

Questioning Strategies

- Why does Shana find prices for equal ounces of juice? To compare rates (or ratios), she finds a common denominator.

- Is there another way to compare rates? You could divide each price by the corresponding number of ounces to get the price per ounce.

Teaching Strategies

Provide students with advertising flyers from different grocery stores. Have students identify unit prices given for various items.

2 EXAMPLE

Questioning Strategies

- What kind of rate do you need to find in part A? the cost-per-lesson unit rate

- How do you know what operation to perform on the numerator and denominator to find a unit rate? Determine what multiplier on the denominator will result in a product of 1. Multiply both numerator and denominator by that multiplier.

Teaching Strategies

Have students use the grocery store advertising pages again to find unit rate in the form of items per dollar, such as 3 apples for $1. Discuss with students how to find the unit rate in terms of price-per-item when given an items-per-price rate. Show students that the two rates are reciprocals.

$$\frac{3 \text{ apples}}{\$1} \text{ or } \frac{\$1 \div 3}{3 \text{ apples} \div 3} = \frac{\$0.33}{1 \text{ apple}}$$

© Houghton Mifflin Harcourt Publishing Company

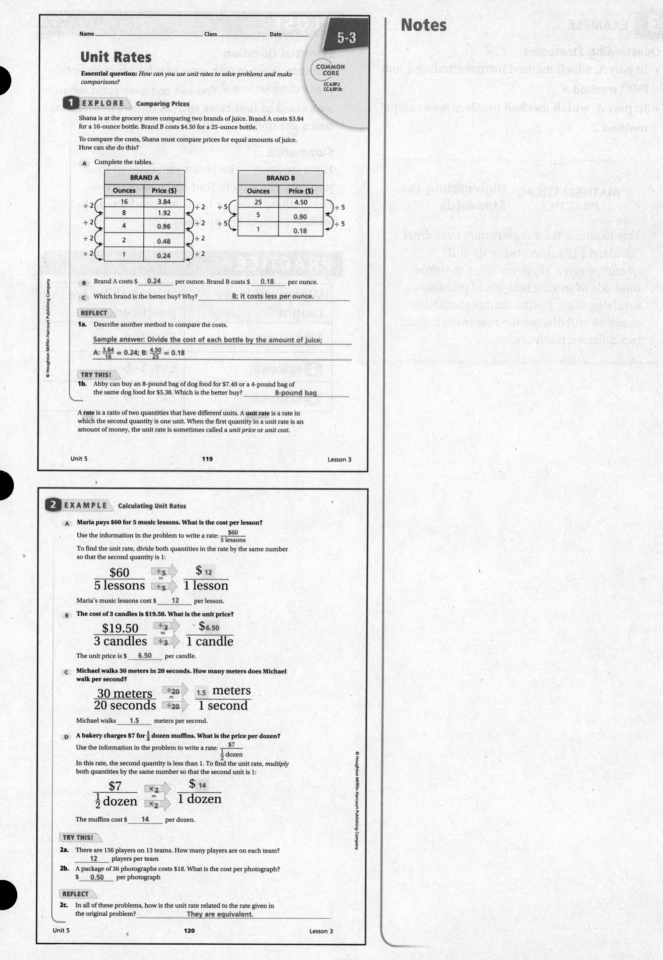

Name_____ Class_____ Date_____

5-3

COMMON CORE
CC.6.RP.2
CC.6.RP.3b

Unit Rates

Essential question: *How can you use unit rates to solve problems and make comparisons?*

1 EXPLORE Comparing Prices

Shana is at the grocery store comparing two brands of juice. Brand A costs $3.84 for a 16-ounce bottle. Brand B costs $4.50 for a 25-ounce bottle.

To compare the costs, Shana must compare prices for equal amounts of juice. How can she do this?

A Complete the tables.

BRAND A	
Ounces	Price ($)
16	3.84
8	1.92
4	0.96
2	0.48
1	0.24

÷2   ÷2
÷2   ÷2
÷2   ÷2
÷2   ÷2

BRAND B	
Ounces	Price ($)
25	4.50
5	0.90
1	0.18

÷5   ÷5
÷5   ÷5

B Brand A costs $ __0.24__ per ounce. Brand B costs $ __0.18__ per ounce.

C Which brand is the better buy? Why? _____ B; it costs less per ounce. _____

REFLECT

1a. Describe another method to compare the costs.

_____ **Sample answer: Divide the cost of each bottle by the amount of juice;** _____

A: $\frac{3.84}{16} = 0.24$; B: $\frac{4.50}{25} = 0.18$

TRY THIS!

1b. Abby can buy an 8-pound bag of dog food for $7.40 or a 4-pound bag of the same dog food for $5.38. Which is the better buy? _____ 8-pound bag

A **rate** is a ratio of two quantities that have different units. A **unit rate** is a rate in which the second quantity is one unit. When the first quantity in a unit rate is an amount of money, the unit rate is sometimes called a *unit price* or *unit cost*.

Unit 5   119   Lesson 3

© Houghton Mifflin Harcourt Publishing Company

---

2 EXAMPLE Calculating Unit Rates

A **Maria pays $60 for 5 music lessons. What is the cost per lesson?**

Use the information in the problem to write a rate: $\frac{\$60}{5 \text{ lessons}}$

To find the unit rate, divide both quantities in the rate by the same number so that the second quantity is 1:

$$\frac{\$60}{5 \text{ lessons}} \quad \overset{÷5}{\underset{÷5}{=}} \quad \frac{\$12}{1 \text{ lesson}}$$

Maria's music lessons cost $ __12__ per lesson.

B **The cost of 3 candles is $19.50. What is the unit price?**

$$\frac{\$19.50}{3 \text{ candles}} \quad \overset{÷3}{\underset{÷3}{=}} \quad \frac{\$6.50}{1 \text{ candle}}$$

The unit price is $ __6.50__ per candle.

C **Michael walks 30 meters in 20 seconds. How many meters does Michael walk per second?**

$$\frac{30 \text{ meters}}{20 \text{ seconds}} \quad \overset{÷20}{\underset{÷20}{=}} \quad \frac{1.5 \text{ meters}}{1 \text{ second}}$$

Michael walks __1.5__ meters per second.

D **A bakery charges $7 for $\frac{1}{2}$ dozen muffins. What is the price per dozen?**

Use the information in the problem to write a rate: $\frac{\$7}{\frac{1}{2} \text{ dozen}}$

In this rate, the second quantity is less than 1. To find the unit rate, *multiply* both quantities by the same number so that the second unit is 1:

$$\frac{\$7}{\frac{1}{2} \text{ dozen}} \quad \overset{×2}{\underset{×2}{=}} \quad \frac{\$14}{1 \text{ dozen}}$$

The muffins cost $ __14__ per dozen.

TRY THIS!

2a. There are 156 players on 13 teams. How many players are on each team?
_____ 12 _____ players per team

2b. A package of 36 photographs costs $18. What is the cost per photograph?
$ __0.50__ per photograph

REFLECT

2c. In all of these problems, how is the unit rate related to the rate given in the original problem? _____ They are equivalent. _____

Unit 5   120   Lesson 3

© Houghton Mifflin Harcourt Publishing Company

Questioning Strategies

- In part A, which method involves finding a unit rate? method 1

- In part A, which method involves fewer steps? method 2

MATHEMATICAL PRACTICE	Highlighting the Standards

This Example is an opportunity to address Standard 2 (Reason abstractly and quantitatively). There are often multiple methods of solving real-world problems involving rates. In this example, students examine and discuss the reasoning behind two different methods.

CLOSE

Essential Question

How can you use unit rates to solve problems and make comparisons? You can compare rates when expressed as unit rates such as dollars per hour or items per dollar.

Summarize

Have students write about unit rates in their journals. Have them find and compare two competitive rates for the same product, including which rate is better and why.

PRACTICE

Where skills are taught	Where skills are practiced
1 EXPLORE	Exs. 1–4
2 EXAMPLE	Exs. 5–6
3 EXAMPLE	Exs. 7–9

© Houghton Mifflin Harcourt Publishing Company

3 EXAMPLE Problem-Solving with Unit Rates

A In a youth soccer league, each team will have 18 players and 3 coaches. This year, 162 players signed up to play soccer. How many coaches are needed?

Method 1 Find the unit rate. How many players per coach?

$$\frac{18 \text{ players}}{3 \text{ coaches}} \xrightarrow[\div 3]{\div 3} \frac{6 \text{ player(s)}}{1 \text{ coach}}$$

There are ——6—— players per coach.

$$\frac{162 \text{ players}}{6 \text{ players per coach}} = 27 \text{ coaches}$$

Method 2 Use equivalent ratios.

$$\frac{18 \text{ players}}{3 \text{ coaches}} \xrightarrow[\times 9]{\times 9} \frac{162 \text{ players}}{27 \text{ coaches}}$$

The soccer league needs ——27—— coaches.

B Tim can mow 4 lawns in 6 hours. How many lawns can he mow in 15 hours?

Find the unit rate.

$$\frac{4 \text{ lawns}}{6 \text{ hours}} \xrightarrow[\div 6]{\div 6} \frac{\frac{2}{3} \text{ lawn(s)}}{1 \text{ hour}}$$

How can you use the unit rate to find how many lawns Tim can mow in 15 hours?

Multiply by 15; $15\left(\frac{2}{3}\right) = 10$

Tim can mow ——10—— lawns in 15 hours.

TRY THIS!

3a. On Tuesday, Donovan earned $9 for 2 hours of babysitting. On Saturday, he babysat for the same family and earned $31.50. How many hours did he babysit on Saturday? ——7—— hours

REFLECT

3b. How could you use estimation to check that your answer to **3a** is reasonable?

Sample answer: Round $9 to $10. Then Donovan earned about $\frac{10}{2} = \$5$/hour

on Sat; $5 · 7 hours = $35, which is close to $31.50.

PRACTICE

The sizes and prices of three brands of laundry detergent are shown in the table. Use the table for 1 and 2.

Brand	Size (oz)	Price ($)
A	32	4.80
B	48	5.76
C	128	17.92

1. What is the unit price for each detergent?

Brand A: $ ——0.15—— per ounce

Brand B: $ ——0.12—— per ounce

Brand C: $ ——0.14—— per ounce

2. Which detergent is the best buy? ——B——

Mason's favorite brand of peanut butter is available in two sizes. Each size and its price are shown in the table. Use the table for 3 and 4.

	Size (oz)	Price ($)
Regular	16	3.36
Family Size	40	7.60

3. What is the unit rate for each size of peanut butter?

Regular: $ ——0.21—— per ounce

Family size: $ ——0.19—— per ounce

4. Which size is the better buy? ——Family size——

For 5 and 6, find the unit rate.

5. Lisa walked 48 blocks in 3 hours.

——16—— blocks per hour

6. Gordon can type 1,800 words in 25 minutes.

——72—— words per minute

7. A particular frozen yogurt has 75 calories in 2 ounces. How many calories are in 8 ounces of the yogurt? ——300—— calories

8. The cost of 10 oranges is $1.00. What is the cost of 5 dozen oranges? $ ——6.00——

9. A carpenter installed 10 windows in 4 hours. Another carpenter installed 50 windows in 20 hours. Are the two carpenters working at the same rate? Explain.

Yes; sample answer: each has a unit rate of 2.5 windows per hour.

Percents

Essential question: How are percents related to fractions and decimals?

COMMON CORE

Standards for Mathematical Content

CC.6.RP.3c Find a percent of a quantity as a rate per 100 (e.g., 30% of a quantity means $\frac{30}{100}$ times the quantity); solve problems involving finding the whole, given a part and the percent.

Vocabulary
percent

Prerequisites
Writing fractions as decimals and vice versa

Math Background
The symbol % is used to indicate *percent*, the ratio that compares a number to 100. To write a ratio given in decimal form as a percent, consider how many hundredths are described by the ratio. To write a ratio given in fraction form as a percent, first write the ratio as an equivalent ratio with a denominator of 100. Rewrite as decimal by using place value to express the number of hundredths.

INTRODUCE

Discuss with students where they may have seen percents in stores, sales flyers, or newspapers. Tell them in this lesson, they will be using the relationships between decimals, fractions, and percents to convert and compare them.

TEACH

1 EXPLORE

Questioning Strategies
• How can you tell from the grids which ratio is greatest? **The grid representing the greatest ratio will have the most squares shaded.**

• How do the shaded squares represent a percent? **The grid has 100 squares, so it shows the number of squares shaded per 100 squares.**

MATHEMATICAL PRACTICE | **Highlighting the Standards**

This explore is an opportunity to address Standard 4 (Model with mathematics). Students use a 10 × 10 grid to represent percents. Students shade squares on the grid to represent the ratios given as fractions and decimals. Using the grid, they model a ratio as a number of shaded squares per 100 squares.

2 EXAMPLE

Questioning Strategies
• How do you use the definition of percent to rewrite a percent as a fraction or decimal? **Use the definition of percent to write it as a ratio comparing the number to 100.**

• Can a percent be greater than 100? **Yes, a percent greater than 100 is a ratio greater than 1.**

Avoid Common Errors
Some students may get confused about where to place the decimal point when rewriting a percent as a decimal. Students may need a brief review of place value.

Tenths: $0.1 = \frac{1}{10}$

Hundredths: $0.01 = \frac{1}{100}$

Thousandths: $0.001 = \frac{1}{1000}$

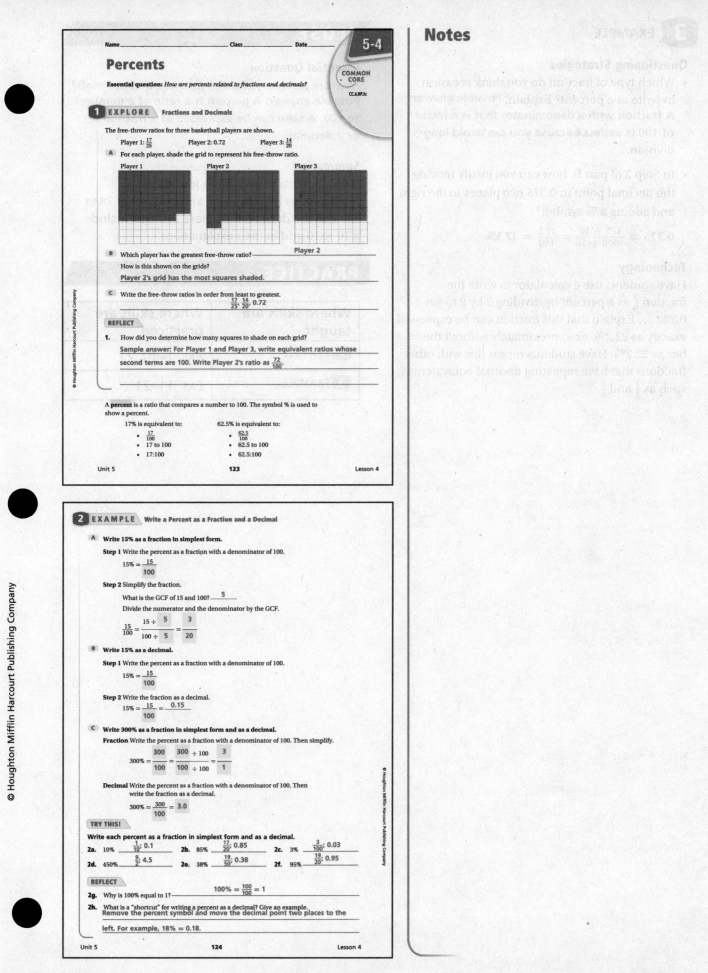

Name_____ Class_____ Date_____

5-4

Percents

Essential question: *How are percents related to fractions and decimals?*

COMMON CORE

CC.6.RP.3c

1 EXPLORE Fractions and Decimals

The free-throw ratios for three basketball players are shown.

Player 1: $\frac{17}{25}$ Player 2: 0.72   Player 3: $\frac{14}{20}$

A For each player, shade the grid to represent his free-throw ratio.

Player 1   Player 2   Player 3

Player 2

B Which player has the greatest free-throw ratio? _____

How is this shown on the grids?

Player 2's grid has the most squares shaded.

C Write the free-throw ratios in order from least to greatest.

$\frac{17}{25}, \frac{14}{20}, 0.72$

REFLECT

1. How did you determine how many squares to shade on each grid?

Sample answer: For Player 1 and Player 3, write equivalent ratios whose

second terms are 100. Write Player 2's ratio as $\frac{72}{100}$.

A **percent** is a ratio that compares a number to 100. The symbol % is used to show a percent.

17% is equivalent to: 62.5% is equivalent to:

- $\frac{17}{100}$ - $\frac{62.5}{100}$
- 17 to 100   - 62.5 to 100
- 17:100   - 62.5:100

2 EXAMPLE Write a Percent as a Fraction and a Decimal

A Write 15% as a fraction in simplest form.

Step 1 Write the percent as a fraction with a denominator of 100.

$15\% = \frac{15}{100}$

Step 2 Simplify the fraction.

What is the GCF of 15 and 100? 5

Divide the numerator and the denominator by the GCF.

$\frac{15}{100} = \frac{15 \div 5}{100 \div 5} = \frac{3}{20}$

B Write 15% as a decimal.

Step 1 Write the percent as a fraction with a denominator of 100.

$15\% = \frac{15}{100}$

Step 2 Write the fraction as a decimal.

$15\% = \frac{15}{100} = 0.15$

C Write 300% as a fraction in simplest form and as a decimal.

Fraction Write the percent as a fraction with a denominator of 100. Then simplify.

$300\% = \frac{300}{100} = \frac{300 \div 100}{100 \div 100} = \frac{3}{1}$

Decimal Write the percent as a fraction with a denominator of 100. Then write the fraction as a decimal.

$300\% = \frac{300}{100} = 3.0$

TRY THIS!

Write each percent as a fraction in simplest form and as a decimal.

2a. 10% $\frac{1}{10}$; 0.1   **2b.** 85% $\frac{17}{20}$; 0.85   **2c.** 3% $\frac{3}{100}$; 0.03

2d. 450% $\frac{9}{2}$; 4.5   **2e.** 38% $\frac{19}{50}$; 0.38   **2f.** 95% $\frac{19}{20}$; 0.95

REFLECT

2g. Why is 100% equal to 1? $100\% = \frac{100}{100} = 1$

2h. What is a "shortcut" for writing a percent as a decimal? Give an example.
Remove the percent symbol and move the decimal point two places to the

left. For example, 18% = 0.18.

© Houghton Mifflin Harcourt Publishing Company

Questioning Strategies

- Which type of fraction do you think is easiest to write as a percent? Explain. **Possible answer: A fraction with a denominator that is a factor of 100 is easiest because you can avoid long division.**

- In Step 2 of part B, how can you justify moving the decimal point in 0.375 two places to the right and adding a % symbol?

$$0.375 = \frac{375 \div 10}{1000 \div 10} = \frac{37.5}{100} = 37.5\%$$

Technology

Have students use a calculator to write the fraction $\frac{2}{9}$ as a percent by dividing 2 by 9 to get 0.222.... Explain that this fraction can be expressed exactly as $22.\overline{2}\%$, or approximately without the bar as 22.2%. Have students repeat this with other fractions that have repeating decimal equivalents, such as $\frac{1}{3}$ and $\frac{5}{6}$.

Essential Question

How are percents related to fractions and decimals? Possible answer: A percent is a ratio of a number to 100. A ratio can be expressed as a fraction or a decimal.

Summarize

Have students write in their journal the relationships between 78% and the ratio of 78 to 100 and the decimal 0.78. Have students include a 10 × 10 grid in their explanations.

Where skills are taught	Where skills are practiced
2 EXAMPLE	Exs. 1–10, 21
3 EXAMPLE	Exs. 11–21

3 EXAMPLE Write Fractions and Decimals as Percents

A Write $\frac{7}{20}$ as a percent.

Method 1 *When the denominator is a factor of 100:*
Write an equivalent fraction with a denominator of 100.

$$\frac{7}{20} = \frac{35}{100}$$

Write the percent.

$$\frac{35}{100} = 35\%$$

B Write $\frac{3}{8}$ as a percent.

Method 2 *When the denominator is NOT a factor of 100:*

Step 1 Use long division to divide the numerator by the denominator. Add a decimal point and zeros to the right of the numerator as needed.

$$\frac{3}{8} = 8)\overline{3.000} \quad 0.375$$
$$-24$$
$$60$$
$$-56$$
$$40$$
$$-40$$
$$0$$

Step 2 Write the quotient. Then move the decimal point two places to the right and add a percent symbol.

$$\frac{3}{8} = 0.375 = 37.5\%$$

TRY THIS!

Write each fraction as a decimal and as a percent.

3a. $\frac{3}{10}$ 0.3; 30%   3b. $\frac{2}{25}$ 0.08; 8%   3c. $\frac{7}{50}$ 0.14; 14%

3d. $\frac{12}{30}$ 0.4; 40%   3e. $\frac{1}{8}$ 0.125; 12.5%   3f. $\frac{350}{100}$ 3.5; 350%

REFLECT

3g. Moving the decimal point two places to the right is equivalent to performing what operation? _____ Multiplying by 100

3h. A given fraction's numerator is greater than its denominator. When this fraction is written as a percent, what will be true about the percent?
_____ The percent will be greater than 100. _____

PRACTICE

1. At Brian's Bookstore, 0.3 of the shelves hold mysteries, 25% of the shelves hold travel books, and $\frac{7}{20}$ of the shelves hold children's books. Which type of book covers the most shelf space in the bookstore?

children's books

Write each percent as a fraction in simplest form and as a decimal.

2. 60%
$\frac{3}{5}$; 0.6

3. 5%
$\frac{1}{20}$; 0.05

4. 37%
$\frac{37}{100}$; 0.37

5. 500%
$\frac{5}{1}$; 5.0

6. 48%
$\frac{12}{25}$; 0.48

7. 66%
$\frac{33}{50}$; 0.66

8. 23%
$\frac{23}{100}$; 0.23

9. 1%
$\frac{1}{100}$; 0.01

10. 8%
$\frac{2}{25}$; 0.08

Write each fraction as a decimal and as a percent.

11. $\frac{27}{50}$
0.54; 54%

12. $\frac{250}{100}$
2.5; 250%

13. $\frac{7}{10}$
0.7; 70%

14. $\frac{24}{30}$
0.8; 80%

15. $\frac{3}{5}$
0.6; 60%

16. $\frac{11}{16}$
0.6875; 68.75%

17. $\frac{9}{20}$
0.45; 45%

18. $\frac{1}{25}$
0.04; 4%

19. $\frac{18}{45}$
0.4; 40%

20. Justine answered 68 questions correctly on an 80-question test.

a. What percent of the questions did Justine answer correctly? _____ 85%

b. To find the percent of questions that Justine answered incorrectly, subtract your answer to a from 100%: 100% − 85% = 15%

What percent of the questions did Justine answer incorrectly? _____ 15%

21. Graph each fraction or percent on the number line.

A. $\frac{4}{5}$ B. 20%   C. $\frac{1}{2}$ D. $\frac{6}{8}$

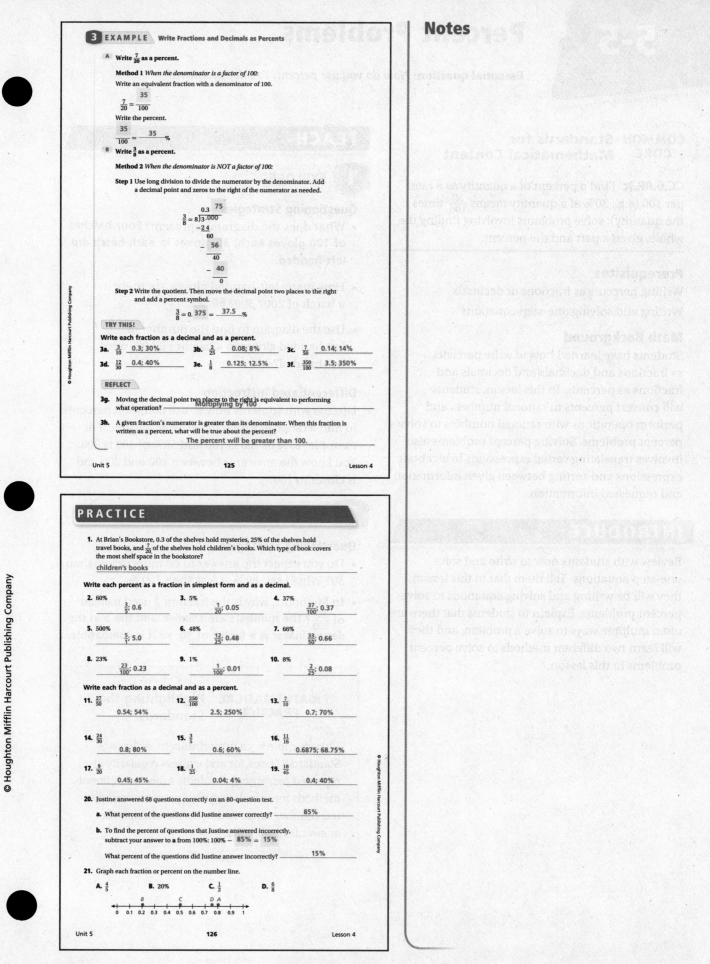

5-5 Percent Problems

Essential question: *How do you use percents to solve problems?*

COMMON CORE Standards for Mathematical Content

CC.6.RP.3c Find a percent of a quantity as a rate per 100 (e.g., 30% of a quantity means $\frac{30}{100}$ times the quantity); solve problems involving finding the whole, given a part and the percent.

Prerequisites

Writing percents as fractions or decimals
Writing and solving one-step equations

Math Background

Students have learned how to write percents as fractions and decimals and decimals and fractions as percents. In this lesson, students will convert percents to rational numbers and perform operations with rational numbers to solve percent problems. Solving percent problems also involves translating verbal expressions to algebraic expressions and sorting between given information and requested information.

INTRODUCE

Review with students how to write and solve one-step equations. Tell them that in this lesson, they will be writing and solving equations to solve percent problems. Explain to students that there are often multiple ways to solve a problem, and they will learn two different methods to solve percent problems in this lesson.

TEACH

1 EXPLORE

Questioning Strategies

- What does the diagram represent? **Four batches of 100 gloves each; 30 gloves in each batch are left-handed.**

- How many left-handed gloves are there in a batch of 200? 300? **60; 90**

- Use the diagram to find the number of left-handed gloves in 4 batches if 60% were left-handed? **240**

Differentiated Instruction

Discuss with students how to use common percents to find a range in which the answer must lie. For example: 25% of 400 is 100 and 50% of 400 is 200. You know the answer is between 100 and 200 and is closer to 100.

2 EXAMPLE

Questioning Strategies

- Do you expect the answer to be more or less than 30? Why? **Less; 80% is less than 100%.**

- In Method 1, why is the fraction $\frac{4}{5}$ used instead of $\frac{80}{100}$? **The numbers are smaller, and the 5 in the denominator is a factor of 30, so it is compatible.**

> **MATHEMATICAL PRACTICE** **Highlighting the Standards**
>
> This example is an opportunity to address Standard 8 (Look for and express regularity in repeated reasoning). Students examine different methods for calculating with percents, and they use number sense to determine whether the answer is reasonable.

© Houghton Mifflin Harcourt Publishing Company

Name _____ Class _____ Date _____

5-5

COMMON
CORE

CC.6.RP.3c

Percent Problems

Essential question: *How do you use percents to solve problems?*

1 EXPLORE Finding Percent of a Number

A sporting-goods store received a shipment of 400 baseball gloves, and 30% were left-handed. How many left-handed gloves were in the shipment?

A You can draw a diagram to solve this problem.

30% means 30 out of ____100____. There were ____30____ left-handed gloves for every 100 baseball gloves.

Complete the diagram to model this situation.

30	30	30	30
100	100	100	100

400

REFLECT

1a. Describe how the diagram models the shipment of gloves.

Each large rectangle represents 100 gloves. There are 4 of these rectangles

because the shipment contained a total of 400 gloves. The small rectangles

represent the 30 out of every 100 gloves that are left-handed.

1b. How can you use the diagram to find the total number of left-handed gloves in the shipment?

30 + 30 + 30 + 30 = 120

B You can use a bar model to solve this problem. The bar represents 100%, or the entire shipment of 400 gloves. Divide the bar into 10 equal parts and label each part.

0%	10%	20%	30%	40%	50%	60%	70%	80%	90%	100%
0	40	80	120	160	200	240	280	320	360	400

REFLECT

1c. How did you determine the labels along the bottom of the bar model?
Sample answer: The bar shows 400 divided into 10 equal parts, so each part

represents 400 ÷ 10 = 40.

1d. How can you use the bar model to find the number of left-handed gloves?
30% corresponds to 120, so there were 120 left-handed gloves.

© Houghton Mifflin Harcourt Publishing Company

When finding the percent of a number, convert the percent to a fraction or decimal and then multiply.

2 EXAMPLE Finding Percent of a Number

A lacrosse team played 30 games and won 80% of the games. How many games did the team win?

To answer this question, you must find 80% of 30.

Method 1 Use a fraction.

Step 1 Write the percent as a fraction in simplest form.

$$80\% = \frac{80}{100} = \frac{4}{5}$$

Step 2 Multiply this fraction by the total number of games.

$$\frac{4}{5} \cdot 30 = \frac{4}{5} \cdot \frac{30}{1} = \frac{120}{5} = 24$$

Method 2 Use a decimal.

Step 1 Write the percent as a decimal: 80% = ____0.8____

Step 2 Multiply this decimal by the total number of games.

$$0.8 \cdot 30 = 24$$

80% of 30 is ____24____. The team won ____24____ games.

TRY THIS!

Find the percent of the number.

2a. 20% of 180
____36____

2b. 80% of 40
____32____

2c. 75% of 480
____360____

2d. 20% of 45
____9____

2e. 25% of 16
____4____

2f. 90% of 80
____72____

REFLECT

2g. When might it be easier to write the percent as a fraction rather than as a decimal? Give an example.

Sample answer: It is easier when the percent can be converted to a fraction

that is easily multiplied by the whole number. For example, to find 75% of 24,

multiply $\frac{3}{4} \cdot 24 = 18$.

© Houghton Mifflin Harcourt Publishing Company

Questioning Strategies

- What value(s) are you given and what value(s) are you asked to find? **Given: percent and part; find: whole**

- What operation is involved in this equation, and what operation is used to solve it? **It is a multiplication equation; it requires division to solve.**

- In part A, what equation could you write if you write the percent as a fraction? $\frac{1}{5}n = 3$

Teaching Strategies

Have students work together to explore other methods for solving percent problems. Students may share their reasoning with the class or others in the group. Allow students to ask and answer questions about each other's methods and operations.

Essential Question

How can you use percents to solve problems?
Possible answer: You can solve percent problems to find the percent, whole, or part by writing and solving an equation in the appropriate form. You can use a decimal or a fraction to represent the percent.

Summarize

Have students describe in their journal a real-life situation in which percents are used. Have them write a percent problem from the situation, and show two different ways to solve it.

Where skills are taught	Where skills are practiced
2 EXAMPLE	Exs. 1–9, 22
3 EXAMPLE	Exs. 10–21

You can use an equation to solve percent problems:

$$\boxed{\text{percent}} \cdot \boxed{\text{whole}} = \boxed{\text{part}}$$

A percent problem may ask you to find any of the three pieces of this equation—the percent, the whole, or the part.

3 EXAMPLE   Finding the Whole

A A girls' softball team has 3 pitchers. The pitchers make up 20% of the team. How many total players are on the softball team?

Identify the pieces of the percent equation. Use the variable n for any piece that is unknown.

$$\boxed{\text{percent}} \cdot \boxed{\text{whole}} = \boxed{\text{part}}$$

$$20\,\% \qquad n \qquad 3$$

Write the percent as a decimal. ____0.2____

Substitute this decimal for the percent and rewrite the equation. ___$0.2n = 3$___

Solve the equation.

$$\frac{0.2n}{0.2} = \frac{3}{0.2} \quad \textit{Divide both sides by} \quad \underline{0.2}.$$

$$n = \underline{15}$$

There are ___15___ players on the softball team.

B 12% of what number is 45?

$$\boxed{\text{percent}} \cdot \boxed{\text{whole}} = \boxed{\text{part}}$$

$$12\,\% \qquad n \qquad 45$$

Write the percent as a decimal. ____0.12____

Substitute this decimal for the percent and rewrite the equation. ___$0.12n = 45$___

Solve the equation.

$$\frac{0.12n}{0.12} = \frac{45}{0.12} \quad \textit{Divide both sides by} \quad \underline{0.12}.$$

$$n = \underline{375}$$

12% of ___375___ is 45.

TRY THIS!

3a. 180 is 30% of ___600___.   **3b.** 25% of ___160___ is 40.

PRACTICE

Find the percent of each number.

1. 5% of 30

____1.5____

2. 80% of 80

____64____

3. 95% of 260

____247____

4. 20% of 90

____18____

5. 32% of 50

____16____

6. 2% of 350

____7____

7. 25% of 56

____14____

8. 3% of 600

____18____

9. 7% of 200

____14____

10. At a shelter, 15% of the dogs are puppies. There are 60 dogs at the shelter. How many are puppies? ___9___ puppies

11. Terry has a box that originally held 64 crayons. She is missing 25% of the crayons. How many crayons are missing? ___16___ crayons

12. In a survey, 230 people were asked their favorite color, and 20% of the people surveyed chose blue. How many people chose blue? ___46___ people

13. Leah is saving money to buy her sister a graduation gift. She needs $44, and she has saved 25% of this amount so far. How much more money must Leah save? $ ___33___

Complete each sentence.

14. 4% of ___1,400___ is 56.

15. 58 is 20% of ___290___.

16. 35% of ___120___ is 42.

17. 360 is 24% of ___1,500___.

18. 92% of ___125___ is 115.

19. 9 is 3% of ___300___.

20. 45 is 20% of ___225___.

21. 8% of ___25___ is 2.

22. Use the circle graph to determine how many hours per day Becky spends on each activity.

School: ___6___ hours

Eating: ___2.4___ hours

Sleep: ___9.6___ hours

Homework: ___2.4___ hours

Free time: ___3.6___ hours

Becky's Day

Eating 10%
Free time 15%
Homework 10%
School 25%

Converting Measurements

Essential question: *How can you use ratios to convert measurements?*

COMMON CORE **Standards for Mathematical Content**

CC.6.RP.3d Use ratio reasoning to convert measurement units; manipulate and transform units appropriately when multiplying or dividing quantities.

Vocabulary
conversion factor

Prerequisites
Measurement units
Converting measurements within a system

Math Background
Measurements using the customary and metric systems are both common in the United States. In this lesson students will convert measurements between the customary and metric systems. A conversion factor is a ratio of two equivalent measurements, such as $\frac{1 \text{ in.}}{2.54 \text{ cm}}$ or $\frac{0.946 \text{ L}}{1 \text{ qt}}$. Multiplying a ratio by a conversion factor does not change the value of the ratio because it is the same as multiplying the ratio by 1.

INTRODUCE

Connect to prior learning by asking students to give examples of customary or metric units of length, weight, and capacity. Write them on the board for review. Tell students that in this lesson, they will multiply ratios by conversion factors in order to convert measurements between the two systems.

TEACH

1 EXPLORE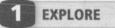

Questioning Strategies
- Which is larger, 1 centimeter or 1 inch? **1 inch**
- Will the number of centimeters be greater or lesser than the number of inches? **Greater; more centimeters are required.**

Teaching Strategies
Students may need to practice reading the table at first. Ask questions such as *"How many meters are in 1 foot?"* to help them get comfortable with reading information from the table. Students may also need to practice identifying which units are for length, weight or mass, and capacity.

2 EXAMPLE

Questioning Strategies
- In part A, what units do you need to convert? **gallons to liters**
- Which unit is larger? **1 gallon = 3.79 liters, so a gallon is larger than a liter.**
- In part B, what units do you need to convert? **Kilograms to pounds**
- Will the number of pounds be greater or less than the number of kilograms? **greater than**

Avoid Common Errors
Some students choose the correct conversion factor and perform some multiplication correctly, but do not even notice if the answer is unreasonable. Encourage students to make sure they know which unit is larger and how the conversion of units is going to affect the number of new units needed.

Name_____ Class_____ Date_____

5-6

Converting Measurements

COMMON CORE
CC.6.RP.3d

Essential question: *How can you use ratios to convert measurements?*

Measurement is a mathematical tool that people use every day. Measurements are used when determining the length, weight, or capacity of an object.

There are several different systems of measurement. The two most common systems are the *customary system* and the *metric system*.

The table below shows equivalencies between the customary and metric systems. You can use these equivalencies to convert a measurement in one system to a measurement in the other system.

Length	Weight/Mass	Capacity
1 inch = 2.54 centimeters	1 ounce ≈ 28.4 grams	1 fluid ounce ≈ 29.6 milliliters
1 foot ≈ 0.305 meters	1 pound ≈ 0.454 kilograms	1 quart ≈ 0.946 liter
1 yard ≈ 0.914 meters		1 gallon ≈ 3.79 liters
1 mile ≈ 1.61 kilometers		

Most conversions are approximate, as indicated by the symbol ≈.

1 EXPLORE Converting Inches to Centimeters

The length of a sheet of a paper is 11 inches. What is this length in centimeters?

You can use a diagram to solve this problem. Each block represents 1 inch.

1 inch = __2.54__ centimeter(s)

How does the diagram help you solve the problem?

Sample answer: The diagram shows that 11 in. is equal to (11 · 2.54) cm.

11 inches = __27.94__ centimeters

TRY THIS!

1. Draw a diagram to find approximately how many grams are equivalent to 6 ounces.

   6 ounces ≈ __170.4__ grams

Another way to convert measurements is by using a ratio called a *conversion factor*. A **conversion factor** is a ratio of two equivalent measurements. Since the two measurements in a conversion factor are equivalent, a conversion factor is a ratio equivalent to 1.

2 EXAMPLE Using Conversion Factors

A **Vicki put 22 gallons of gasoline in her car. About how many liters of gasoline did she put in her car?**

Step 1 Find the conversion factor.

_____3.79_____ liter(s) ≈ 1 gallon

Write as a ratio: $\dfrac{3.79 \text{ liter(s)}}{1 \text{ gallon}}$

Step 2 Convert the given measurement.

gallons · conversion factor = liters

22 gallons · $\dfrac{3.79 \text{ liter(s)}}{1 \text{ gallon}}$ ≈ 83.38 liters

Vicki put about __83.38__ liters of gasoline in her car.

B **While lifting weights, John adds 11.35 kilograms to his bar. About how many pounds did he add to his bar?**

Step 1 Find the conversion factor.

1 pound ≈ _____0.454_____ kilogram(s)

Write as a ratio: $\dfrac{1 \text{ pound}}{0.454 \text{ kilogram(s)}}$

Step 2 Convert the given measurement.

kilograms · conversion factor = pounds

11.35 kilograms · $\dfrac{1 \text{ pound}}{0.454 \text{ kilogram(s)}}$ ≈ 25 pounds

John has added about __25__ pounds to his bar.

TRY THIS!

2a. 6 quarts ≈ __5.676__ liters

2b. 14 feet ≈ __4.27__ meters

2c. 255.6 grams ≈ __9__ ounces

2d. 7 liters ≈ __7.40__ quarts

© Houghton Mifflin Harcourt Publishing Company

3 EXAMPLE

Questioning Strategies

- What units do you need to convert?
  feet to meters

- What is wrong with Leo's solution method
  in Reflect **3a**? The conversion factor is for
  converting feet to meters, but Leo is trying to use
  it with square feet and square meters, which are
  different units.

MATHEMATICAL PRACTICE   **Highlighting the Standards**

This example is an opportunity to address
Standard 1 (Make sense of problems and
persevere in solving them). Students solve
a real-world problem in which they need
to analyze the information given and the
relationship between units in different
measurement systems. Students need to
translate information from a table into a
conversion factor and use it properly to solve
the problem.

CLOSE

Essential Question

*How can you use ratios to convert measurements
from one unit to another?* Possible answer:
Use a table of equivalent measures to set up
a conversion factor, and multiply it to convert
from one unit to another.

Summarize

Have students write in their journal lists of units
that can be converted back and forth and pairs of
units from the two systems that cannot. Encourage
students to check that they are listing pairs of the
same type of measure, such as length unit to length
unit, not weight unit to length unit.

PRACTICE

Where skills are taught	Where skills are practiced
1 EXPLORE	Exs. 1–5, 19
2 EXAMPLE	Exs. 6–17
3 EXAMPLE	Ex. 18

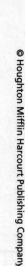

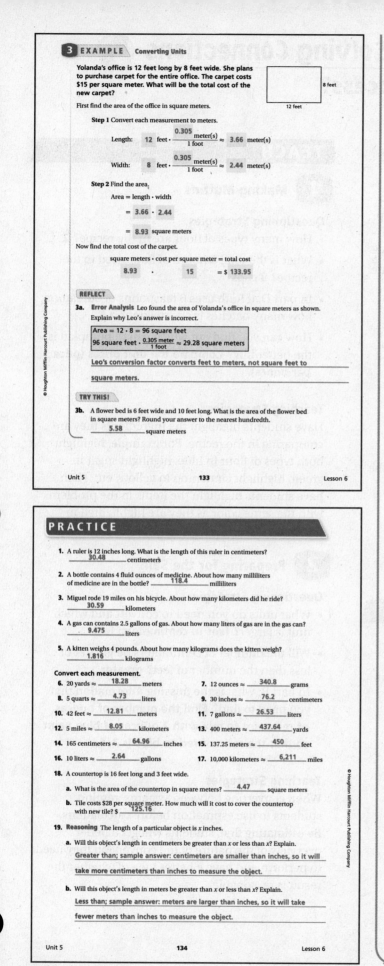

3 EXAMPLE Converting Units

Yolanda's office is 12 feet long by 8 feet wide. She plans to purchase carpet for the entire office. The carpet costs $15 per square meter. What will be the total cost of the new carpet?

8 feet
12 feet

First find the area of the office in square meters.

Step 1 Convert each measurement to meters.

Length: 12 feet $\cdot \dfrac{0.305 \text{ meter(s)}}{1 \text{ foot}} \approx 3.66$ meter(s)

Width: 8 feet $\cdot \dfrac{0.305 \text{ meter(s)}}{1 \text{ foot}} \approx 2.44$ meter(s)

Step 2 Find the area.

Area = length · width

$= 3.66 \cdot 2.44$

$= 8.93$ square meters

Now find the total cost of the carpet.

square meters · cost per square meter = total cost

$8.93 \cdot 15 = \$133.95$

REFLECT

3a. Error Analysis Leo found the area of Yolanda's office in square meters as shown. Explain why Leo's answer is incorrect.

> Area = 12 · 8 = 96 square feet
> 96 square feet · $\dfrac{0.305 \text{ meter}}{1 \text{ foot}} \approx 29.28$ square meters

Leo's conversion factor converts feet to meters, not square feet to
square meters.

TRY THIS!

3b. A flower bed is 6 feet wide and 10 feet long. What is the area of the flower bed in square meters? Round your answer to the nearest hundredth.

5.58 square meters

PRACTICE

1. A ruler is 12 inches long. What is the length of this ruler in centimeters?
   30.48 centimeters

2. A bottle contains 4 fluid ounces of medicine. About how many milliliters of medicine are in the bottle? 118.4 milliliters

3. Miguel rode 19 miles on his bicycle. About how many kilometers did he ride?
   30.59 kilometers

4. A gas can contains 2.5 gallons of gas. About how many liters of gas are in the gas can?
   9.475 liters

5. A kitten weighs 4 pounds. About how many kilograms does the kitten weigh?
   1.816 kilograms

Convert each measurement.

6. 20 yards ≈ 18.28 meters
7. 12 ounces ≈ 340.8 grams
8. 5 quarts ≈ 4.73 liters
9. 30 inches ≈ 76.2 centimeters
10. 42 feet ≈ 12.81 meters
11. 7 gallons ≈ 26.53 liters
12. 5 miles ≈ 8.05 kilometers
13. 400 meters ≈ 437.64 yards
14. 165 centimeters ≈ 64.96 inches
15. 137.25 meters ≈ 450 feet
16. 10 liters ≈ 2.64 gallons
17. 10,000 kilometers ≈ 6,211 miles

18. A countertop is 16 feet long and 3 feet wide.

   a. What is the area of the countertop in square meters? 4.47 square meters

   b. Tile costs $28 per square meter. How much will it cost to cover the countertop with new tile? $ 125.16

19. **Reasoning** The length of a particular object is x inches.

   a. Will this object's length in centimeters be greater than x or less than x? Explain.

   Greater than; sample answer: centimeters are smaller than inches, so it will

   take more centimeters than inches to measure the object.

   b. Will this object's length in meters be greater than x or less than x? Explain.

   Less than; sample answer: meters are larger than inches, so it will take

   fewer meters than inches to measure the object.

Notes

Problem Solving Connections
Sweet Success?

© Houghton Mifflin Harcourt Publishing Company

COMMON CORE Standards for Mathematical Content

CC.6.RP.1 Understand the concept of a ratio and use ratio language to describe a ratio relationship between two quantities.

CC.6.RP.2 Understand the concept of a unit rate $\frac{a}{b}$ associated with a ratio $a:b$ with $b \neq 0$, and use rate language in the context of a ratio relationship.

CC.6.RP.3a Make tables of equivalent ratios relating quantities with whole number measurements, find missing values in the tables, and plot the pairs of values on the coordinate plane. Use tables to compare ratios.

CC.6.RP.3b Solve unit rate problems including those involving unit pricing and constant speed.

CC.6.RP.3c Find a percent of a quantity as a rate per 100 (e.g., 30% of a quantity means $\frac{30}{100}$ times the quantity); solve problems involving finding the whole, given a part and the percent.

CC.6.RP.3d Use ratio reasoning to convert measurement units; manipulate and transform units appropriately when multiplying or dividing quantities.

INTRODUCE

Ask students to imagine they are going on a ski trip and ask them to think of ways to raise funds. Record students' responses on the board. Explain to students that this project is going to explore some fundraising ideas and use mathematical concepts that they have learned in this unit.

TEACH

1 Making Muffins

Questioning Strategies

- How many types of flour are in the recipe? **2**

- What is the total amount of flour used in the recipe? **8 cups**

- In part D, if Ruth uses 6 teaspoons of cinnamon, how many batches is she making? **1.5**

- How can you find out which can of pumpkin is the better buy? **Compare the unit prices (price per ounce).**

Teaching Strategies

Have students highlight the ingredients they are comparing in the recipe. For example, highlight both types of flour in blue, highlight sugar in green, highlight cinnamon in yellow, etc. Then have students highlight the items in the problem with the same color as they are highlighted in the recipe.

2 Preparing for the Sale

Questioning Strategies

- What units do you need to convert and which unit is larger? **feet to centimeters; feet**

- Will the number of centimeters be greater or less than the number of feet? **greater**

- In part B, what is the missing information that you need to find? **Find the number of ounces of red paint to mix with 2 ounces of blue paint so that the ratio of red to blue is 3:4.**

Teaching Strategies

When converting between systems, remind students to use estimation before calculations. By estimating first, students will get a better overview of the nature of the conversion they need to perform and have a better idea of whether the result is reasonable.

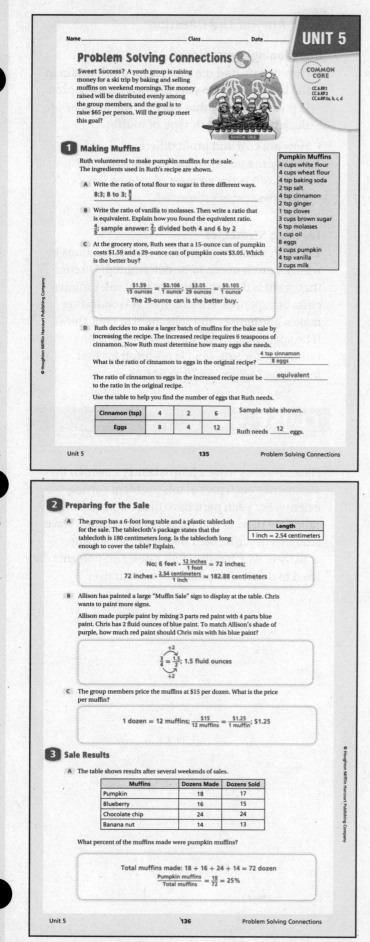

Name_____ Class_____ Date_____

UNIT 5

COMMON CORE
CC.6.RP.1
CC.6.RP.2
CC.6.RP.3a, b, c, d

Problem Solving Connections

Sweet Success? A youth group is raising money for a ski trip by baking and selling muffins on weekend mornings. The money raised will be distributed evenly among the group members, and the goal is to raise $65 per person. Will the group meet this goal?

1 Making Muffins

Ruth volunteered to make pumpkin muffins for the sale. The ingredients used in Ruth's recipe are shown.

Pumpkin Muffins
4 cups white flour
4 cups wheat flour
4 tsp baking soda
2 tsp salt
4 tsp cinnamon
2 tsp ginger
1 tsp cloves
3 cups brown sugar
6 tsp molasses
1 cup oil
8 eggs
4 cups pumpkin
4 tsp vanilla
3 cups milk

A Write the ratio of total flour to sugar in three different ways.

8:3; 8 to 3; $\frac{8}{3}$

B Write the ratio of vanilla to molasses. Then write a ratio that is equivalent. Explain how you found the equivalent ratio.

$\frac{4}{6}$; sample answer: $\frac{2}{3}$; divided both 4 and 6 by 2

C At the grocery store, Ruth sees that a 15-ounce can of pumpkin costs $1.59 and a 29-ounce can of pumpkin costs $3.05. Which is the better buy?

$$\frac{\$1.59}{15 \text{ ounces}} = \frac{\$0.106}{1 \text{ ounce}}; \frac{\$3.05}{29 \text{ ounces}} = \frac{\$0.105}{1 \text{ ounce}}$$

The 29-ounce can is the better buy.

D Ruth decides to make a larger batch of muffins for the bake sale by increasing the recipe. The increased recipe requires 6 teaspoons of cinnamon. Now Ruth must determine how many eggs she needs.

What is the ratio of cinnamon to eggs in the original recipe? $\frac{4 \text{ tsp cinnamon}}{8 \text{ eggs}}$

The ratio of cinnamon to eggs in the increased recipe must be ___equivalent___ to the ratio in the original recipe.

Use the table to help you find the number of eggs that Ruth needs.

Cinnamon (tsp)	4	2	6
Eggs	8	4	12

Sample table shown.

Ruth needs ___12___ eggs.

2 Preparing for the Sale

A The group has a 6-foot long table and a plastic tablecloth for the sale. The tablecloth's package states that the tablecloth is 180 centimeters long. Is the tablecloth long enough to cover the table? Explain.

Length
1 inch = 2.54 centimeters

No; 6 feet · $\frac{12 \text{ inches}}{1 \text{ foot}}$ = 72 inches;

72 inches · $\frac{2.54 \text{ centimeters}}{1 \text{ inch}}$ ≈ 182.88 centimeters

B Allison has painted a large "Muffin Sale" sign to display at the table. Chris wants to paint more signs.

Allison made purple paint by mixing 3 parts red paint with 4 parts blue paint. Chris has 2 fluid ounces of blue paint. To match Allison's shade of purple, how much red paint should Chris mix with his blue paint?

$\frac{3}{4} \overset{\div 2}{=} \frac{1.5}{2}$; 1.5 fluid ounces

C The group members price the muffins at $15 per dozen. What is the price per muffin?

1 dozen = 12 muffins; $\frac{\$15}{12 \text{ muffins}} = \frac{\$1.25}{1 \text{ muffin}}$ $1.25

3 Sale Results

A The table shows results after several weekends of sales.

Muffins	Dozens Made	Dozens Sold
Pumpkin	18	17
Blueberry	16	15
Chocolate chip	24	24
Banana nut	14	13

What percent of the muffins made were pumpkin muffins?

Total muffins made: 18 + 16 + 24 + 14 = 72 dozen

$\frac{\text{Pumpkin muffins}}{\text{Total muffins}} = \frac{18}{72} = 25\%$

3 Sale Results

Questioning Strategies

- How do you find the percent of pumpkin muffins sold in part A? **Divide the number of dozens of pumpkin muffins sold by the total number of dozens sold, and write the quotient in the form of a percent.**

- In part C, how can you find the percent of muffins that did not sell? **Subtract the number of dozens sold from the total number of dozens made to get the number of dozens that did not sell. Divide the number that did not sell by the total number that were made, and write the quotient in the form of a percent.**

Avoid Common Errors

In part A, some students may use the wrong column from the table, resulting in the percent that describes a whole divided by a part instead of a part divided by a whole. Encourage students to identify the information given and the information needed in terms of the part, the whole, and the percent before they begin calculations.

4 Answer the Question

Questioning Strategies

- How do you find the income for each muffin in the last column? **In part 2, the price per dozen is given. Multiply that price by the number of dozens sold for each type of muffin.**

- How are cost and profit different? **Cost is the money the youth spend to make the muffins, and profit is the amount of income left over after the cost is subtracted.**

Teaching Strategies

Talk with students about real-world situations in which a profit needs to be determined. Discuss that profit is determined from total sales minus costs or expenses. For example: A woodcarver makes birdhouses and sells them at craft shows. If he spends $6.75 for supplies and sells one birdhouse for $20, what is his profit for that birdhouse? **$20 − $6.75 = $13.25**

CLOSE

Journal

Have students write a journal entry in which they summarize each part of this problem solving activity. For each part, have them explain how ratios are used to find missing information. Have students describe their own problem solving activity in which ratios, unit rates, and percents are used to determine profits for a fundraiser.

© Houghton Mifflin Harcourt Publishing Company

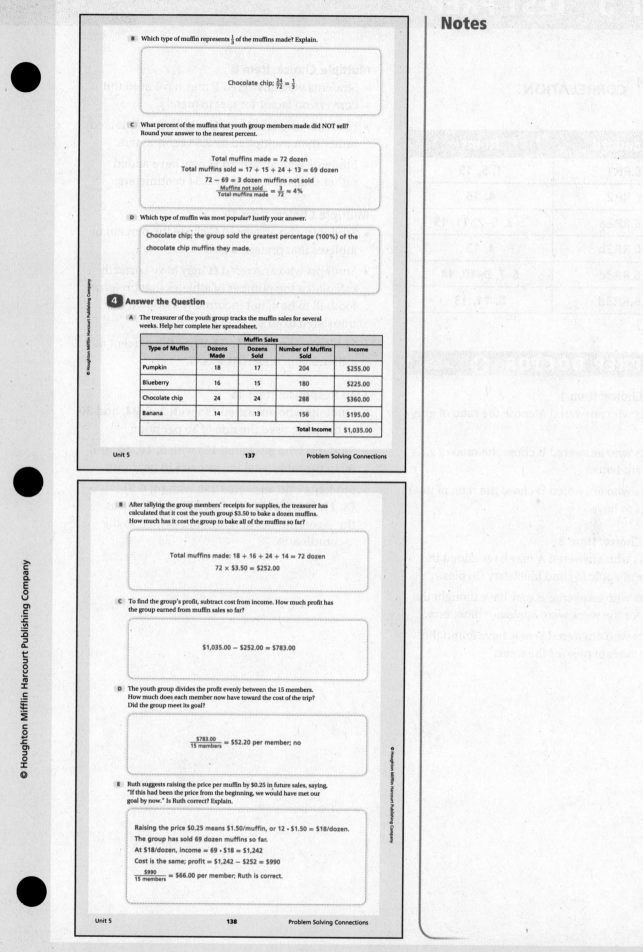

B Which type of muffin represents $\frac{1}{3}$ of the muffins made? Explain.

Chocolate chip; $\frac{24}{72} = \frac{1}{3}$

C What percent of the muffins that youth group members made did NOT sell? Round your answer to the nearest percent.

Total muffins made = 72 dozen

Total muffins sold = 17 + 15 + 24 + 13 = 69 dozen

72 − 69 = 3 dozen muffins not sold

$\frac{\text{Muffins not sold}}{\text{Total muffins made}} = \frac{3}{72} \approx 4\%$

D Which type of muffin was most popular? Justify your answer.

Chocolate chip; the group sold the greatest percentage (100%) of the chocolate chip muffins they made.

4 Answer the Question

A The treasurer of the youth group tracks the muffin sales for several weeks. Help her complete her spreadsheet.

Muffin Sales				
Type of Muffin	Dozens Made	Dozens Sold	Number of Muffins Sold	Income
Pumpkin	18	17	204	$255.00
Blueberry	16	15	180	$225.00
Chocolate chip	24	24	288	$360.00
Banana	14	13	156	$195.00
			Total Income	$1,035.00

B After tallying the group members' receipts for supplies, the treasurer has calculated that it cost the youth group $3.50 to bake a dozen muffins. How much has it cost the group to bake all of the muffins so far?

Total muffins made: 18 + 16 + 24 + 14 = 72 dozen

72 × $3.50 = $252.00

C To find the group's profit, subtract cost from income. How much profit has the group earned from muffin sales so far?

$1,035.00 − $252.00 = $783.00

D The youth group divides the profit evenly between the 15 members. How much does each member now have toward the cost of the trip? Did the group meet its goal?

$\frac{\$783.00}{15 \text{ members}} = \$52.20$ per member; no

E Ruth suggests raising the price per muffin by $0.25 in future sales, saying, "If this had been the price from the beginning, we would have met our goal by now." Is Ruth correct? Explain.

Raising the price $0.25 means $1.50/muffin, or 12 · $1.50 = $18/dozen.

The group has sold 69 dozen muffins so far.

At $18/dozen, income = 69 · $18 = $1,242

Cost is the same; profit = $1,242 − $252 = $990

$\frac{\$990}{15 \text{ members}} = \$66.00$ per member; Ruth is correct.

COMMON CORE CORRELATION

Standard	Items
CC.6.RP.1	1, 5, 15
CC.6.RP.2	4, 15
CC.6.RP.3a	2–3, 6–7, 11, 15
CC.6.RP.3b	4, 15
CC.6.RP.3c	6–7, 9–10, 14
CC.6.RP.3d	8, 11, 13

TEST PREP DOCTOR ✚

Multiple Choice: Item 1
- Students who answered **A** chose the ratio of girls to boys.
- Students who answered **B** chose the ratio of girls to total students.
- Students who answered **D** chose the ratio of total students to boys.

Multiple Choice: Item 3
- Students who answered **A** may have added the number of apple (5) and blueberry (3) pies.
- Students who answered **B** may have thought the 15 pies for the week were apple not blueberry.
- Students who answered **D** may have found the total number of pies for the week.

Multiple Choice: Item 8
- Students who answered **F** may have used the conversion factor for feet to meters.
- Students who answered **G** may have subtracted rather than multiplied by 2.54 centimeters.
- Students who answered **H** may have added rather than multiplied by 2.54 centimeters.

Multiple Choice: Item 10
- Students who answered **G** chose the percent of athletes that preferred golf.
- Students who answered **H** may have correctly calculated the number of athletes that preferred football to be 4, but incorrectly assumed that translated to 40%.
- Students who answered **J** chose the percent of athletes who preferred soccer.

Free Response: Item 15
- Students who answered 15a with **3, 6, 24, and 30** in the table used the rate of $6 per hour.
- Students who answered 15a with **5, 10, 40, and 50** in the table used the rate of $10 per hour.
- Students who answered 15b with **(4, 0.5), (8, 1), (24, 3), (32, 4), (40, 5)** used Hours as the *y*-coordinates and Amount earned as the *x*-coordinates.

UNIT 5 TEST PREP

Name _____ Class _____ Date _____

MULTIPLE CHOICE

1. The ratio of boys to girls in a classroom is 15 to 12. What is the ratio of boys to total students in the classroom?

A. 12:15   (C.) 15:27

B. 12:27   D. 27:15

2. Each day, the cafeteria staff at Brookview Middle School orders 80 pints of white milk and 30 pints of chocolate milk. Which ratio is equivalent to the ratio of white milk to chocolate milk?

F. 8:11   H. 3:8

(G.) 8:3   J. 3:11

3. A baker makes 5 apple pies for every 3 blueberry pies. Last week the baker made 15 blueberry pies. How many apple pies did the baker make?

A. 8   (C.) 25

B. 9   D. 40

4. Bagel prices at four different bakeries are shown below. Which is the best buy?

(F.) Bakery 1: A dozen bagels costs $7.79.

G. Bakery 2: 6 bagels cost $4.09.

H. Bakery 3: Bagels cost $0.75 each.

J. Bakery 4: 2 bagels cost $1.55.

5. Which is another way to write the ratio 8:3?

A. 3 to 8   C. 8 to 11

B. $\frac{3}{8}$ (D.) 8 to 3

6. Which is **not** equivalent to $\frac{45}{75}$?

F. $\frac{9}{15}$ H. 60%

G. $\frac{15}{25}$ (J.) 70%

7. Which shows the ratio "44 to 200" written as a percent, a decimal, and a fraction in simplest form?

A. 44%, 0.44, $\frac{44}{50}$

B. 44%, 0.22, $\frac{22}{100}$

C. 22%, 0.2, $\frac{22}{100}$

(D.) 22%, 0.22, $\frac{11}{50}$

8. The length of a poster is 16 inches.

Length
1 inch = 2.54 centimeters

What is the length of this poster in centimeters?

F. 6.30 centimeters

G. 13.46 centimeters

H. 18.54 centimeters

(J.) 40.64 centimeters

9. A certain shade of orange requires a 3 to 2 ratio of yellow to red paint. You have 6 gallons of red paint. How much yellow paint do you need?

A. 4 gallons

B. 5 gallons

(C.) 9 gallons

D. 12 gallons

10. Out of 20 athletes surveyed, 10 athletes chose soccer as their favorite sport, 6 chose golf, and the others chose football. What percent of the athletes chose football?

(F.) 20%

G. 30%

H. 40%

J. 50%

© Houghton Mifflin Harcourt Publishing Company

11. In Miranda's flower garden, 65% of the flowers are tulips. What fraction of Miranda's flowers are tulips?

A. $\frac{100}{65}$ C. $\frac{65}{1}$

(B.) $\frac{13}{20}$ D. $\frac{7}{40}$

FREE RESPONSE

12. Use the tables to compare the ratios $\frac{7}{8}$ and $\frac{11}{12}$.

7	14	21	28	35
8	16	24	32	40

11	22	33	44	55
12	24	36	48	60

$\frac{7}{8} < \frac{11}{12}$

13. Paula's dog, Toby, weighs 95 pounds.

Weight/Mass
1 pound ≈ 0.454 kilogram

a. To find Toby's weight in kilograms, what conversion factor should you use?

$\frac{0.454 \text{ kilogram}}{1 \text{ pound}}$

b. Explain why multiplying a quantity by a conversion factor does not change the quantity's value.

The terms in a conversion factor

are equivalent measurements, so a

conversion factor is equivalent to 1.

c. Find Toby's weight in kilograms.

43.13 kg

14. Samantha correctly answered 38 out of 55 questions on a test. She must score 70% or greater to pass the test. Did she pass? Justify your answer.

No; $\frac{38}{55} \approx 69\%$

15. To earn money, Peter shovels driveways in the winter. He earns $24 in 3 hours.

a. Complete the table.

Hours	0.5	1	3	4	5
Amount Earned ($)	4	8	24	32	40

b. Write the information in the table as ordered pairs. Use Hours as the x-coordinates and Amount earned as the y-coordinates.

(0.5, 4), (1, 8), (3, 24), (4, 32), (5, 40)

c. Graph the ordered pairs from **b** and connect the points.

d. What is Peter's unit rate in dollars per hour? How are the table and the graph above related to this unit rate?

$\frac{8}{1}$; for each column in the table, the

ratio of Amount earned to Hours is

equivalent to $\frac{8}{1}$; for each point (x, y)

on the graph, $\frac{y}{x}$ is equivalent to $\frac{8}{1}$.

e. How can you use the graph to find the amount of money Peter earns in 6 hours?

Find the point whose x-coord. is 6.

The y-coord. of this point is the

amount Peter earns in 6 hours.

f. How can you use the unit rate to find the amount of money Peter earns in 6 hours?

Multiply the unit rate by 6.

© Houghton Mifflin Harcourt Publishing Company

Geometry

Unit Vocabulary

heptagon	(6-4)
hexagon	(6-4)
net	(6-6)
octagon	(6-4)
pentagon	(6-4)
pyramid	(6-6)
regular polygon	(6-4)
rhombus	(6-2)
surface area	(6-6)
vertex	(6-4)

UNIT 6

Geometry

Unit Focus

In this unit you will learn about two- and three-dimensional figures. You will learn how to find the areas of polygons like triangles and quadrilaterals. You will find the volume of a prism. You will use nets to find surface area. You will apply all of these measurements in both real-world and mathematical situations.

Unit at a Glance

COMMON CORE

Lesson	Standards for Mathematical Content
6-1 Area of Triangles	CC.6.G.1
6-2 Area of Quadrilaterals	CC.6.G.1
6-3 Area of Polygons	CC.6.G.1
6-4 Polygons in the Coordinate Plane	CC.6.G.3
6-5 Volume of Prisms	CC.6.G.2
6-6 Nets and Surface Area	CC.6.G.4
Problem Solving Connections	
Test Prep	

UNIT 6

Unit 6   141   Geometry

Unpacking the Common Core State Standards

Use the table to help you understand the Standards for Mathematical Content that are taught in this unit. Refer to the lessons listed after each standard for exploration and practice.

COMMON CORE **Standards for Mathematical Content**	**What It Means For You**
CC.6.G.1 Find the area of right triangles, other triangles, …; apply these techniques in the context of solving real-world and mathematical problems. Lesson 6-1	You will find the areas of triangles to solve both real-world and mathematical problems.
CC.6.G.1 Find the area of … special quadrilaterals, …; apply these techniques in the context of solving real-world and mathematical problems. Lesson 6-2	You will find the areas of special quadrilaterals to solve both real-world and mathematical problems.
CC.6.G.1 Find the area of … polygons by composing into rectangles or decomposing into triangles and other shapes; apply these techniques in the context of solving real-world and mathematical problems. Lesson 6-3	You will learn a variety of methods to find the areas of polygons to solve both real-world and mathematical problems.
CC.6.G.3 Draw polygons in the coordinate plane given coordinates for the vertices; use coordinates to find the length of a side joining points with the same first coordinate or the same second coordinate. Apply these techniques in the context of solving real-world or mathematical problems. Lesson 6-4	You will graph polygons in the coordinate plane, given coordinates for the vertices. You will use coordinates to find the length of a polygon's side.
CC.6.G.2 Find the volume of a right rectangular prism with fractional edge lengths by packing it with unit cubes of the appropriate unit fraction edge lengths, and show that the volume is the same as would be found by multiplying the edge lengths of the prism. Apply the formulas $V = lwh$ and $V = bh$ to find volumes of right rectangular prisms with fractional edge lengths in the context of solving real-world and mathematical problems. Lesson 6-5	You will find the volume of a right rectangular prism with fractional edge lengths to solve both real-world and mathematical problems.
CC.6.G.4 Represent three-dimensional figures using nets made up of rectangles and triangles, and use these nets to find the surface area of these figures. Apply these techniques in the context of solving real-world and mathematical problems. Lesson 6-6	You will use nets to find the surface area of three-dimensional figures and use this technique to solve real-world and mathematical problems.

Unpacking the Common Core State Standards

This page lists and explains the Standards for Mathematical Content that are addressed in this unit. For information about the Standards for Mathematical Practice, which are integrated throughout the text, see Teacher Edition pages vii–xiii.

UNIT 6

Notes

6-1 Area of Triangles

Essential question: *How do you find the area of a triangle?*

© Houghton Mifflin Harcourt Publishing Company

COMMON CORE Standards for Mathematical Content

CC.6.G.1 Find the area of right triangles, other triangles, ...; apply these techniques in the context of solving real-world and mathematical problems.

Prerequisites
Area of rectangles

Math Background
Students should be familiar with finding the area of a rectangle. In this lesson, students will derive the formula for area of a triangle from the formula for area of a rectangle. A diagonal of a rectangle divides the rectangle into two triangles, both of which have the same base length and height as the rectangle. Therefore, the formula for the area of a triangle is $\frac{1}{2}$ that of the formula for a rectangle with the same base and height.

INTRODUCE

Have students draw a 6-by-4 rectangle on grid paper and find the area of the rectangle: 24 sq. units. Then have them draw a diagonal of the rectangle. Discuss with students that the area of each triangle formed would be half that of the rectangle, or 12 sq. units.

TEACH

1 EXPLORE

Questioning Strategies
- Does it matter which way you draw the diagonal? no
- How can you show that the diagonal cuts the rectangle into equal triangles? Cut along the diagonal and match up the two equal parts.

2 EXPLORE

Questioning Strategies
- Does it matter what type of triangle is drawn in part A? any triangle
- What angle will the cut make with the opposite side in part C? *Directly across to the opposite side* means that it should form a right angle with the opposite side.

Teaching Strategies
Have students compare their original triangle shapes to see that a variety of triangle shapes will give the same results. Ask students if they can think of any non-right triangle that would give different results. Try any triangles that the students want to test until they are convinced that the same results will occur with any non-right triangle.

3 EXAMPLE

Questioning Strategies
- How can you tell which dimension is the height? The height must form a right angle with the base.
- Why is the area expressed in square units? Because area is a two-dimensional measure that involves multiplication of two units: e.g., $cm \times cm = cm^2$.

Avoid Common Errors
Sometimes students forget to multiply by $\frac{1}{2}$ when finding the area of a triangle. Remind students to write all the steps in the solution: (1) write the formula for area of a triangle, (2) substitute values for the given information, and (3) simplify.

Name_____ Class_____ Date_____

6-1

Area of Triangles

Essential question: *How do you find the area of a triangle?*

COMMON CORE
CC.6.G.1

1 EXPLORE Area of a Right Triangle

A Draw a large rectangle on grid paper.

What is the formula for the area of a rectangle? $A =$ ___bh___

B Draw one diagonal of your rectangle.

The diagonal divides the rectangle into __two right triangles__. Each one represents __half__ of the rectangle.

Use this information and the formula for area of a rectangle to write a formula for the area of a right triangle. $A = \frac{1}{2}bh$

REFLECT

1. In the formula for the area of a right triangle, what do b and h represent?

   __the lengths of the sides that form the right angle__

2 EXPLORE Area of a Triangle

A Draw a large triangle on grid paper. Do not draw a right triangle.

B Cut out your triangle. Then trace around it to make a copy of your triangle. Cut out the copy.

C Cut one of your triangles into two pieces by cutting through one angle directly across to the opposite side. Now you have three triangles — one large triangle and two smaller triangles.

When added together, the areas of the two smaller triangles equal the __area__ of the large triangle.

D Arrange the three triangles into a rectangle. What fraction of the rectangle does the large triangle represent? __$\frac{1}{2}$__

The area of the rectangle is $A = bh$. What is the area of the large triangle? $A = \frac{1}{2}bh$

How does this formula compare to the formula for the area of a right triangle that you found in ① ?

__They are the same.__

Unit 6   143   Lesson 1

REFLECT

2. In the formula for the area of a triangle, what do b and h represent?

   __b: length of the triangle's base; h: distance from the base to the opposite vertex__

Area of a Triangle

$A = \frac{1}{2}bh$

3 EXAMPLE Finding the Area of a Triangle

Find the area of each triangle.

A

8 m
20 m

$b =$ ___20___ meters
$h =$ ___8___ meters

Use the formula to find the area. $A = \frac{1}{2}bh$

$= \frac{1}{2}\left(20 \text{ meters}\right)\left(8 \text{ meters}\right)$

$= 80$ square meters

B

5 in.
12 in.

$b =$ ___12___ inches
$h =$ ___5___ inches

Use the formula to find the area. $A = \frac{1}{2}bh$

$= \frac{1}{2}\left(12 \text{ inches}\right)\left(5 \text{ inches}\right)$

$= 30$ square inches

TRY THIS!

Find the area of each triangle.

3a.

12 m
25 m

$A =$ ___150 m²___

3b.

14 in.
8.5 in.

$A =$ ___59.5 in²___

Unit 6   144   Lesson 1

Questioning Strategies

- How do you know which dimension is the base? The base is always a side of the triangle. The height must be perpendicular to the base.

- What happens to the area of the triangle if you double the height? The area is twice the original area.

MATHEMATICAL PRACTICE **Highlighting the Standards**

This example is an opportunity to address Standard 4 (Model with mathematics). Students solve a real-world problem by modeling the pennant with a triangle, and using a formula to find the area. Students model the pennant with a triangle and they model the area with a formula.

CLOSE

Essential Question

How do you find the area of a triangle?

Use the formula for the area of a triangle: $A = \frac{1}{2}bh$. Multiply $\frac{1}{2}$ times the length of the base times the height.

Summarize

Have students explain in their journal the relationship between the area of a triangle and the area of a rectangle. Have them include an example.

Have students begin a chart of area formulas like the one shown below and include formula for the area of a triangle.

Figure	2-D or 3-D?	Formula
Triangle	2-D	$A = \frac{1}{2}bh$ b is base length. h is height.

PRACTICE

Where skills are taught	Where skills are practiced
3 EXAMPLE	EXS. 1–8
4 EXAMPLE	EXS. 9–12

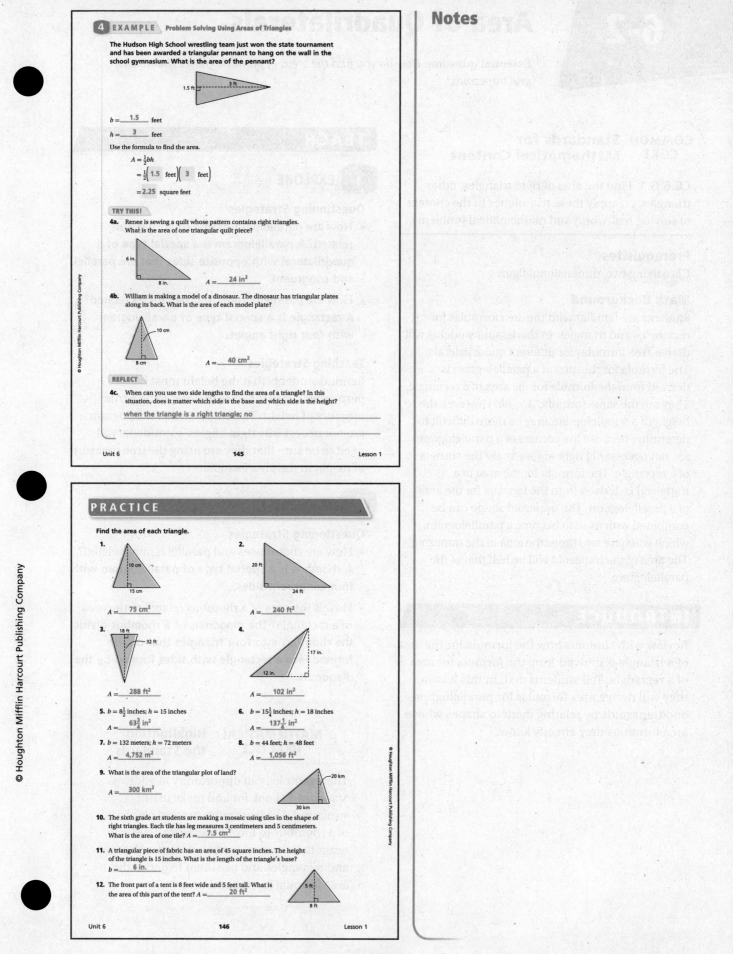

4 EXAMPLE Problem Solving Using Areas of Triangles

The Hudson High School wrestling team just won the state tournament and has been awarded a triangular pennant to hang on the wall in the school gymnasium. What is the area of the pennant?

$b = \underline{\quad 1.5 \quad}$ feet

$h = \underline{\quad 3 \quad}$ feet

Use the formula to find the area.

$A = \frac{1}{2}bh$

$\quad = \frac{1}{2}\left(\underline{1.5}\ \text{feet}\right)\left(\underline{3}\ \text{feet}\right)$

$\quad = \underline{2.25}$ square feet

TRY THIS!

4a. Renee is sewing a quilt whose pattern contains right triangles. What is the area of one triangular quilt piece?

$A = \underline{\quad 24\ in^2 \quad}$

4b. William is making a model of a dinosaur. The dinosaur has triangular plates along its back. What is the area of each model plate?

$A = \underline{\quad 40\ cm^2 \quad}$

REFLECT

4c. When can you use two side lengths to find the area of a triangle? In this situation, does it matter which side is the base and which side is the height?

when the triangle is a right triangle; no

PRACTICE

Find the area of each triangle.

1.

$A = \underline{\quad 75\ cm^2 \quad}$

2.

$A = \underline{\quad 240\ ft^2 \quad}$

3.

$A = \underline{\quad 288\ ft^2 \quad}$

4.

$A = \underline{\quad 102\ in^2 \quad}$

5. $b = 8\frac{1}{2}$ inches; $h = 15$ inches

$A = \underline{\quad 63\frac{3}{4}\ in^2 \quad}$

6. $b = 15\frac{1}{4}$ inches; $h = 18$ inches

$A = \underline{\quad 137\frac{1}{4}\ in^2 \quad}$

7. $b = 132$ meters; $h = 72$ meters

$A = \underline{\quad 4,752\ m^2 \quad}$

8. $b = 44$ feet; $h = 48$ feet

$A = \underline{\quad 1,056\ ft^2 \quad}$

9. What is the area of the triangular plot of land?

$A = \underline{\quad 300\ km^2 \quad}$

10. The sixth grade art students are making a mosaic using tiles in the shape of right triangles. Each tile has leg measures 3 centimeters and 5 centimeters. What is the area of one tile? $A = \underline{\quad 7.5\ cm^2 \quad}$

11. A triangular piece of fabric has an area of 45 square inches. The height of the triangle is 15 inches. What is the length of the triangle's base?

$b = \underline{\quad 6\ in. \quad}$

12. The front part of a tent is 8 feet wide and 5 feet tall. What is the area of this part of the tent? $A = \underline{\quad 20\ ft^2 \quad}$

Notes

Area of Quadrilaterals

Essential question: *How do you find the areas of parallelograms, rhombuses, and trapezoids?*

COMMON CORE

Standards for Mathematical Content

CC.6.G.1 Find the area of right triangles, other triangles, ...; apply these techniques in the context of solving real-world and mathematical problems.

Prerequisites

Classifying two-dimensional figures

Math Background

Students are familiar with the area formulas for rectangles and triangles. In this lesson, students will derive area formulas for different quadrilaterals. The formula for the area of a parallelogram is derived from the formula for the area of a rectangle. They are the same formula, $A = bh$. However, the height of a parallelogram may be more difficult to determine because the corners of a parallelogram are not necessarily right angles as are the corners of a rectangle. The formula for the area of a trapezoid is derived from the formula for the area of a parallelogram. The trapezoid shape can be combined with itself to become a parallelogram, which will have two times the area of the trapezoid. The area of the trapezoid will be half that of the parallelogram.

INTRODUCE

Review with students how the formula for the area of a triangle is derived from the formula for area of a rectangle. Tell students that, in this lesson, they will derive area formulas for parallelograms and trapezoids by relating them to shapes whose area formulas they already know.

TEACH

1 EXPLORE

Questioning Strategies

• How are parallelograms and quadrilaterals related? A parallelogram is a special type of quadrilateral with opposite sides that are parallel and congruent.

• How are parallelograms and rectangles related? A rectangle is a special type of parallelogram with four right angles.

Teaching Strategies

Remind students that the height must be perpendicular to the base in order to be a true measure of height. The angles in a parallelogram are not necessarily right angles, so students will need to be sure that they are using the true measure of height in the area formula.

2 EXAMPLE

Questioning Strategies

• How are rhombuses and parallelograms related? A rhombus is a special type of parallelogram with four congruent sides.

• How is the area of a rhombus related to the area of a rectangle? The diagonals of a rhombus divide the rhombus into four triangles that can be formed into a rectangle with sides formed by the diagonals.

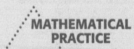

MATHEMATICAL PRACTICE   **Highlighting the Standards**

This example is an opportunity to address Standard 7 (Look for and make use of structure). Students move around pieces of a rhombus to form a rectangle. Students examine relationships between rhombuses and rectangles and use them to derive the area formula for a rhombus.

© Houghton Mifflin Harcourt Publishing Company

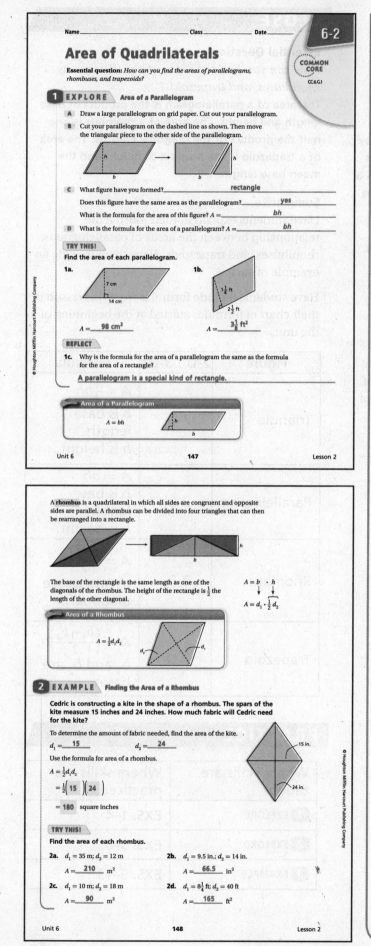

Name _____ **Class** _____ **Date** _____

6-2

COMMON CORE
CC.6.G.1

Area of Quadrilaterals

Essential question: *How can you find the areas of parallelograms, rhombuses, and trapezoids?*

1 EXPLORE — Area of a Parallelogram

A Draw a large parallelogram on grid paper. Cut out your parallelogram.

B Cut your parallelogram on the dashed line as shown. Then move the triangular piece to the other side of the parallelogram.

C What figure have you formed? _____ rectangle

Does this figure have the same area as the parallelogram? _____ yes

What is the formula for the area of this figure? $A =$ _____ bh

D What is the formula for the area of a parallelogram? $A =$ _____ bh

TRY THIS!

Find the area of each parallelogram.

1a.

7 cm
14 cm

$A =$ _____ 98 _____ cm²

1b.

$1\frac{1}{4}$ ft
$2\frac{1}{2}$ ft

$A =$ _____ $3\frac{1}{8}$ ft²

REFLECT

1c. Why is the formula for the area of a parallelogram the same as the formula for the area of a rectangle?

_____ A parallelogram is a special kind of rectangle. _____

Area of a Parallelogram

$A = bh$

h
b

Unit 6   147   Lesson 2

A **rhombus** is a quadrilateral in which all sides are congruent and opposite sides are parallel. A rhombus can be divided into four triangles that can then be rearranged into a rectangle.

b
h

The base of the rectangle is the same length as one of the diagonals of the rhombus. The height of the rectangle is $\frac{1}{2}$ the length of the other diagonal.

$A = b \cdot h$
$A = d_1 \cdot \frac{1}{2} d_2$

Area of a Rhombus

$A = \frac{1}{2} d_1 d_2$

d_2 d_1

2 EXAMPLE — Finding the Area of a Rhombus

Cedric is constructing a kite in the shape of a rhombus. The spars of the kite measure 15 inches and 24 inches. How much fabric will Cedric need for the kite?

To determine the amount of fabric needed, find the area of the kite.

$d_1 =$ _____ 15 _____ $d_2 =$ _____ 24 _____

Use the formula for area of a rhombus.

$A = \frac{1}{2} d_1 d_2$

$= \frac{1}{2} \left(15 \right) \left(24 \right)$

$=$ _____ 180 _____ square inches

15 in.
24 in.

TRY THIS!

Find the area of each rhombus.

2a. $d_1 = 35$ m; $d_2 = 12$ m

$A =$ _____ 210 _____ m²

2b. $d_1 = 9.5$ in.; $d_2 = 14$ in.

$A =$ _____ 66.5 _____ in²

2c. $d_1 = 10$ m; $d_2 = 18$ m

$A =$ _____ 90 _____ m²

2d. $d_1 = 8\frac{1}{4}$ ft; $d_2 = 40$ ft

$A =$ _____ 165 _____ ft²

Unit 6   148   Lesson 2

© Houghton Mifflin Harcourt Publishing Company

Questioning Strategies

- How are trapezoids and quadrilaterals related? A trapezoid is a quadrilateral with one pair of parallel sides.

- How is the area of the trapezoid related to the area of a parallelogram? A trapezoid and its copy can be arranged side-by-side in such a way that it forms a parallelogram. The parallelogram has a height equal to that of the trapezoid and a base equal to the sum of the trapezoid bases.

- How can you tell which base is b_1 and which is b_2? It does not matter because you use the sum.

Teaching Strategies

Tell students that the formula for the area of a trapezoid is actually very close to the formula for the area of a parallelogram. The bases of a parallelogram are congruent, but the bases of a trapezoid are not. You can use the formula for the area of a parallelogram, $A = bh$, to find the area of the trapezoid as long as you substitute the *mean* of the trapezoid base lengths for b: $A = \left(\frac{b_1 + b_2}{2}\right)h$.

Essential Question

How can you find the areas of parallelograms, rhombuses, and trapezoids?
The area of a parallelogram is the product of base length and height. The area of a rhombus is one half the product of the diagonal lengths. The area of a trapezoid is the product of height and the mean base length.

Summarize

Have students explain in their journal the relationship between the areas of parallelograms, rhombuses, and trapezoids. Have them include an example of each.

Have students include formulas from this lesson in their chart of formulas started at the beginning of the unit.

Figure	2-D / 3-D?	Formula
Triangle	2-D	$A = \frac{1}{2}bh$ b is base length. h is height.
Parallelogram	2-D	$A = bh$ b is base length. h is height.
Rhombus	2-D	$A = \frac{d_1 \cdot d_2}{2}$ d_1 and d_2 are diagonals.
Trapezoid	2-D	$A = \left(\frac{b_1 + b_2}{2}\right)h$ b_1 and b_2 are bases.

PRACTICE

Where skills are taught	Where skills are practiced
1 EXPLORE	EXS. 1–4
2 EXPLORE	EXS. 5–8
3 EXAMPLE	EXS. 9–13

To find the formula for the area of a trapezoid, notice that two copies of the same trapezoid fit together to form a parallelogram. Therefore, the area of the trapezoid is $\frac{1}{2}$ the area of the parallelogram.

The height of the parallelogram is the same as the height of the trapezoid. The base of the parallelogram is the sum of the two bases of the trapezoid.

$A = \underset{\downarrow}{b} \cdot h$

$A = (b_1 + b_2) \cdot h$

Area of a Trapezoid

$A = \frac{1}{2}h(b_1 + b_2)$

3 EXAMPLE Finding the Area of a Trapezoid

A section of a deck is in the shape of a trapezoid. What is the area of this section of the deck?

$b_1 = \underline{17}$ $b_2 = \underline{39}$ $h = \underline{16}$

Use the formula for area of a trapezoid.

$A = \frac{1}{2}h(b_1 + b_2)$

$= \frac{1}{2} \cdot 16 \left(17 + 39 \right)$

$= \frac{1}{2} \cdot 16 \left(56 \right)$ *Add inside the parentheses.*

$= 8 \cdot 56$ *Multiply $\frac{1}{2}$ and 16.*

$= 448$ square feet   *Multiply.*

TRY THIS!

3a. Another section of the deck is also shaped as a trapezoid. For this section, the length of one base is 27 feet, and the length of the other base is 34 feet. The height is 12 feet. What is the area of this section of the deck? $A = \underline{366}$ ft²

REFLECT

3b. Does it matter which of the trapezoid's bases is substituted for b_1 and which is substituted for b_2? Why or why not?

No; the sum $b_1 + b_2$ will have the same value regardless of which base is

b_1 and which is b_2.

Unit 6   149   Lesson 2

PRACTICE

Find the area of each parallelogram.

1.
6 cm
14 cm
$A = \underline{84}$ cm²

2.
8 cm
21 cm
$A = \underline{168}$ cm²

3. $b = 13$ meters; $h = 7$ meters
$A = \underline{91}$ m²

4. $b = 12\frac{3}{4}$ inches; $h = 2\frac{1}{2}$ inches
$A = \underline{31\frac{7}{8}}$ in²

Find the area of each rhombus.

5.
16 m
9 m
$A = \underline{72}$ m²

6.
21 m
32 m
$A = \underline{336}$ m²

7. $d_1 = 18$ feet; $d_2 = 7.25$ feet
$A = \underline{65.25}$ ft²

8. $d_1 = 8$ inches; $d_2 = 2\frac{1}{2}$ inches
$A = \underline{10}$ in²

Find the area of each trapezoid.

9.
42 in.
24 in.
36 in.
$A = \underline{936}$ in²

10.
36 in.
18 in.
52 in.
$A = \underline{792}$ in²

11. $b_1 = 9$ meters
$b_2 = 15$ meters
$h = 8$ meters
$A = \underline{96}$ m²

12. $b_1 = 11$ meters
$b_2 = 14$ meters
$h = 10$ meters
$A = \underline{125}$ m²

13. Find the area of the figure. Explain how you found your answer.

Area of rectangle = 12 · 18 = 216 ft²

Area of trapezoid = $\frac{1}{2}(10 + 18) \cdot 6 = 84$ ft²

Total area = 216 + 84 = 300 ft²

10 ft
6 ft
12 ft
18 ft

Unit 6   150   Lesson 2

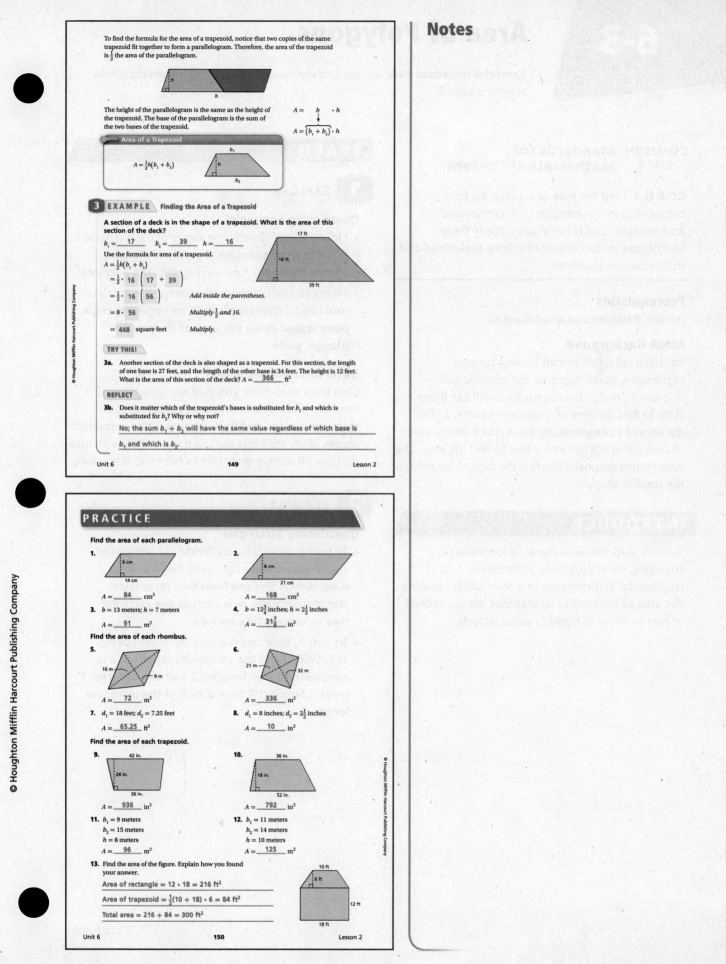

Area of Polygons

Essential question: *How do you find the area of a polygon by breaking it into simple shapes?*

COMMON CORE

Standards for Mathematical Content

CC.6.G.1 Find the area of ... polygons by composing into rectangles or decomposing into triangles and other shapes; apply these techniques in the context of solving real-world and mathematical problems.

Prerequisites

Area of triangles and quadrilaterals

Math Background

Students are familiar with finding the area of triangles, parallelograms, rhombuses, and trapezoids. In this lesson, students will use these skills to find the area of composite figures. To find the area of a composite figure, divide it into smaller shapes for which you know how to find the area. The area of the composite figure is the sum of the areas of the smaller shapes.

INTRODUCE

Review with students the area formulas for triangles, parallelograms, rhombuses, and trapezoids. Tell students that they will be finding the area of unfamiliar figures that are composed of two or more of these familiar shapes.

TEACH

1 EXPLORE

Questioning Strategies

• How can you classify the shape of each tangram piece? **2 large triangles, 1 medium triangle, 2 small triangles, 1 parallelogram, and 1 square**

• How can you compare the sizes of the smallest and largest triangle pieces? **The largest triangle piece is four times the area of the smallest triangle piece.**

Differentiated Instruction

Give each student or group of students a set of tangram pieces. Have students complete some tangram puzzles and find the area of the composite shape. Show students that all the composite shapes that use all the tangram pieces have the same area.

2 EXAMPLE

Questioning Strategies

• In part A, how can you divide the composite figure into smaller figures to find the area? **A horizontal line can form two rectangles stacked vertically, or a vertical line can form two rectangles side-by-side.**

• In part A, how can you find the length of the unlabeled side? **The composite length of 6 is composed of two lengths: 3 and an unknown length. Subtract 3 from 6 to find the unknown length.**

© Houghton Mifflin Harcourt Publishing Company

continued

Name_____ Class_____ Date_____

6-3

COMMON
CORE
CC.6.G.1

Area of Polygons

Essential question: *How can you find the area of a polygon by breaking it into simpler shapes?*

1 EXPLORE Area Using Tangrams

The area of the small square is 1 square unit. Find the area of each of the other tangram pieces.

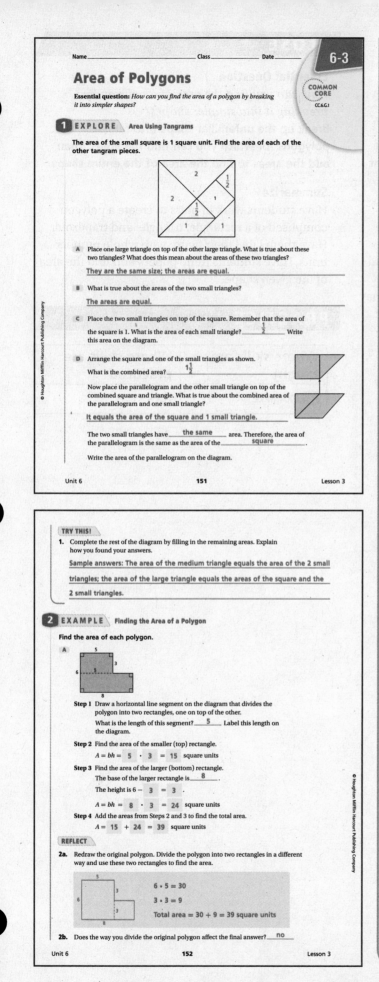

A Place one large triangle on top of the other large triangle. What is true about these two triangles? What does this mean about the areas of these two triangles?

They are the same size; the areas are equal.

B What is true about the areas of the two small triangles?

The areas are equal.

C Place the two small triangles on top of the square. Remember that the area of the square is 1. What is the area of each small triangle? __$\frac{1}{2}$__ Write this area on the diagram.

D Arrange the square and one of the small triangles as shown. What is the combined area? __$1\frac{1}{2}$__

Now place the parallelogram and the other small triangle on top of the combined square and triangle. What is true about the combined area of the parallelogram and one small triangle?

It equals the area of the square and 1 small triangle.

The two small triangles have __the same__ area. Therefore, the area of the parallelogram is the same as the area of the __square__ .

Write the area of the parallelogram on the diagram.

Unit 6   151   Lesson 3

TRY THIS!

1. Complete the rest of the diagram by filling in the remaining areas. Explain how you found your answers.

Sample answers: The area of the medium triangle equals the area of the 2 small

triangles; the area of the large triangle equals the areas of the square and the

2 small triangles.

2 EXAMPLE Finding the Area of a Polygon

Find the area of each polygon.

A

Step 1 Draw a horizontal line segment on the diagram that divides the polygon into two rectangles, one on top of the other.

What is the length of this segment? __5__ Label this length on the diagram.

Step 2 Find the area of the smaller (top) rectangle.

$A = bh =$ __5__ · __3__ = __15__ square units

Step 3 Find the area of the larger (bottom) rectangle.

The base of the larger rectangle is __8__ .

The height is 6 − __3__ = __3__ .

$A = bh =$ __8__ · __3__ = __24__ square units

Step 4 Add the areas from Steps 2 and 3 to find the total area.

$A =$ __15__ + __24__ = __39__ square units

REFLECT

2a. Redraw the original polygon. Divide the polygon into two rectangles in a different way and use these two rectangles to find the area.

6 · 5 = 30

3 · 3 = 9

Total area = 30 + 9 = 39 square units

2b. Does the way you divide the original polygon affect the final answer? __no__

Unit 6   152   Lesson 3

Questioning Strategies

- In part B, what are two ways to divide the figure to find its area? **Divide it into two rectangles or subtract a rectangular area from a square.**

- In part C, how can you find the base and height of the triangle? **Subtract 7 from 13 for the height and subtract 8 from 16 for the base.**

Differentiated Learning

To avoid missing pieces of the composite shape when finding the areas of the pieces, suggest to students that they highlight each piece as they find the area and place a check in the shape when they have included its area in the total. This practice may help students organize their work as they find the area of each piece of the composite shape.

MATHEMATICAL PRACTICE   **Highlighting the Standards**

This example is an opportunity to address Standard 1 (Make sense of problems and persevere in solving them). Students analyze a composite figure, determine a plan for dividing the figure into pieces for which they can find the area, find the individual areas, and add them together for a total area.

CLOSE

Essential Question

How can you find the area of a polygon by breaking it into simpler shapes?
Break up the unfamiliar shape into familiar polygons for which you can find the areas. Then add the areas to find the area of the entire shape.

Summarize

Have students work in pairs to create a polygon composed of a rectangle, triangle, and trapezoid. Have them label their figure with whole number units. Have students trade papers and find the area of the given shape.

PRACTICE

Where skills are taught	Where skills are practiced
2 EXAMPLE	EXS. 1–5

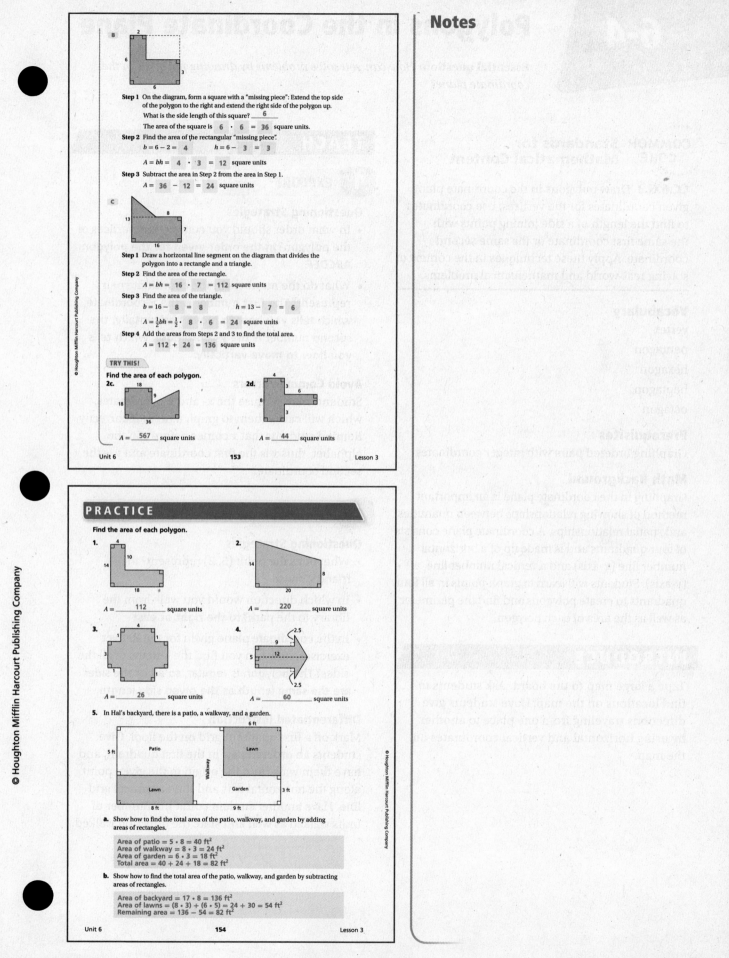

B

Step 1 On the diagram, form a square with a "missing piece": Extend the top side of the polygon to the right and extend the right side of the polygon up.

What is the side length of this square? __6__

The area of the square is $6 \cdot 6 = 36$ square units.

Step 2 Find the area of the rectangular "missing piece".

$b = 6 - 2 = $ __4__ $\qquad h = 6 - $ __3__ $ = $ __3__

$A = bh = $ __4__ $\cdot$ __3__ $ = $ __12__ square units

Step 3 Subtract the area in Step 2 from the area in Step 1.

$A = $ __36__ $ - $ __12__ $ = $ __24__ square units

C

Step 1 Draw a horizontal line segment on the diagram that divides the polygon into a rectangle and a triangle.

Step 2 Find the area of the rectangle.

$A = bh = $ __16__ $\cdot$ __7__ $ = $ __112__ square units

Step 3 Find the area of the triangle.

$b = 16 - $ __8__ $ = $ __8__ $\qquad h = 13 - $ __7__ $ = $ __6__

$A = \frac{1}{2}bh = \frac{1}{2} \cdot$ __8__ $\cdot$ __6__ $ = $ __24__ square units

Step 4 Add the areas from Steps 2 and 3 to find the total area.

$A = $ __112__ $ + $ __24__ $ = $ __136__ square units

TRY THIS!

Find the area of each polygon.

2c.

$A = $ __567__ square units

2d.

$A = $ __44__ square units

PRACTICE

Find the area of each polygon.

1.

$A = $ __112__ square units

2.

$A = $ __220__ square units

3.

$A = $ __26__ square units

4.

$A = $ __60__ square units

5. In Hal's backyard, there is a patio, a walkway, and a garden.

a. Show how to find the total area of the patio, walkway, and garden by adding areas of rectangles.

Area of patio = $5 \cdot 8 = 40$ ft^2
Area of walkway = $8 \cdot 3 = 24$ ft^2
Area of garden = $6 \cdot 3 = 18$ ft^2
Total area = $40 + 24 + 18 = 82$ ft^2

b. Show how to find the total area of the patio, walkway, and garden by subtracting areas of rectangles.

Area of backyard = $17 \cdot 8 = 136$ ft^2
Area of lawns = $(8 \cdot 3) + (6 \cdot 5) = 24 + 30 = 54$ ft^2
Remaining area = $136 - 54 = 82$ ft^2

6-4 Polygons in the Coordinate Plane

Essential question: *How can you solve problems by drawing polygons in the coordinate plane?*

COMMON CORE Standards for Mathematical Content

CC.6.G.3 Draw polygons in the coordinate plane given coordinates for the vertices; use coordinates to find the length of a side joining points with the same first coordinate or the same second coordinate. Apply these techniques in the context of solving real-world and mathematical problems.

Vocabulary

vertex

pentagon

hexagon

heptagon

octagon

Prerequisites

Graphing ordered pairs with integer coordinates

Math Background

Graphing in the coordinate plane is an important method of showing relationships between quantities and spatial relationships. A coordinate plane consists of four quadrants and is made up of a horizontal number line (x-axis) and a vertical number line (y-axis). Students will learn to graph points in all four quadrants to create polygons and find the perimeter as well as the area of each polygon.

INTRODUCE

Tape a large map to the board. Ask students to find locations on the map. Have students give directions traveling from one place to another by using horizontal and vertical coordinates on the map.

TEACH

1 EXPLORE

Questioning Strategies

- In what order should you connect the vertices of the polygon? **In the order given for the polygon, ABCDEF.**

- What do the numbers in the coordinate pair represent? **The first number is the x-coordinate, which tells you how to move horizontally; the second number is the y-coordinate, which tells you how to move vertically.**

Avoid Common Errors

Students may confuse the x- and y-coordinates, which will cause them to graph a point incorrectly. Remind students that x comes before y in the alphabet, thus x is the first coordinate and y is the second coordinate.

2 EXAMPLE

Questioning Strategies

- What does the point (5, 2) represent? **the friend's house**

- In which direction would you walk from the library to the park? **to the right or east**

- In the coordinate plane given for the Reflect exercises, how can you find the lengths of all the sides? **The polygon is regular, so all of the sides are the same length as the given side length.**

Differentiated Instruction

Mark off a first quadrant grid on the floor. Give students an ordered pair in the first quadrant, and have them walk from the origin to the given point along the horizontal axis and then a vertical grid line. Have another student count the number of units walked as well and state the direction walked.

© Houghton Mifflin Harcourt Publishing Company

Name_____ Class_____ Date_____

Polygons in the Coordinate Plane

COMMON CORE CC.6.G.3

Essential question: *How can you solve problems by drawing polygons in the coordinate plane?*

A **vertex** is a point common to two sides of an angle, a polygon, or a three-dimensional figure. The *vertices* of a polygon can be represented by ordered pairs, and the polygon can then be drawn in the coordinate plane.

1 EXPLORE Polygons in the Coordinate Plane

A clothing designer makes letters for varsity jackets by graphing the letters as polygons on a coordinate plane. One of the letters is polygon *ABCDEF* with the following vertices.

$A(3, -2)$, $B(3, -4)$, $C(-3, -4)$, $D(-3, 4)$,
$E(-1, 4)$, $F(-1, -2)$

Graph the points on the coordinate plane and connect them in order.

What letter is formed? _____ L

Polygons are named by the number of their sides and angles. A **regular polygon** is a polygon in which all sides have the same length and all angles have the same measure.

Polygon	Sides and Angles	Regular	Not Regular
Triangle	3		
Quadrilateral	4		
Pentagon	5		
Hexagon	6		
Heptagon	7		
Octagon	8		

2 EXAMPLE Finding Perimeter in the Coordinate Plane

This afternoon, Tommy walked from his home to the library. He then walked to the park. From the park, he visited a friend's house, and the two of them walked to a nearby goldfish pond. Tommy left the goldfish pond and stopped at the store before returning home.

A The coordinates of each location are given. Graph and connect the points to show Tommy's path.

Home (0, 0)
Library (0, 4)
Park (5, 4)
Friend's house (5, 2)
Goldfish pond (7, 2)
Store (7, 0)

B Each grid unit represents one block. What is the distance from Tommy's home to the library?

You can use coordinates to find the distance between two points.

If two points have the same *x*-coordinate, find the distance by subtracting the *y*-coordinates.

The distance from Tommy's home at $(0, 0)$ to the library at $(0, 4)$ is $4 - 0 =$ **4** blocks.

C What is the distance from Tommy's friend's house to the goldfish pond?

If two points have the same *y*-coordinate, find the distance by subtracting the *x*-coordinates.

The distance from Tommy's friend's house at $(5, 2)$ to the goldfish pond at $(7, 2)$ is **7** – **5** = **2** blocks.

TRY THIS!

2a. What does the perimeter of the polygon represent?

the total distance Tommy walked

2b. Calculate the remaining distances. Then find the perimeter.

Library to park ___5___ blocks   Park to friend's house ___2___ blocks

Goldfish pond to store ___2___ blocks   Store to home ___7___ blocks

Perimeter = ___22___ blocks

Questioning Strategies

- What two shapes can you use to find the area of the composite figure? **parallelogram and rectangle**

- If point C were moved to (3, 6) and point D were moved to (8, 6), how would the area change? **The area would increase by 5 square feet.**

Differentiated Learning

Challenge students to find other ways to find the area of the composite figure. In this example, if the triangle with vertices *A*, *B*, and (3, 0) were moved to *F*, *E*, and (8, 0), the area of the composite figure can be calculated as a square, $5^2 = 25$ sq. units.

| MATHEMATICAL PRACTICE | Highlighting the Standards |

This example is an opportunity to address Standard 2 (Model with mathematics). Students are given a real-world problem to model in a coordinate plane. Students need to plan a solution method for finding the area of a composite figure based on using area formulas they know and information that can be obtained from the model.

Essential Question

How can you solve problems by drawing polygons in the coordinate plane?
Plot the vertices of composite polygons in the coordinate plane. Find the areas of smaller shapes that compose the larger polygon. Add the areas to find the total area of the composite figure.

Summarize

Have students plot the vertices of a composite polygon made from two or more of the following shapes: triangle, parallelogram, rhombus, or trapezoid. Have students list the vertices of the composite polygon and the vertices of each smaller shape. Have them show how to find the area of each smaller shape and the total area of the composite polygon.

Where skills are taught	Where skills are practiced
1 EXPLORE	EXS. 1–4
2 EXAMPLE	EX. 5
3 EXAMPLE	EXS. 5–7

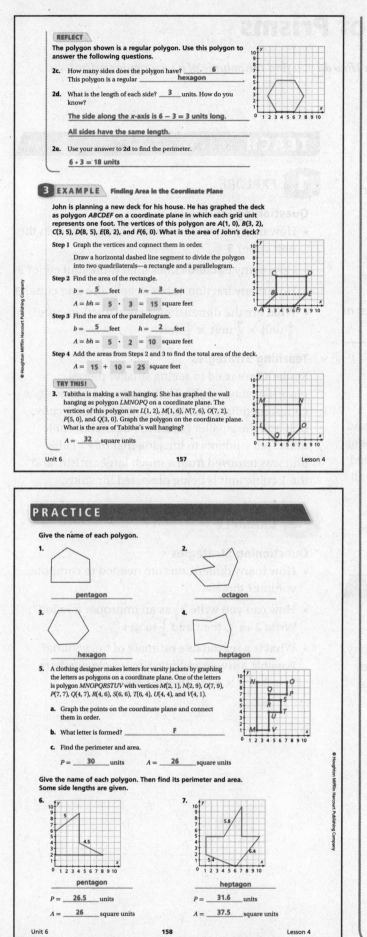

REFLECT

The polygon shown is a regular polygon. Use this polygon to answer the following questions.

2c. How many sides does the polygon have? _____6_____
This polygon is a regular _____hexagon_____

2d. What is the length of each side? __3__ units. How do you know?

The side along the x-axis is 6 − 3 = 3 units long.

All sides have the same length.

2e. Use your answer to **2d** to find the perimeter.

6 • 3 = 18 units

3 EXAMPLE Finding Area in the Coordinate Plane

John is planning a new deck for his house. He has graphed the deck as polygon *ABCDEF* on a coordinate plane in which each grid unit represents one foot. The vertices of this polygon are *A*(1, 0), *B*(3, 2), *C*(3, 5), *D*(8, 5), *E*(8, 2), and *F*(6, 0). What is the area of John's deck?

Step 1 Graph the vertices and connect them in order.

Draw a horizontal dashed line segment to divide the polygon into two quadrilaterals—a rectangle and a parallelogram.

Step 2 Find the area of the rectangle.

$b =$ __5__ feet $h =$ __3__ feet

$A = bh =$ __5__ • __3__ = __15__ square feet

Step 3 Find the area of the parallelogram.

$b =$ __5__ feet $h =$ __2__ feet

$A = bh =$ __5__ • __2__ = __10__ square feet

Step 4 Add the areas from Steps 2 and 3 to find the total area of the deck.

$A =$ __15__ + __10__ = __25__ square feet

TRY THIS!

3. Tabitha is making a wall hanging. She has graphed the wall hanging as polygon *LMNOPQ* on a coordinate plane. The vertices of this polygon are *L*(1, 2), *M*(1, 6), *N*(7, 6), *O*(7, 2), *P*(5, 0), and *Q*(3, 0). Graph the polygon on the coordinate plane. What is the area of Tabitha's wall hanging?

$A =$ __32__ square units

Unit 6   157   Lesson 4

PRACTICE

Give the name of each polygon.

1. _____pentagon_____

2. _____octagon_____

3. _____hexagon_____

4. _____heptagon_____

5. A clothing designer makes letters for varsity jackets by graphing the letters as polygons on a coordinate plane. One of the letters is polygon *MNOPQRSTUV* with vertices *M*(2, 1), *N*(2, 9), *O*(7, 9), *P*(7, 7), *Q*(4, 7), *R*(4, 6), *S*(6, 6), *T*(6, 4), *U*(4, 4), and *V*(4, 1).

a. Graph the points on the coordinate plane and connect them in order.

b. What letter is formed? _____F_____

c. Find the perimeter and area.

$P =$ __30__ units $A =$ __26__ square units

Give the name of each polygon. Then find its perimeter and area. Some side lengths are given.

6. _____pentagon_____

$P =$ __26.5__ units

$A =$ __26__ square units

7. _____heptagon_____

$P =$ __31.6__ units

$A =$ __37.5__ square units

Unit 6   158   Lesson 4

Volume of Prisms

Essential question: How do you find the volume of a rectangular prism?

© Houghton Mifflin Harcourt Publishing Company

COMMON CORE Standards for Mathematical Content

CC.6.G.2 Find the volume of a right rectangular prism with fractional edge lengths by packing it with unit cubes of the appropriate unit fraction edge lengths, and show that the volume is the same as would be found by multiplying the edge lengths of the prism. Apply the formulas $V = lwh$ and $V = Bh$ to find volumes of right rectangular prisms with fractional edge lengths in the context of solving real-world and mathematical problems.

Prerequisites

Definition and properties of prisms

Math Background

Students should be familiar with the definition and properties of prisms. A prism is a three-dimensional figure with two parallel and congruent faces called bases. The other faces connecting the bases are all rectangles. A prism is named by the shape of its bases. For example, a triangular prism has bases that are triangles. In this lesson, students learn to find the volume of rectangular prisms.

INTRODUCE

Review with students the definition and properties of rectangular prisms. Recall with students that volume is a measure of the capacity of a three-dimensional figure. Tell students they will learn how to find the volume of rectangular prisms in this lesson.

TEACH

1 EXPLORE

Questioning Strategies

- How many rows of fraction cubes are there in the unit cube? **3**
- How many fraction cubes high is the unit cube? **3**
- How many fraction cubes deep is the unit cube? **3**
- What are the dimensions of one fraction cube? $\frac{1}{3}$ unit $\times \frac{1}{3}$ unit $\times \frac{1}{3}$ unit

Teaching Strategies

Students are used to seeing smaller pieces represent single units. They might need assistance comprehending that the large cube is the 1 cubic unit and the smaller pieces are fractional cubic units. Tell students to imagine that this 1 cubic unit was removed from a much larger prism, and the 1 cubic unit is being dissected for study.

2 EXAMPLE

Questioning Strategies

- How many dimensions are needed to compute volume? **three**
- How can you write $2\frac{1}{4}$ as an improper fraction? Write 2 as $\frac{8}{4}$, then add $\frac{1}{4}$ to get $\frac{9}{4}$.
- What is a reasonable estimate of the volume? Possible answer: rounding to whole numbers, $V \approx 3 \times 2 \times 5$, or 30 cubic meters.

© Houghton Mifflin Harcourt Publishing Company

Name_____ Class_____ Date_____

6-5

COMMON CORE
CC&G.2

Volume of Prisms

Essential question: *How do you find the volume of a rectangular prism?*

1 EXPLORE Volume of a Prism

A cube with edge length 1 unit and volume 1 cubic unit is filled with smaller cubes as shown.

A How many small cubes are there? ___27___

How does the combined volume of the small cubes compare to the volume of the large cube?

The volumes are equal.

Number of small cubes		Volume of one small cube	=	Volume of large cube

| 27 | · | ? | = | 1 |

What is the volume of one small cube? $\frac{1}{27}$ cubic unit(s).

B Each edge of the large cube contains ___3___ small cubes.

Number of small cubes per edge		Edge length of one small cube	=	Edge length of large cube

| 3 | · | ? | = | 1 |

What is the edge length of one small cube? $\frac{1}{3}$ unit(s).

C Combine your results from **A** and **B** to complete the following sentence.

Each small cube has edge length $\frac{1}{3}$ unit(s) and volume $\frac{1}{27}$ cubic unit(s).

D Remember that the formula for volume of a cube with edge length ℓ is $V = \ell \cdot \ell \cdot \ell$, or $V = \ell^3$.

Show how to find the volume of one small cube using this formula.

$V = \frac{1}{3} \cdot \frac{1}{3} \cdot \frac{1}{3} = \frac{1}{27}$

Unit 6   159   Lesson 5

E Several of the small cubes are arranged into a medium-sized cube as shown.

Show two different ways to find the volume of the medium-sized cube.

1) There are 8 small cubes and each has volume $\frac{1}{27}$; $8 \cdot \frac{1}{27} = \frac{8}{27}$

2) Each small cube has edge length $\frac{1}{3}$, and there are 2 small cubes along each edge. Therefore the edge length of the medium-sized cube is $2 \cdot \frac{1}{3} = \frac{2}{3}$, and the volume of the medium-sized cube is $\frac{2}{3} \cdot \frac{2}{3} \cdot \frac{2}{3} = \frac{8}{27}$.

Volume of a Rectangular Prism

$V = \ell wh$, or $V = Bh$
(where B represents the area of the prism's base; $B = \ell w$.)

2 EXAMPLE Finding Volume

Find the volume of the rectangular prism.

$\ell = $ ___3___ meters $w = 2\frac{1}{4}$ meters $h = 4\frac{1}{2}$ meters

$V = \ell wh$

$= 3 \cdot 2\frac{1}{4} \cdot 4\frac{1}{2}$

$= 3 \cdot \frac{9}{4} \cdot \frac{9}{2}$ *Write each mixed number as an improper fraction.*

$= \frac{243}{8}$ *Multiply.*

$= 30\frac{3}{8}$ cubic meters   *Write as a mixed number in simplest form.*

REFLECT

2a. Show how to use the formula $V = Bh$ to find the volume.

$B = $ area of base $= 3 \cdot 2\frac{1}{4} = 3 \cdot \frac{9}{4} = \frac{27}{4}$

$Bh = \frac{27}{4} \cdot 4\frac{1}{2} = \frac{27}{4} \cdot \frac{9}{2} = \frac{243}{8} = 30\frac{3}{8}$

Unit 6   160   Lesson 5

Questioning Strategies

- Can you multiply the dimensions in any order to find the volume? Explain. **Yes, multiplication is commutative.**

- If the side lengths are given in meters, what will be the units of the volume? **cubic meters**

MATHEMATICAL PRACTICE **Highlighting the Standards**

This example is an opportunity to address Standard 7 (Look for and make use of structure). Students see that the formula for the volume of a prism holds for whole-number side lengths as well as fractional side lengths, including mixed-number lengths.

CLOSE

Essential Question

How do you find the volume of a rectangular prism?

Find the product of the length, width, and height of the rectangular prism. Express volume in cubic units.

Summarize

Have students include formulas from this lesson in their chart of formulas which they started at the beginning of the unit.

Figure	2-D / 3-D?	Formula
Triangle	2-D	$A = \frac{1}{2}bh$ b is base length. h is height.
Parallelogram	2-D	$A = bh$ b is base length. h is height.
Rhombus	2-D	$A = \frac{d_1 \cdot d_2}{2}$ d_1 and d_2 are diagonals.
Trapezoid	2-D	$A = \left(\frac{b_1 + b_2}{2}\right)h$ b_1 and b_2 are bases.
Rectangular Prism	3-D	$V = \ell wh$ ℓ is length, w is width, and h is height.

PRACTICE

Where skills are taught	Where skills are practiced
2 EXAMPLE	EXS. 1–6, 9
3 EXAMPLE	EXS. 7–9

© Houghton Mifflin Harcourt Publishing Company

TRY THIS!

Find the volume of each rectangular prism.

2b.

$2\frac{1}{2}$ inches

4 inches

$7\frac{1}{2}$ inches

$V = \underline{\quad 75 \quad}$ cubic inches

2c. length = $5\frac{1}{4}$ inches
width = $3\frac{1}{2}$ inches
height = 3 inches

$V = \underline{\quad 55\frac{1}{8} \quad}$ cubic inches

3 EXAMPLE Problem-Solving by Finding Volume

A rectangular city swimming pool is 25 meters long, $17\frac{1}{2}$ meters wide, and has an average depth of $1\frac{1}{2}$ meters. What is the volume of the pool?

$1\frac{1}{2}$ m

$17\frac{1}{2}$ m

25 m

Label the rectangular prism to represent the pool.

$\ell = \underline{\quad 25 \quad}$ meters $w = \underline{\quad 17\frac{1}{2} \quad}$ meters $h = \underline{\quad 1\frac{1}{2} \quad}$ meters

$V = \ell wh$

$= 25 \cdot 17\frac{1}{2} \cdot 1\frac{1}{2}$

$= 25 \cdot \frac{35}{2} \cdot \frac{3}{2}$ *Write each mixed number as an improper fraction.*

$= \frac{2,625}{4}$ *Multiply.*

$= 656\frac{1}{4}$ cubic meters   *Write as a mixed number in simplest form.*

TRY THIS!

3a. Miguel has a turtle aquarium that measures $18\frac{1}{2}$ inches by $12\frac{1}{2}$ inches by 4 inches. What is the volume of the aquarium?

$V = \underline{\quad 925 \quad}$ cubic inches

REFLECT

3b. How can you use estimation to check the reasonableness of your answer to 3a?

Sample answer: Round $18\frac{1}{2}$ to 20, $12\frac{1}{2}$ to 10, and 4 to 5; $20 \cdot 10 \cdot 5 = 1,000$,

which is close to 925.

PRACTICE

Find the volume of each rectangular prism.

1.

5 m

10 m

3 m

$V = \underline{\quad 150 \quad}$ cubic meters

2.

8 m

7 m

4 m

$V = \underline{\quad 224 \quad}$ cubic meters

3.

5 cm

$4\frac{1}{4}$ cm

$2\frac{3}{4}$ cm

$V = \underline{\quad 58\frac{7}{16} \quad}$ cubic centimeters

4.

$8\frac{1}{4}$ m

$8\frac{3}{8}$ m

6 m

$V = \underline{\quad 414\frac{9}{16} \quad}$ cubic meters

5.

7.5 ft

9.25 ft

4 ft

$V = \underline{\quad 277.5 \quad}$ cubic feet

6.

$6\frac{1}{2}$ in.

$4\frac{1}{2}$ in.

18 in.

$V = \underline{\quad 526\frac{1}{2} \quad}$ cubic inches

7. A block of wood measures 4.5 centimeters by 3.5 centimeters by 7 centimeters. What is the volume of the block of wood?

$V = \underline{\quad 110.25 \quad}$ cubic centimeters

8. A restaurant buys a freezer in the shape of a rectangular prism. The dimensions of the freezer are shown. What is the volume of the freezer?

36 in.

24 in.

72 in.

$V = \underline{\quad 62,208 \quad}$ cubic inches

9. Conjecture The length, width, and height of a rectangular prism are doubled. How many times greater is the volume compared to the original prism?

The volume is 8 times greater than the original volume.

© Houghton Mifflin Harcourt Publishing Company

6-6 Nets and Surface Area

Essential question: *How can you use nets to find surface area?*

COMMON **Standards for**
CORE **Mathematical Content**

CC.6.G.4 Represent three-dimensional figures using nets made up of rectangles and triangles, and use the nets to find the surface area of these figures. Apply these techniques in the context of solving real-world and mathematical problems.

Vocabulary

net

surface area

Prerequisites

Area of a triangle

Math Background

Students should be familiar with finding perimeter and area of polygons. In this lesson, students will learn to make nets and find surface areas. A net is a two-dimensional pattern of shapes that can be folded into a three-dimensional figure. The shapes in the net become the faces of the three-dimensional figure. You can use the net to find the surface area of the three-dimensional figure by adding up the areas of the faces.

INTRODUCE

Have students bring a box from home (e.g., cereal box, shoe box, snack box) that they may cut up. Have them cut the box along the edges, without cutting any faces off, unfold it, and lay it on a flat surface. Discuss with students that each box was a rectangular prism and that each cut-up box should have 6 faces. Tell students that the cut-up box can be considered a *net*, and it represents the *surface area* of the rectangular prism.

TEACH

1 EXPLORE

Questioning Strategies

- How are the patterns alike? They each have 6 squares.

- How are the patterns different? The arrangement of the squares is different.

Differentiated Instruction

Have students use grid paper and make different nets that can fold up into cubes of various dimensions. Have students keep track of which nets fold into a cube and which nets do not, including why they do not.

2 EXPLORE

Questioning Strategies

- How many faces does the net have? 6

- Which faces have the same dimensions? Why? Top and bottom; left and right; front and back; opposite faces are congruent.

- Why are the areas of the faces in square units? The area of each face involves multiplying two dimensions.

Avoid Common Errors

Some students may forget one or more of the faces when determining the surface area. Have students write the area of each face on the appropriate face on the net. Tell students to make sure they have 6 separate area measures before adding them together for the total surface area.

© Houghton Mifflin Harcourt Publishing Company

Name_____ Class_____ Date_____

6-6

Nets and Surface Area

COMMON
CORE
CC.6.G.4

Essential question: *How can you use nets to find surface areas?*

A **net** is a two-dimensional pattern of shapes that can be folded into a three-dimensional figure. The shapes in the net become the faces of the three-dimensional figure.

1 EXPLORE Nets of a Cube

A Copy the following nets on graph paper and cut them out along the blue lines.

Net A   Net B

One of these nets can be folded along the black lines to make a cube. Which net will NOT make a cube? ____B____

B See if you can find another net that can be folded into a cube.

Draw a net that you think will make a cube on your graph paper, and then cut it out. Can you fold it into a cube?

C Compare your results with several of your classmates. How many different nets for a cube did you and your classmates find?
Check students' answers.

REFLECT

How do you know that each net cannot be folded into a cube without actually cutting and folding it?

1a.

1b.

The net has only 5 faces, but a   The net folds into a "loop" of
cube has 6.   squares.

1c. What shapes will appear in a net for a rectangular prism that is not a cube? How many of these shapes will there be?
rectangles; 6

© Houghton Mifflin Harcourt Publishing Company

The **surface area** of a three-dimensional figure is the sum of the areas of its faces. A net can be helpful when finding surface area.

2 EXPLORE Surface Area of a Rectangular Prism

The gift wrap department of a store has specially sized boxes to wrap sweaters. Use the box's dimensions to label the dimensions of the net. Then find the surface area of the box.

3 inches
10 inches
15 inches

3 inches
10 inches   10 inches
3 inches
15 inches   15 inches
3 inches

Complete the table to find the surface area.

Face	Base (in.)	Height (in.)	Area (in²)
Top	15	10	150
Bottom	15	10	150
Front	15	3	45
Back	15	3	45
Right	10	3	30
Left	10	3	30
		Total	450

The surface area of the sweater box is ____450____ square inches.

REFLECT

2a. How did you find the area of each face?

Each face is a rectangle, so use the formula $A = bh$.

2b. If the box had been a cube, how would finding the surface area have been easier?

Each of the 6 faces of a cube has the same area, so you can find the area of one face and multiply by 6.

© Houghton Mifflin Harcourt Publishing Company

Questioning Strategies

- How are rectangular prisms and rectangular pyramids alike and how are they different? **Both are three-dimensional and both have faces that are polygons. Prisms have two bases; pyramids have only one base. Rectangular prisms have 6 faces; rectangular pyramids have 5 faces.**

- How do the triangular faces of the square prism compare? **All four triangular faces are congruent.**

- How many faces would a triangular prism have? **4**

MATHEMATICAL PRACTICE   **Highlighting the Standards**

This explore is an opportunity to address Standard 7 (Attend to precision). Students need to be careful when labeling the dimensions on their nets. They need to calculate the areas of all of the faces carefully and make sure they have calculated the area of all of the faces.

CLOSE

Essential Question
How can you use nets to find surface area?
Find the sum of the areas of all faces on the net.

Summarize
Have students use grid paper to create nets for the following three-dimensional figures:

- Rectangular prism
- Square prism
- Triangular prism

- Rectangular pyramid
- Square pyramid
- Triangular pyramid

PRACTICE

Where skills are taught	Where skills are practiced
1 EXPLORE	EXS. 1–2
2 EXPLORE	EXS. 3–4
3 EXPLORE	EXS. 5–6

A **pyramid** is a three-dimensional figure whose base is a polygon and whose other faces are all triangles. A pyramid is named by its base. A pyramid whose base is a triangle is a triangular pyramid. A pyramid whose base is a square is a square pyramid, and so on.

3 EXPLORE   Surface Area of a Pyramid

Find the surface area of the pyramid.

A How many faces does the pyramid have? __5__

B What polygon forms the base of the pyramid?

square

What is the formula for the area of this polygon?

$A = bh$, or b^2

C What polygon forms each of the other faces?
What is the formula for the area of this polygon?

triangle; $A = \frac{1}{2} bh$

D Complete the net by labeling its dimensions.

E Complete the table to find the surface area.

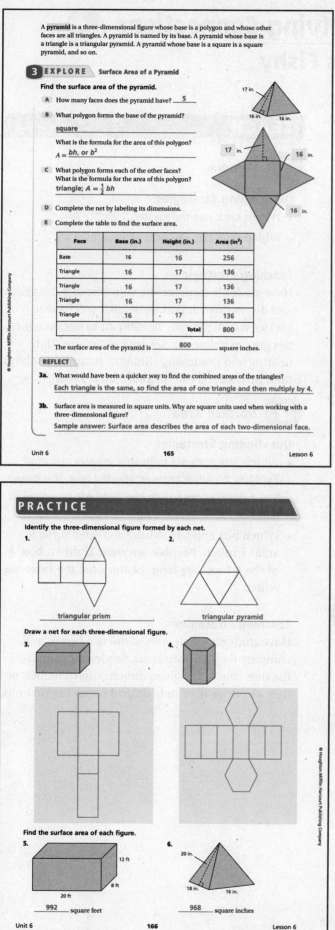

Face	Base (in.)	Height (in.)	Area (in²)
Base	16	16	256
Triangle	16	17	136
Triangle	16	17	136
Triangle	16	17	136
Triangle	16	17	136
		Total	800

The surface area of the pyramid is ____800____ square inches.

REFLECT

3a. What would have been a quicker way to find the combined areas of the triangles?

Each triangle is the same, so find the area of one triangle and then multiply by 4.

3b. Surface area is measured in square units. Why are square units used when working with a three-dimensional figure?

Sample answer: Surface area describes the area of each two-dimensional face.

PRACTICE

Identify the three-dimensional figure formed by each net.

1.

triangular prism

2.

triangular pyramid

Draw a net for each three-dimensional figure.

3.

4.

Find the surface area of each figure.

5.

12 ft
8 ft
20 ft

____992____ square feet

6.

20 in.
18 in.
16 in.

____968____ square inches

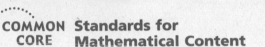

UNIT 6

Problem Solving Connections
Something's Fishy

COMMON Standards for
CORE Mathematical Content

CC.6.G.1 Find the area of right triangles, other triangles, ...; apply these techniques in the context of solving real-world and mathematical problems.

CC.6.G.2 Find the volume of a right rectangular prism with fractional edge lengths by packing it with unit cubes of the appropriate unit fraction edge lengths, and show that the volume is the same as would be found by multiplying the edge lengths of the prism. Apply the formulas $V = lwh$ and $V = Bh$ to find volumes of right rectangular prisms with fractional edge lengths in the context of solving real-world and mathematical problems.

CC.6.G.3 Draw polygons in the coordinate plane given coordinates for the vertices; use coordinates to find the length of a side joining points with the same first coordinate or the same second coordinate. Apply these techniques in the context of solving real-world and mathematical problems.

CC.6.G.4 Represent three-dimensional figures using nets made up of rectangles and triangles, and use the nets to find the surface area of these figures. Apply these techniques in the context of solving real-world and mathematical problems.

INTRODUCE

Discuss with students what kinds of decisions are involved in getting an aquarium and some fish. Include topics about the accessories, such as the air filter, the light, the heater, and some other optional items, such as a stand for the aquarium and decorations. Tell students that they will be making decisions about such items based on geometry concepts learned in this unit.

TEACH

1 Volume

Questioning Strategies
- Which tank has the greater height? **A**
- Which tank has the greater length? **B**

Teaching Strategies
Have students estimate the volumes of the tanks and discuss which tank they think will have a greater volume. It may be difficult to decide which has greater volume based on predictions, but hearing and discussing students' reasoning behind their predictions can be informative for all.

2 Surface Area

Questioning Strategies
- Which box appears to have a greater volume? Explain. **Possible answer: Heater box: the base has a greater area than the light-kit box, and it is almost as tall as the light-kit box.**
- Which box appears to have a greater surface area? Explain. **Possible answers: Light-kit box: 4 of the 6 faces are long; heater box: the faces are wider.**

Teaching Strategies
Have students create nets of the two boxes, and compare their surface areas. Students can make the nets true to the given dimensions in inches, or they can draw their nets on grid paper in grid units.

Name_____ Class_____ Date_____

UNIT 6

COMMON CORE
CC.6.G.1
CC.6.G.2
CC.6.G.3
CC.6.G.4

Problem Solving Connections

Something's Fishy As a birthday surprise for their son Wyatt, Mr. and Mrs. Watson plan to purchase a large aquarium, its accessories, and all of Wyatt's favorite species of tropical fish. Once they have decided on an aquarium, Mr. Watson will build a stand for it, and then they will decide how many fish to buy.

1 Volume

After looking at several different aquariums, Mr. and Mrs. Watson have decided to purchase either tank A or tank B.

A Find the volume of tank A.

Tank A — 5 feet, $3\frac{3}{4}$ feet, $3\frac{1}{2}$ feet

$V = \ell wh$

$= 5 \cdot 3\frac{3}{4} \cdot 3\frac{1}{2}$

$= 5 \cdot \frac{15}{4} \cdot \frac{7}{2}$

$= \frac{525}{8} = 65\frac{5}{8}$ cubic feet

B Find the volume of tank B.

Tank B — $5\frac{1}{2}$ feet, 3 feet, $3\frac{3}{4}$ feet

$V = \ell wh$

$= 5\frac{1}{2} \cdot 3\frac{3}{4} \cdot 3$

$= \frac{11}{2} \cdot \frac{15}{4} \cdot 3$

$= \frac{495}{8} = 61\frac{7}{8}$ cubic feet

C The Watsons decide to purchase the tank with the greater volume. Which tank is this? How much greater is its volume than that of the other tank?

A; $65\frac{5}{8} - 61\frac{7}{8} = \frac{525}{8} - \frac{495}{8}$

$= \frac{30}{8}$

$= 3\frac{6}{8}$

$= 3\frac{3}{4}$ cubic feet

D A box of fish food is 2.25 inches long, 1.5 inches wide, and 4 inches tall. What is the volume of the box of fish food?

$V = \ell wh$

$= 2.25 \cdot 1.5 \cdot 4$

$= 13.5$ cubic inches

E The filter system for the aquarium is in the shape of a rectangular prism. It measures $8\frac{1}{2}$ inches long, $8\frac{1}{2}$ inches wide, and 15 inches high. What is the volume of the filter system?

$V = \ell wh$

$= 8\frac{1}{2} \cdot 8\frac{1}{2} \cdot 15$

$= \frac{17}{2} \cdot \frac{17}{2} \cdot 15$

$= \frac{4,335}{4}$

$= 1,083\frac{3}{4}$ cubic inches

2 Surface Area

Mrs. Watson is wrapping the accessories for the aquarium. She will find the surface area of each box to determine how much gift wrap she needs.

Aquarium Light Kit — 7.5 in., 2 in., 3 in.

A Find the surface area of the box for the light kit.

Top: $7.5 \cdot 2 = 15$

Bottom: $7.5 \cdot 2 = 15$

Left: $2 \cdot 3 = 6$

Right: $2 \cdot 3 = 6$

Front: $7.5 \cdot 3 = 22.5$

Back: $7.5 \cdot 3 = 22.5$

$15 + 15 + 6 + 6 + 22.5 + 22.5 = 87$ square inches

3 Area and Perimeter

Questioning Strategies

- Will the aquarium backdrop fit on the aquarium? Explain. Yes, it has the same dimensions as the front and back faces of the aquarium.

- In part B, where is the molding going to be placed? around three sides of the plywood; front and two sides

Avoid Common Errors

Some students may have a difficult time visualizing the construction of the aquarium stand and its top, which serves as the base for the tank to rest on. Have students sketch the aquarium stand as shown below, and label it with the known measurements.

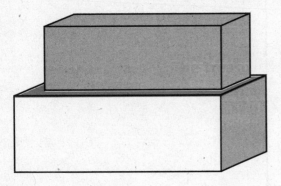

4 Answer the Question

Questioning Strategies

- What are the units of volume that you have for the fish tank from part 1? cubic feet

- How can you find the number of gallons of water that will fill the tank? Convert cubic feet to cubic inches, and then convert cubic inches to gallons.

- How can you find the number of fish that can survive in the tank based on the recommendation of 12 gallons per fish? Write and solve a proportion, or divide the number of gallons by 12.

Teaching Strategies

Discuss with students some real-world situations in which volume, perimeter, area, or surface area are used to make decisions and constructions. For example: Suppose you are installing a new above-ground swimming pool. How much area will the pool take up in the yard? How much water will be needed to fill the pool? How much fencing would be needed to enclose the pool area?

CLOSE

Journal

Have students write a journal entry in which they describe the dimensions of a real-world object and make decisions about how to make it and any accessories for it. Remind them to state the project's problem in their own words and to describe their solution. Also, ask students to outline the main steps they used to reach their solution.

© Houghton Mifflin Harcourt Publishing Company

B Find the surface area of the box for the heater.

Top: $3 \cdot 4 = 12$

Bottom: $3 \cdot 4 = 12$

Left: $6 \cdot 3 = 18$

Right: $6 \cdot 3 = 18$

Front: $6 \cdot 4 = 24$

Back: $6 \cdot 4 = 24$

$12 + 12 + 18 + 18 + 24 + 24 = 108$ square inches

3 Area and Perimeter

A A rectangular backdrop for the aquarium measures 5 feet by 3.5 feet. What is the area that the back drop will cover?

$A = bh$

$= 5 \cdot 3.5$

$= 17.5$ square feet

B Mr. Watson has a solid rectangular piece of birch plywood for the top of the aquarium stand. The plywood is 6 feet long and $4\frac{3}{4}$ feet wide. He plans to attach decorative trim around the front and side edges. How much trim does he need?

$4\frac{3}{4} + 6 + 4\frac{3}{4} = 14\frac{6}{4}$

$= 15\frac{2}{4} = 15\frac{1}{2}$ feet

C Mr. Watson removes a rectangle from the top back edge of the stand, as shown, to allow space for electrical cords. Will the aquarium still fit on the stand in front of this space? Explain.

Yes; the distance from the front of the stand to the front of the space is $4\frac{3}{4} - \frac{1}{2} = 4\frac{1}{4}$ feet. The corresponding dimension of the tank is $3\frac{3}{4}$ feet.

D What is the area of the top of the stand? Explain how you found your answer.

28 square feet

Sample explanation:

Original piece of wood: $6 \cdot 4\frac{3}{4} = 28\frac{1}{2}$ square feet

Removed rectangle: $\frac{1}{2} \cdot 1 = \frac{1}{2}$ square foot

$28\frac{1}{2} - \frac{1}{2} = 28$ square feet

E Find the area of the top of the stand using a different method than the one you used in **D**.

Sample answer: Divide into three rectangles.

Areas of left and right rectangles: $2\frac{1}{2} \cdot 4\frac{3}{4} = 11\frac{7}{8}$

Area of center rectangle: $4\frac{1}{4} \cdot 1 = 4\frac{1}{4}$ square feet

$11\frac{7}{8} + 11\frac{7}{8} + 4\frac{1}{4} = 28$ square feet

4 Answer the Question

A One gallon of water fills 231 cubic inches of space. About how many gallons of water are needed to fill the aquarium? (*Hint*: There are 1,728 cubic inches in a cubic foot.)

$V = 65\frac{5}{8}$ cubic feet $\cdot 1,728 = 113,400$ cubic inches

$\frac{113,400}{231} \approx 491$ gallons

B It is recommended that there be at least 12 gallons of water in the aquarium for each fish. Using this rule, what is the maximum number of fish the Watsons should purchase for the aquarium?

$\frac{491}{12} = 40$ fish

C If the Watsons had purchased the smaller tank, what would be the maximum number of fish they should purchase?

$V = 61\frac{7}{8}$ cubic feet $\cdot 1,728 = 106,920$ cubic inches

$\frac{106,920}{231} \approx 463$ gallons of water

$\frac{463}{12} = 38$ fish

COMMON CORE CORRELATION

Standard	Items
CC.6.G.1	1–8
CC.6.G.2	11–12
CC.6.G.3	8
CC.6.G.4	3, 9–10, 13

TEST PREP DOCTOR ⊕

Multiple Choice: Item 2

- Students who answered **F** may have added 30 and 24.
- Students who answered **G** may have added (30 + 30 + 30 + 24).
- Students who answered **J** may not have divided by 2.

Multiple Choice: Item 7

- Students who answered **A** may have multiplied 18 and 8.
- Students who answered **C** may have multiplied 18 and 15.
- Students who answered **D** may have multiplied 15 by the sum of the two bases, but forgot to divide by 2.

Multiple Choice: Item 8

- Students who answered **F** may have found the product of 6 and 4, instead of 5 and 6.
- Students who answered **H** may have found the product of 5 and 7, instead of 5 and 6.
- Students who answered **J** may have found the product of 6 and 7, instead of 5 and 6.

Multiple Choice: Item 10

- Students who answered **F** may have found the area of only the top and bottom: (12)(8)(2).
- Students who answered **G** may have found the area of only 4 sides: (12)(8)(2) + (8)(5)(2).
- Students who answered **J** may have found the volume of the figure, instead of the surface area.

Free Response: Item 11

- Students who answered **45** may have divided the volume by 18 but not by 9.
- Students who answered **90** may have divided the volume by 9 but not by 18.

Notes

Name _____ Class _____ Date _____

MULTIPLE CHOICE

1. New tiles are being laid in the school hallway. The tiles measure 1 foot by 1 foot. The hallway is 75 feet long and 9 feet wide. How many tiles will be needed to cover the floor of the hallway?

   A. 84 tiles   (C) 675 tiles

   B. 168 tiles   D. 6,075 tiles

2. A triangular street sign has a base of 30 inches and a height of 24 inches.

   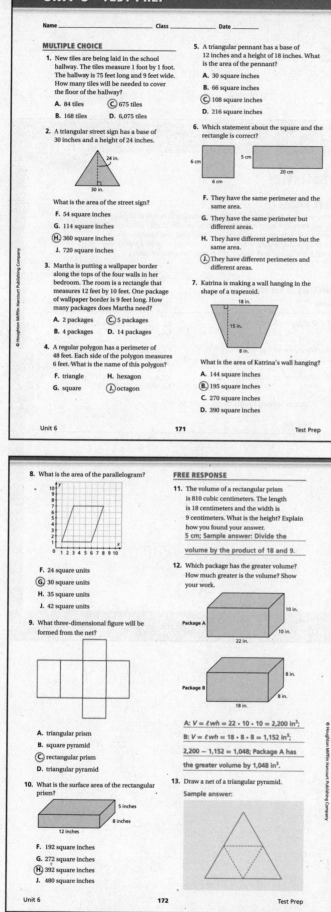

   What is the area of the street sign?

   F. 54 square inches

   G. 114 square inches

   (H) 360 square inches

   J. 720 square inches

3. Martha is putting a wallpaper border along the tops of the four walls in her bedroom. The room is a rectangle that measures 12 feet by 10 feet. One package of wallpaper border is 9 feet long. How many packages does Martha need?

   A. 2 packages   (C) 5 packages

   B. 4 packages   D. 14 packages

4. A regular polygon has a perimeter of 48 feet. Each side of the polygon measures 6 feet. What is the name of this polygon?

   F. triangle   H. hexagon

   G. square   (J) octagon

5. A triangular pennant has a base of 12 inches and a height of 18 inches. What is the area of the pennant?

   A. 30 square inches

   B. 66 square inches

   (C) 108 square inches

   D. 216 square inches

6. Which statement about the square and the rectangle is correct?

   F. They have the same perimeter and the same area.

   G. They have the same perimeter but different areas.

   H. They have different perimeters but the same area.

   (J) They have different perimeters and different areas.

7. Katrina is making a wall hanging in the shape of a trapezoid.

   What is the area of Katrina's wall hanging?

   A. 144 square inches

   (B) 195 square inches

   C. 270 square inches

   D. 390 square inches

8. What is the area of the parallelogram?

   F. 24 square units

   (G) 30 square units

   H. 35 square units

   J. 42 square units

9. What three-dimensional figure will be formed from the net?

   A. triangular prism

   B. square pyramid

   (C) rectangular prism

   D. triangular pyramid

10. What is the surface area of the rectangular prism?

    5 inches
    8 inches
    12 inches

    F. 192 square inches

    G. 272 square inches

    (H) 392 square inches

    J. 480 square inches

FREE RESPONSE

11. The volume of a rectangular prism is 810 cubic centimeters. The length is 18 centimeters and the width is 9 centimeters. What is the height? Explain how you found your answer.

    5 cm; Sample answer: Divide the

    volume by the product of 18 and 9.

12. Which package has the greater volume? How much greater is the volume? Show your work.

    Package A   10 in.
                 10 in.
    22 in.

    Package B   8 in.
                 8 in.
    18 in.

    A: $V = \ell wh = 22 \cdot 10 \cdot 10 = 2,200$ in³;

    B: $V = \ell wh = 18 \cdot 8 \cdot 8 = 1,152$ in³;

    $2,200 - 1,152 = 1,048$; Package A has

    the greater volume by 1,048 in³.

13. Draw a net of a triangular pyramid.

    Sample answer:

Statistics

Unit Vocabulary

box plot	(7-3)
dot plot	(7-1)
histogram	(7-1)
interquartile range (IQR)	(7-3)
lower quartile	(7-3)
mean	(7-2)
mean absolute deviation (MAD)	(7-3)
measure of center	(7-2)
measure of variability	(7-3)
median	(7-2)
statistical question	(7-1)
statistics	(7-1)
upper quartile	(7-3)

UNIT 7

Statistics

Unit Focus
In this unit, you will learn to identify statistical and non-statistical questions. You will draw dot plots and histograms to visually display data sets. Then you will calculate measures of center – the mean and median. You will also analyze the spread of data sets by drawing box plots, finding the interquartile range, and finding the mean absolute deviation.

Unit at a Glance
COMMON CORE

Lesson	Standards for Mathematical Content
7-1 Displaying Numerical Data	CC.6.SP.1, CC.6.SP.2, CC.6.SP.4, CC.6.SP.5a, CC.6.SP.5b
7-2 Measures of Center	CC.6.SP.2, CC.6.SP.3, CC.6.SP.5c, CC.6.SP.5d
7-3 Measures of Variability	CC.6.SP.2, CC.6.SP.3, CC.6.SP.4, CC.6.SP.5c, CC.6.SP.5d
Problem Solving Connections	
Test Prep	

UNIT 7

Unit 7   173   Statistics

©Houghton Mifflin Harcourt Publishing Company

Unpacking the Common Core State Standards

This page lists and explains the Standards for Mathematical Content that are addressed in this unit. For information about the Standards for Mathematical Practice, which are integrated throughout the text, see Teacher Edition pages vii–xiii.

Unpacking the Common Core State Standards

Use the table to help you understand the Standards for Mathematical Content that are taught in this unit. Refer to the lessons listed after each standard for exploration and practice.

COMMON CORE Standards for Mathematical Content	What It Means For You
CC.6.SP.1 Recognize a statistical question as one that anticipates variability in the data related to the question and accounts for it in the answers. Lesson 7-1	You will identify statistical and non-statistical questions.
CC.6.SP.2 Understand that a set of data collected to answer a statistical question has a distribution which can be described by its center, spread, and overall shape. Lessons 7-1, 7-2, 7-3	You will display data in histograms, dot plots, and box plots; calculate the mean and median of a data set as measures of center; and find the interquartile range and mean absolute deviation of a data set.
CC.6.SP.3 Recognize that a measure of center for a numerical data set summarizes all of its values with a single number, while a measure of variation describes how its values vary with a single number. Lessons 7-2, 7-3	You will calculate mean and median and use them to describe a typical value of a data set. You will calculate interquartile range and mean absolute deviation to describe variability of a data set.
CC.6.SP.4 Display numerical data in ... dot plots, histograms, and box plots. Lessons 7-1, 7-3	You will display numerical data in histograms, dot plots, and box plots.
CC.6.SP.5a Summarize numerical data sets in relation to their context, such as by: Reporting the number of observations. Lessons 7-1, 7-3	You will count the number of values in a data set.
CC.6.SP.5b Summarize numerical data sets in relation to their context, such as by: Describing the nature of the attribute under investigation, including how it was measured and its units of measurement. Lesson 7-1	You will identify the type of data measured and its unit of measurement.
CC.6.SP.5c Summarize numerical data sets in relation to their context, such as by: Giving quantitative measures of center (median and/or mean) and variability (interquartile range and/or mean absolute deviation), as well as describing any overall pattern and any striking deviations from the overall pattern with reference to the context in which the data were gathered. Lessons 7-2, 7-3	You will calculate mean, median, interquartile range, and mean absolute deviation for a data set.
CC.6.SP.5d Summarize numerical data sets in relation to their context, such as by: Relating the choice of measures of center and variability to the shape of the data distribution and the context in which the data were gathered. Lessons 7-2, 7-3	You will compare mean and median and use at least one of them to describe a typical value of a data set. You will compare interquartile range and mean absolute deviation and choose which one describes better the variability of the data set.

Notes

_____

_____

_____

_____

_____

_____

_____

_____

_____

_____

Displaying Numerical Data

Essential question: *How can you summarize and display numerical data?*

COMMON CORE **Standards for Mathematical Content**

CC.6.SP.1 Recognize a statistical question as one that anticipates variability in the data related to the question and accounts for it in the answers.

CC.6.SP.2 Understand that a set of data collected to answer a statistical question has a distribution which can be described by its … overall shape.

CC.6.SP.4 Display numerical data in plots on a number line, including dot plots, histograms, … .

CC.6.SP.5a Summarize numerical data sets in relation to their content, such as by: Reporting the number of observations.

CC.6.SP.5b Summarize numerical data sets in relation to their content, such as by: Describing the nature of the attribute under investigation, including how it was measured and its units of measurement.

Vocabulary

statistics

statistical question

dot plot

histogram

Prerequisites

Graphing on a number line

Math Background

Statistical questions have answers that are varied. You can represent numerical data in dot plots or histograms. The dots in a dot plot represent individual numerical data values, but the bars in a histogram represent a range of values.

INTRODUCE

Ask the following question to students in the class and record all the answers: *What are all the numbers in your home address?* Discuss with students that answers to statistical questions will vary. Tell students that, in this lesson, they will learn two ways to display numerical data.

TEACH

1 EXPLORE

Questioning Strategies

• What does it mean when answers to a statistical question have variability? **It means that there are many possible answers; the answers vary.**

• How are the answers to statistical questions different from the answers to non-statistical questions? **A non-statistical question has one answer, while a statistical question has many answers.**

Teaching Strategies

To help students distinguish between statistical and non-statistical questions, have them circle key words in each question. For statistical questions, they should look for plural words such as *students*. For non-statistical questions, they should look for single names and singular nouns and pronouns.

2 EXAMPLE

Questioning Strategies

• What is the first step when making a dot plot? **Possible answer: Find the least and the greatest value in the data, and make a number line to include all values in the data set.**

• How do you plot more than one dot for a given number? **Stack the dots above the number.**

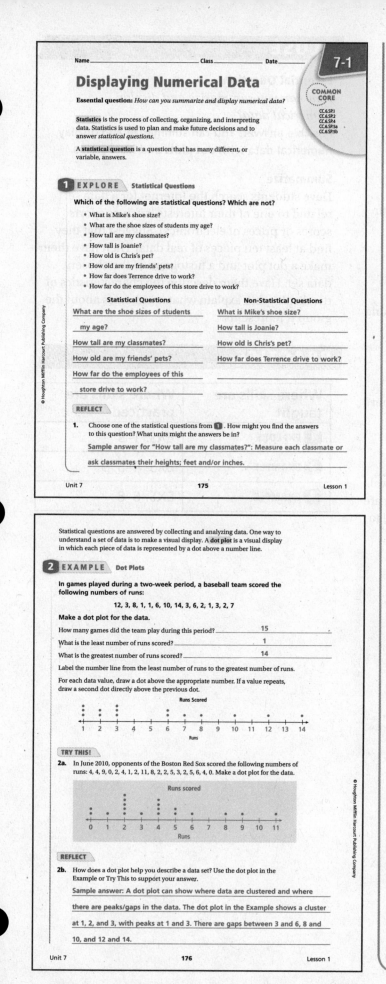

Name_____ Class_____ Date_____

7-1

Displaying Numerical Data

COMMON
CORE

CC.6.SP.1
CC.6.SP.2
CC.6.SP.4
CC.6.SP.5a
CC.6.SP.5b

Essential question: *How can you summarize and display numerical data?*

Statistics is the process of collecting, organizing, and interpreting data. Statistics is used to plan and make future decisions and to answer *statistical questions.*

A **statistical question** is a question that has many different, or variable, answers.

1 EXPLORE   Statistical Questions

Which of the following are statistical questions? Which are not?

- What is Mike's shoe size?
- What are the shoe sizes of students my age?
- How tall are my classmates?
- How tall is Joanie?
- How old is Chris's pet?
- How old are my friends' pets?
- How far does Terrence drive to work?
- How far do the employees of this store drive to work?

Statistical Questions	Non-Statistical Questions
What are the shoe sizes of students my age?	What is Mike's shoe size?
How tall are my classmates?	How tall is Joanie?
How old are my friends' pets?	How old is Chris's pet?
How far do the employees of this store drive to work?	How far does Terrence drive to work?

REFLECT

1. Choose one of the statistical questions from **1**. How might you find the answers to this question? What units might the answers be in?

Sample answer for "How tall are my classmates?": Measure each classmate or

ask classmates their heights; feet and/or inches.

Unit 7   175   Lesson 1

Statistical questions are answered by collecting and analyzing data. One way to understand a set of data is to make a visual display. A **dot plot** is a visual display in which each piece of data is represented by a dot above a number line.

2 EXAMPLE   Dot Plots

In games played during a two-week period, a baseball team scored the following numbers of runs:

12, 3, 8, 1, 1, 6, 10, 14, 3, 6, 2, 1, 3, 2, 7

Make a dot plot for the data.

How many games did the team play during this period? _____15_____

What is the least number of runs scored? _____1_____

What is the greatest number of runs scored? _____14_____

Label the number line from the least number of runs to the greatest number of runs.

For each data value, draw a dot above the appropriate number. If a value repeats, draw a second dot directly above the previous dot.

Runs Scored

(dot plot from 1 to 14, labeled "Runs")

TRY THIS!

2a. In June 2010, opponents of the Boston Red Sox scored the following numbers of runs: 4, 4, 9, 0, 2, 4, 1, 2, 11, 8, 2, 2, 5, 3, 2, 5, 6, 4, 0. Make a dot plot for the data.

Runs scored

(dot plot from 0 to 11, labeled "Runs")

REFLECT

2b. How does a dot plot help you describe a data set? Use the dot plot in the Example or Try This to support your answer.

Sample answer: A dot plot can show where data are clustered and where

there are peaks/gaps in the data. The dot plot in the Example shows a cluster

at 1, 2, and 3, with peaks at 1 and 3. There are gaps between 3 and 6, 8 and

10, and 12 and 14.

Unit 7   176   Lesson 1

Teaching Strategies

Discuss with students some characteristics of dot plots in terms of what they mean in context:

- Shape – general center and spread
- Clustering – value(s) around which all values tend to group
- Peak – a data value that occurs frequently
- Gap – data value that does not occur
- Symmetry – property in which data values occur as a reflection on both sides of some center

3 EXAMPLE

Questioning Strategies

- How is making a histogram different from making a dot plot? **The bars in a histogram represent a range of data values, an interval, instead of a single data value that a dot represents in a dot plot.**
- Why do the bars of a histogram touch each other? **They represent consecutive intervals.**

Avoid Common Errors

Students may not be sure which way to include data values that match the endpoints of an interval. Explain to them that the intervals in a histogram are inclusive; the interval includes data values equal to the endpoint.

MATHEMATICAL PRACTICE **Highlighting the Standards**

This example is an opportunity to address Standard 2 (Reason abstractly and quantitatively.). Students must be able to consider the data set as a whole spread and use number sense to decide on the appropriate size and number of intervals for a histogram.

CLOSE

Essential Question

How can you summarize and display numerical data?

Possible answer: You can summarize and display numerical data with dot plots and histograms.

Summarize

Have students search the Internet for a data set related to one of their interests (such as sports scores or prices of electronics). Suggest that they find at least ten pieces of real data. Then have them make a dot plot and a histogram of the chosen data set. Have them describe the characteristics of the display and explain what it indicates about the group it represents.

PRACTICE

Where skills are taught	Where skills are practiced
1 EXPLORE	EXS. 1–3
2 EXAMPLE	EXS. 4–5, 9
3 EXAMPLE	EXS. 6–8

2c. The *frequency* of a data value is the number of times it occurs in a data set. How can you tell the frequency of a data value by looking at a dot plot?

Count the number of dots above the data value.

It is sometimes more convenient to show data that has been divided into intervals than to display individual data values. A **histogram** is a type of bar graph whose bars represent the frequencies of data within intervals.

3 EXAMPLE Histograms

Make a histogram for the data given in **2**:
12, 3, 8, 1, 1, 6, 10, 14, 3, 6, 2, 1, 3, 2, 7

Step 1 Make a frequency table.

Divide the data into equally-sized intervals of 4. Complete the frequency table.

Interval	Frequency – How many data values are in this interval?
1–4	8
5– 8	4
9–12	2
13 –16	1

Step 2 Make a histogram.

The intervals are listed along the horizontal axis. For each interval, draw a bar to show the number of runs in that interval. The bars should have equal widths. They should touch but not overlap.

Runs Scored

REFLECT

3. How is the histogram similar to the dot plot in **2**? How does it differ?

Both show that most data lie between 1 and 4. The shapes are similar, but

because the hist. shows intervals, it looks more skewed left than the dot

plot. The dot plot shows each data value, so you can tell there are peaks at

1 and 3 and that the greatest value lies at 14. The hist. does not provide this

information. The dot plot shows "gaps" in the data (e.g., between 3 and 6),

but the hist. does not. The hist. does not show the number of data values.

PRACTICE

Tell whether each question is statistical or non-statistical.

1. What are the incomes of your neighbors? —— statistical

2. How old are the homes on your street? —— statistical

3. What is your favorite movie? —— non-statistical

The dot plot shows the number of runs scored by a baseball team in games played during the month of April. Use the dot plot for 4–9.

Runs Scored

4. What does each dot represent? the number of runs scored
by the team in one game

5. How many games did the team play in April? —— 18

6. Make a frequency table and histogram for the data.

Interval	Frequency
0–4	9
5–9	7
10–14	1
15–19	1

Baseball Games in April

7. What size are the intervals used to make the histogram? —— 5

8. Give an example of information provided by the dot plot that is not provided by the histogram.

Sample answer: There is a gap between 9 and 13, which means there was

no game in which the team scored 10, 11, or 12 runs.

9. The numbers of runs scored by the same team in games played during May are: 3, 5, 2, 5, 4, 7, 1, 0, 6, 4, 8, 5, 3, 2, 4, 5, 9. Add these data to the dot plot.

Describe the shape of the data. Are there any data values that do not fit the overall shape? If so, which ones?

Almost all of the data are between 0 and 9, with peaks at 2, 4, and 5;

13 and 17 do not fit.

Measures of Center

Essential question: How can you use measures of center to describe a data set?

COMMON CORE Standards for Mathematical Content

CC.6.SP.2 Understand that a set of data collected to answer a statistical question has a distribution which can be described by its center...

CC.6.SP.3 Display numerical data in plots on a number line, including dot plots, histograms, ...

CC.6.SP.5c Summarize numerical data sets in relation to their content, such as by: Giving quantitative measures of center (median and/or mean) ... as well as describing any overall pattern and any striking deviations from the overall pattern with reference to the context in which the data were gathered.

CC.6.SP.5d Summarize numerical data sets in relation to their content, such as by: Relating the choice of measures of center ... to the shape of the data distribution and the context in which the data were gathered.

Vocabulary

mean
measure of center
median

Prerequisites

Rational number operations

Math Background

The mean and median are two commonly used measures of center. The mean, often called the average, is found by "leveling" the data values, or by dividing the sum of values by the number of values. The median is the value that is in the middle of an ordered data set. The median can be a better choice as a measure of center when you need a typical value from a data set that has outliers, or values that are much different from most of the others.

INTRODUCE

Have students think of or find examples from media that use the words *mean* or *average*, such as reports of the average precipitation, the mean income of a city, or the grade point average of a student. Explain that the mean or average usually represents the most typical of a set of data.

TEACH

1 EXPLORE

Questioning Strategies

- Among how many groups are you dividing the counters? Explain. You are dividing among 5 stacks because there are 5 people.

- Does 2 seem to be the mean of this data set? Yes, when divided up evenly among the 5 stacks, each one gets 2 counters.

- What does a mean of 2 represent in this context? The mean number of siblings for the people in this group is 2.

MATHEMATICAL PRACTICE **Highlighting the Standards**

This explore is an opportunity to address Standard 4 (Model with mathematics). Students use counters to model the data values in a real-world data set. Students model finding the mean by rearranging the counters so that all stacks have the same number of counters.

---

2 EXAMPLE

Questioning Strategies

- How do you represent numbers that repeat when you are ordering the data? Include each one.

- Would the median be the same if you ordered the set from greatest to least? Yes, the middle is still in the same place.

Teaching Strategies

To help students visualize the middle of the data, have them write each number on a separate index card. Have them order the cards and then ask them to find the middle. For part A, they should be able to pick out the card in the middle. For part B, they should point out that the middle is between fifth and sixth cards.

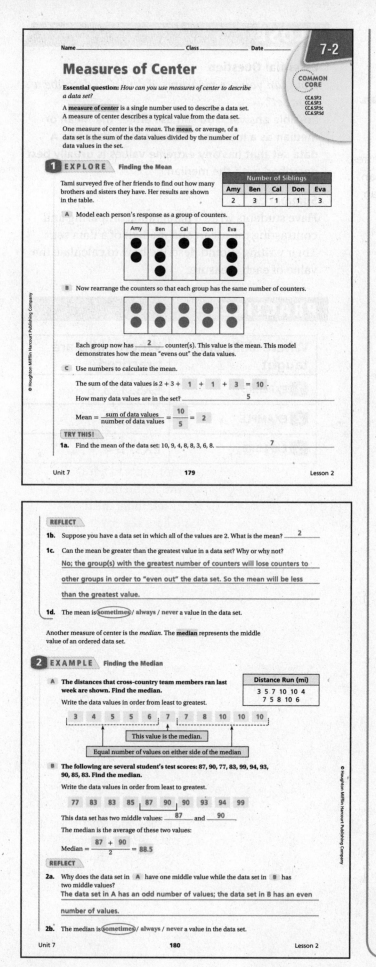

Name _____ Class _____ Date _____

7-2

Measures of Center

COMMON CORE
CC.6.SP.2
CC.6.SP.3
CC.6.SP.5c
CC.6.SP.5d

Essential question: *How can you use measures of center to describe a data set?*

A **measure of center** is a single number used to describe a data set. A measure of center describes a typical value from the data set.

One measure of center is the *mean*. The **mean**, or average, of a data set is the sum of the data values divided by the number of data values in the set.

1 EXPLORE   Finding the Mean

Tami surveyed five of her friends to find out how many brothers and sisters they have. Her results are shown in the table.

Number of Siblings				
Amy	Ben	Cal	Don	Eva
2	3	1	1	3

A Model each person's response as a group of counters.

B Now rearrange the counters so that each group has the same number of counters.

Each group now has ___2___ counter(s). This value is the mean. This model demonstrates how the mean "evens out" the data values.

C Use numbers to calculate the mean.

The sum of the data values is $2 + 3 + 1 + 1 + 3 = 10$.

How many data values are in the set? ___5___

$\text{Mean} = \dfrac{\text{sum of data values}}{\text{number of data values}} = \dfrac{10}{5} = 2$

TRY THIS!

1a. Find the mean of the data set: 10, 9, 4, 8, 8, 3, 6, 8. ___7___

REFLECT

1b. Suppose you have a data set in which all of the values are 2. What is the mean? ___2___

1c. Can the mean be greater than the greatest value in a data set? Why or why not?

No; the group(s) with the greatest number of counters will lose counters to other groups in order to "even out" the data set. So the mean will be less than the greatest value.

1d. The mean is (sometimes) / always / never a value in the data set.

Another measure of center is the *median*. The **median** represents the middle value of an ordered data set.

2 EXAMPLE   Finding the Median

A The distances that cross-country team members ran last week are shown. Find the median.

Distance Run (mi)
3 5 7 10 10 4
7 5 8 10 6

Write the data values in order from least to greatest.

3   4   5   5   6   7   7   8   10   10   10

[This value is the median.]

[Equal number of values on either side of the median]

B The following are several student's test scores: 87, 90, 77, 83, 99, 94, 93, 90, 85, 83. Find the median.

Write the data values in order from least to greatest.

77   83   83   85   87   90   90   93   94   99

This data set has two middle values: ___87___ and ___90___

The median is the average of these two values:

$\text{Median} = \dfrac{87 + 90}{2} = 88.5$

REFLECT

2a. Why does the data set in **A** have one middle value while the data set in **B** has two middle values?

The data set in A has an odd number of values; the data set in B has an even number of values.

2b. The median is (sometimes) / always / never a value in the data set.

3 EXPLORE

Questioning Strategies

- How do the mean and median compare?
  The mean is about $40 greater than the median.

- Which data value is very different from all the others? $750

- How does the data value $750 affect the measures of center? It makes the mean much greater than most of the values. It doesn't affect the median because the middle value is not affected.

MATHEMATICAL PRACTICE   Highlighting the Standards

This explore is an opportunity to address Standard 3 (Construct viable arguments and critique the reasoning of others). Students discuss how measures of center are affected by outliers. They must decide which measure of center is better for the situation, and then provide an argument supporting their decision.

CLOSE

Essential Question

How can you use measures of center to describe a data set?
Possible answer: You can use either the mean or median as a measure of center for a data set. A data set that has any extreme values is usually best described with the median.

Summarize

Have students write a paragraph comparing and contrasting the mean and median of a data set. Their writing should describe how to calculate the value of each measure.

PRACTICE

Where skills are taught	Where skills are practiced
1 EXPLORE	EXS. 1, 3, 5
2 EXAMPLE	EXS. 1, 3
3 EXPLORE	EXS. 1–4

TRY THIS!

2c. Find the median of the data set in **1a**: 10, 9, 4, 8, 8, 3, 6, 8. How does the median compare to the mean?

median = 8; mean = 7; about the same

The mean and median of a data set may be equal, very close to each other, or very different from each other. For data sets where the mean and median differ greatly, one likely describes the data set better than the other.

3 EXPLORE   Mean or Median?

The monthly earnings of several teenagers are $200, $320, $275, $250, $750, $350, and $310.

A Find the mean.

$$\frac{200 + 320 + 275 + 250 + 750 + 350 + 310}{7} = \frac{2,455}{7} \approx 350.71$$

B Write the data values in order from least to greatest and find the median.

200 250 275 (310) 320 350 750

C The mean and the median differ by about $ _40_ . Why?

The mean is affected by the data value 750, which is much greater than the

other data values. The median is not affected by this value.

D Which measure of center better describes a typical teenager's monthly earnings—the mean or the median? Explain.

Median; sample explanation: The mean is greater than all but one of the data

values because of the value 750. The median is a more central value.

TRY THIS!

3a. Luka's final exam scores for this semester are 70, 72, 99, 72, and 69. Find the mean and median. Which is a better description of Luka's typical exam score?

Mean = 76.4; median = 72; median

REFLECT

3b. Luka's parents ask Luka how his final exams went. Luka says, "My average exam score was about 76." Is Luka being truthful? Is Luka misleading his parents? Explain.

He is being truthful because his mean score really is about 76. However,

all but one of his scores are less than 76, so he is misleading his parents.

PRACTICE

Several students' scores on a history test are shown. Use these data for 1 and 2.

1. Mean ≈ _79_   Median = _83_

History Test Scores
73 45 88 90 90 81 83

2. Which measure better describes the typical score for these students? Explain.

Median; the mean is affected by the low score of 45.

The points scored by a basketball team in its last 6 games are shown. Use these data for 3 and 4.

Points Scored
73 77 85 84 35 115

3. Mean ≈ _78_   Median = _80.5_

4. Which measure better describes the typical number of points scored? Explain.

Both describe the number of points equally well.

5. Error Analysis For two weeks, the school librarian recorded the number of library books returned each morning. The data are shown in the dot plot.

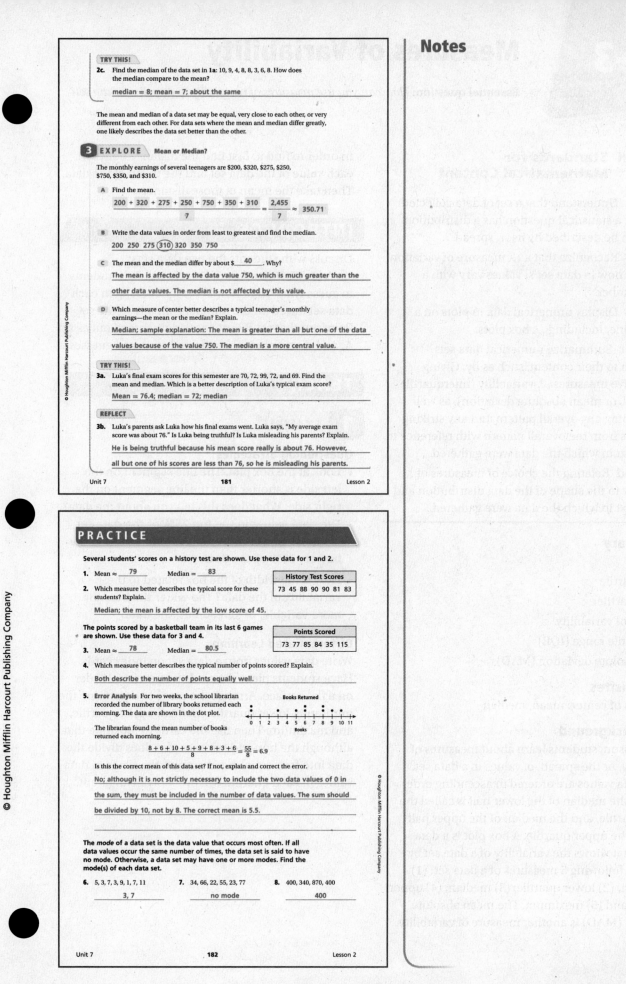

Books Returned

The librarian found the mean number of books returned each morning.

$$\frac{8 + 6 + 10 + 5 + 9 + 8 + 3 + 6}{8} = \frac{55}{8} = 6.9$$

Is this the correct mean of this data set? If not, explain and correct the error.

No; although it is not strictly necessary to include the two data values of 0 in

the sum, they must be included in the number of data values. The sum should

be divided by 10, not by 8. The correct mean is 5.5.

The *mode* of a data set is the data value that occurs most often. If all data values occur the same number of times, the data set is said to have no mode. Otherwise, a data set may have one or more modes. Find the mode(s) of each data set.

6. 5, 3, 7, 3, 9, 1, 7, 11   **7.** 34, 66, 22, 55, 23, 77   **8.** 400, 340, 870, 400

_3, 7_   _no mode_   _400_

Essential question: *How can you use measures of variability to describe a data set?*

© Houghton Mifflin Harcourt Publishing Company

CC.6.SP.2 Understand that a set of data collected to answer a statistical question has a distribution which can be described by its ... spread...

CC.6.SP.3 Recognize that a ... measure of variation describes how [a data set's] values vary with a single number.

CC.6.SP.4 Display numerical data in plots on a number line, including ... box plots.

CC.6.SP.5c Summarize numerical data sets in relation to their content, such as by: Giving quantitative measures ... variability (interquartile range and/or mean absolute deviation), as well as describing any overall pattern and any striking deviations from the overall pattern with reference to the context in which the data were gathered.

CC.6.SP.5d Relating the choice of measures of ... variability to the shape of the data distribution and the context in which the data were gathered.

Vocabulary

box plot
lower quartile
upper quartile
measure of variability
interquartile range (IQR)
mean absolute deviation (MAD)

Prerequisites

Measures of center: mean, median

Math Background

In this lesson, students learn about measures of variability, or the spread, of values in a data set. When data values are ordered in ascending order of value, the median of the lower half is called the lower quartile, and the median of the upper half is called the upper quartile. A box plot is a data display that shows the variability of a data set by using the following 5 measures of a data set: (1) minimum; (2) lower quartile; (3) median; (4) upper quartile; and (5) maximum. The mean absolute deviation (MAD) is another measure of variability.

In order to find it, first find the distance between each value of the data set and the mean of the data. Then take the mean of those distances.

INTRODUCE

Discuss with students the two data sets: set A {0, 40, 20} and set B {19, 21, 20}. Ask students to guess what other number might belong in each data set based on the numbers already in the set. Point out that set B is not as widely spread out as set A, and discuss how that affected students' guesses.

TEACH

1 EXAMPLE

Questioning Strategies

- Look at the box plot. The line segment on the left side is shorter than the line segment on the right side. What does this tell you about the data? **The data values in the top 25% of the data set are more spread out than the data values in the bottom 25% of the data.**

- How is the width of the box related to the variability of the data? **The wider the box, the more variable, or spread out, the data.**

Differentiated Learning

Write data values from a data set on index cards. Have students place the cards in numerical order on a flat surface. Arrange the cards to determine the minimum, lower quartile, median, upper quartile, and maximum. Then use the cards to illustrate that although the box-and-whisker plot does divide the data into four equal-sized groups, the range of data values in each quartile will probably be different.

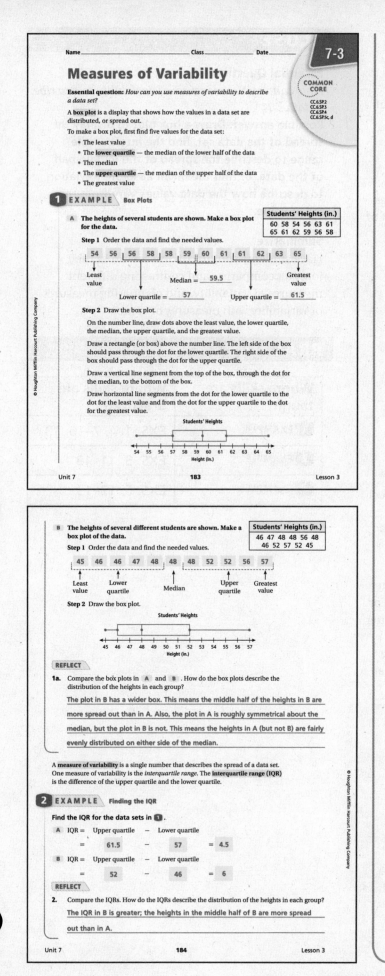

Name _____ **Class** _____ **Date** _____

7-3

Measures of Variability

COMMON CORE

CC.6.SP.2
CC.6.SP.3
CC.6.SP.4
CC.6.SP.5c, d

Essential question: *How can you use measures of variability to describe a data set?*

A **box plot** is a display that shows how the values in a data set are distributed, or spread out.

To make a box plot, first find five values for the data set:

- The least value
- The **lower quartile** — the median of the lower half of the data
- The median
- The **upper quartile** — the median of the upper half of the data
- The greatest value

1 EXAMPLE Box Plots

A The heights of several students are shown. Make a box plot for the data.

Students' Heights (in.)
60	58	54	56	63	61
65	61	62	59	56	58

Step 1 Order the data and find the needed values.

54 56 56 58 58 59 60 61 61 62 63 65

Least value

Median = 59.5

Greatest value

Lower quartile = 57

Upper quartile = 61.5

Step 2 Draw the box plot.

On the number line, draw dots above the least value, the lower quartile, the median, the upper quartile, and the greatest value.

Draw a rectangle (or box) above the number line. The left side of the box should pass through the dot for the lower quartile. The right side of the box should pass through the dot for the upper quartile.

Draw a vertical line segment from the top of the box, through the dot for the median, to the bottom of the box.

Draw horizontal line segments from the dot for the lower quartile to the dot for the least value and from the dot for the upper quartile to the dot for the greatest value.

Students' Heights

54 55 56 57 58 59 60 61 62 63 64 65
Height (in.)

© Houghton Mifflin Harcourt Publishing Company

Unit 7 183 Lesson 3

B The heights of several different students are shown. Make a box plot of the data.

Students' Heights (in.)
46	47	48	48	56	48
46	52	57	52	45	

Step 1 Order the data and find the needed values.

45 46 47 48 48 48 48 52 52 56 57

Least value

Lower quartile

Median

Upper quartile

Greatest value

Step 2 Draw the box plot.

Students' Heights

45 46 47 48 49 50 51 52 53 54 55 56 57
Height (in.)

REFLECT

1a. Compare the box plots in A and B . How do the box plots describe the distribution of the heights in each group?

The plot in B has a wider box. This means the middle half of the heights in B are more spread out than in A. Also, the plot in A is roughly symmetrical about the median, but the plot in B is not. This means the heights in A (but not B) are fairly evenly distributed on either side of the median.

A **measure of variability** is a single number that describes the spread of a data set. One measure of variability is the *interquartile range*. The **interquartile range (IQR)** is the difference of the upper quartile and the lower quartile.

2 EXAMPLE Finding the IQR

Find the IQR for the data sets in 1 .

A IQR = Upper quartile – Lower quartile

= 61.5 – 57 = 4.5

B IQR = Upper quartile – Lower quartile

= 52 – 46 = 6

REFLECT

2. Compare the IQRs. How do the IQRs describe the distribution of the heights in each group?

The IQR in B is greater; the heights in the middle half of B are more spread out than in A.

© Houghton Mifflin Harcourt Publishing Company

Unit 7 184 Lesson 3

Questioning Strategies

- What does the IQR help you measure?
It measures how spread out the middle half of the data is.

- How do you find the IQR from a box plot?
Find the distance between the left and right sides of the box.

- The IQR for data set X is very small. What does this tell you about data set X? The middle half of the data values are clustered close together.

- How can you "see" the IQR on a box plot?
The IQR is equal to the width of the box.

Teaching Strategies

Remind students that the IQR is a distance and it cannot be negative. Therefore, students should always subtract the least value from the greatest value.

3 EXAMPLE

Questioning Strategies

- Which measure of center is used to find the MAD? mean

- How do values that are far from the mean affect the MAD? If there are outlying values either much greater than or much less than the mean value of the data set, the MAD will also be increased or decreased, respectively.

- You have learned that some data sets are better described by the median than by the mean. For these data sets, do you think the spread is better described by the IQR or the MAD? Explain. IQR; the MAD is found using the mean. If the mean does not describe the data set well, then the MAD will not either.

MATHEMATICAL PRACTICE   **Highlighting the Standards**

This example is an opportunity to address Standard 6 (Attend to precision.). Students have to be careful in their calculation of the MAD, making sure that each distance from the mean is calculated correctly to find the positive number that represents the distance.

CLOSE

Essential Question

How can you use measures of variability to describe a data set?
Possible answer: Draw a box plot to display the spread of the data set, find the interquartile range to describe the spread of the middle half of the data, or find the mean absolute deviation to describe how the data values vary from the mean value.

Summarize

Have students summarize this lesson in their journal, comparing and contrasting different measures of variability, and comparing measures of variability with measures of center.

PRACTICE

Where skills are taught	Where skills are practiced
1 EXAMPLE	EXS. 1–4, 7–10, 13
2 EXAMPLE	EXS. 5, 11, 13
3 EXAMPLE	EXS. 6, 12–13

Another measure of variability is the *mean absolute deviation*. The **mean absolute deviation (MAD)** is the mean distance between each data value and the mean of the data set.

3 EXAMPLE Mean Absolute Deviation

Find the MAD for the data sets in **1**.

A   60, 58, 54, 56, 63, 61, 65, 61, 62, 59, 56, 58

Step 1 Find the mean. Round to the nearest whole number.

$$\frac{60 + 58 + 54 + 56 + 63 + 61 + 65 + 61 + 62 + 59 + 56 + 58}{12} \approx 59$$

Step 2 Complete the table.

Height	60	58	54	56	63	61	65	61	62	59	56	58
Distance from Mean	1	1	5	3	4	2	6	2	3	0	3	1

Step 3 To calculate the MAD, find the mean of the values in the second row of the table. Round to the nearest whole number.

$$\frac{1 + 1 + 5 + 3 + 4 + 2 + 6 + 2 + 3 + 0 + 3 + 1}{12} \approx 3$$

B   46, 47, 48, 48, 56, 48, 46, 52, 57, 52, 45

Step 1 Find the mean. Round to the nearest whole number.

$$\frac{46 + 47 + 48 + 48 + 56 + 48 + 46 + 52 + 57 + 52 + 45}{11} \approx 50$$

Step 2 Complete the table.

Height	46	47	48	48	56	48	46	52	57	52	45
Distance from Mean	4	3	2	2	6	2	4	2	7	2	5

Step 3 To calculate the MAD, find the mean of the values in the second row of the table. Round to the nearest whole number.

$$\frac{4 + 3 + 2 + 2 + 6 + 2 + 4 + 2 + 7 + 2 + 5}{11} \approx 4$$

REFLECT

3. Compare the MADs. How do the MADs describe the distribution of the heights in each group?

The MAD in B is greater; in general, the heights in B are farther from the

mean than the heights in A.

PRACTICE

The RBIs (Runs Batted In) for 15 players from the 2010 Seattle Mariners are shown. Use this data set for 1–6.

Mariners' RBIs
15 51 35 25 58 33 64
43 33 29 14 13 11 4 10

1. Find the median. __29__

2. Find the lower quartile. __13__

3. Find the upper quartile. __43__

4. Make a box plot for the data.

Mariners' RBIs

0 5 10 15 20 25 30 35 40 45 50 55 60 65 70 75 80
RBIs

5. Find the IQR. Round to the nearest whole number. __30__

6. Find the MAD. Round to the nearest whole number. __15__

The RBIs for 15 players from the 2010 Baltimore Orioles are shown. Use this data set for 7–12.

Orioles' RBIs
55 76 15 28 39 31 69
60 72 32 20 12 9 14 9

7. Find the median. __31__

8. Find the lower quartile. __14__

9. Find the upper quartile. __60__

10. Make a box plot for the data.

Orioles' RBIs

0 5 10 15 20 25 30 35 40 45 50 55 60 65 70 75 80
RBIs

11. Find the IQR. Round to the nearest whole number. __46__

12. Find the MAD. Round to the nearest whole number. __21__

13. Using the information from 1–12, make a statement that compares the RBIs for the two teams.

Sample answer: Mariners have RBIs more similar to each other than the

Orioles do.

COMMON CORE Standards for Mathematical Content

CC.6.SP.1 Recognize a statistical question as one that anticipates variability in the data related to the question and accounts for it in the answers. …

CC.6.SP.2 Understand that a set of data collected to answer a statistical question has a distribution which can be described by its center, spread, and overall shape.

CC.6.SP.3 Recognize that a measure of center for a numerical data set summarizes all of its values with a single number, while a measure of variation describes how its values vary with a single number.

CC.6.SP.4 Display numerical data in plots on a number line, including dot plots, histograms, and box plots.

CC.6.SP.5a Summarize numerical data sets in relation to their content, such as by: Reporting the number of observations.

CC.6.SP.5b Summarize numerical data sets in relation to their content, such as by: Describing the nature of the attribute under investigation, including how it was measured and its units of measurement.

CC.6.SP.5c Summarize numerical data sets in relation to their content, such as by: Giving quantitative measures of center (median and/or mean) … as well as describing any overall pattern and any striking deviations from the overall pattern with reference to the context in which the data were gathered.

CC.6.SP.5d Summarize numerical data sets in relation to their content, such as by: Relating the choice of measures of center … to the shape of the data distribution and the context in which the data were gathered.

INTRODUCE

Ask students to consider ways that measures of center and measures of variability can be used in a business situation. For example, you can use these statistical measures to help you determine the greatest price that most people are willing to pay for a given item. Explain to students that they will calculate and use measures of center and variability to make business decisions for Farmer Fred's chicken farm.

TEACH

1 Display Numerical Data

Questioning Strategies

- What can you determine about the weights of chickens in each pen from the dot plots? **More of the weights of pen A are heavier than the weights of pen B.**

- What can you determine from the histograms about the weights of chickens in each pen? **The weights for pen A are skewed to the right, so many of the chickens in pen A are in the heaviest category.**

Teaching Strategies

Caution students to take care not to accidentally skip a data value when making a dot plot. After plotting, have students check that the number of dots in the dot plot matches the number of data values.

2 Measures of Center

Questioning Strategies

- Which pen has the greater mean of weights of chickens? **pen A**

- Which pen has the greater median of weights of chickens? **pen A**

Avoid Common Errors

Remind students to list each value of a data set as many times as it appears when calculating mean or median.

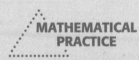

MATHEMATICAL PRACTICE Highlighting the Standards

This part of the project is an opportunity to address Standard 5 (Use appropriate tools strategically). Students can use a scientific calculator to check their work, or they can use a graphing calculator to find all the required measures.

Name_____ Class_____ Date_____

Problem Solving Connections

COMMON CORE
CC.6.SP.1,
CC.6.SP.2,
CC.6.SP.3,
CC.6.SP.4,
CC.6.SP.5a, b, c, d

You Big Chicken! Farmer Fred has been conducting an experiment with two pens of chickens. Since they were chicks, the chickens in pen A have been eating Premium Star chicken feed, while the chickens in pen B have been eating Rapid Growth chicken feed. Help Farmer Fred decide which feed produces larger chickens.

1 Display Numerical Data

A Farmer Fred will weigh the chickens in both pens at the end of his experiment. Is the question "How much do the chickens in each pen weigh?" a statistical question? Why or why not?

Yes; there are several answers.

B The weights that Farmer Fred records are shown in the tables.

Pen A – Premium Star Chickens' Weights (lb)				
6.4	5.2	7.5	8.3	5.6
7.6	8.1	7.7	6.2	6.4
8.1	4.8	5.5	6.6	6.7
4.9	5.1	8.1	7.9	7.5

Pen B – Rapid Growth Chickens' Weights (lb)				
6.6	5.1	7.7	8.1	5.7
5.7	4.5	7.4	6.1	6.3
7.9	4.9	5.6	6.4	6.8
4.7	5.3	6.0	8.0	6.6

How many chickens are in each pen? ____20____

What units are used to measure the chickens' weights? ____pounds____

C Make a dot plot of each data set.

Pen A – Premium Star

Weights (lb)
4   4.5   5   5.5   6   6.5   7   7.5   8   8.5   9

Pen B – Rapid Growth

Weights (lb)
4   4.5   5   5.5   6   6.5   7   7.5   8   8.5   9

D Make a frequency table and histogram of the data for pen A.

Pen A – Premium Star	
Interval	Frequency
4.5–5.4	4
5.5–6.4	5
6.5–7.4	2
7.5–8.4	9

Pen A – Premium Star

Frequency
Weight (lb)
4.5–5.4   5.5–6.4   6.5–7.4   7.5–8.4

E Make a frequency table and histogram of the data for pen B.

Pen B – Rapid Growth	
Interval	Frequency
4.5–5.4	5
5.5–6.4	7
6.5–7.4	4
7.5–8.4	4

Pen B – Rapid Growth

Frequency
Weight (lb)
4.5–5.4   5.5–6.4   6.5–7.4   7.5–8.4

2 Measures of Center

A Find the mean and median weights of the chickens in pen A. Round to the nearest tenth if necessary.

The sum of the data values is 134.2; mean $= \frac{134.2}{20} \approx 6.7$

Ordered data set:

4.8, 4.9, 5.1, 5.2, 5.5, 5.6, 6.2, 6.4, 6.4, 6.6, 6.7, 7.5, 7.5, 7.6, 7.7, 7.9, 8.1, 8.1, 8.1, 8.3

Middle values = 6.6 and 6.7; median $= \frac{6.6 + 6.7}{2} \approx 6.7$

B Find the mean and median weights of the chickens in pen B. Round to the nearest tenth if necessary.

The sum of the data values is 125.4; mean $= \frac{125.4}{20} \approx 6.3$

Ordered data set:

4.5, 4.7, 4.9, 5.1, 5.3, 5.6, 5.7, 5.7, 6.0, 6.1, 6.3, 6.4, 6.6, 6.6, 6.8, 7.4, 7.7, 7.9, 8.0, 8.1

Middle values = 6.1 and 6.3; median $= \frac{6.1 + 6.3}{2} = 6.2$

3 Measures of Variability

Questioning Strategies

- What does the measure of variability tell you about the chickens' weights? **It will tell you which feed gives more consistent weights.**

- How does the box plot help you make conclusions about the variability of the weights? **The box plot with the narrower box tells you which set of weights has less variability.**

Avoid Common Errors

Students may mistakenly pick the box plot with larger width as the better feed. Remind them that a narrower width indicates a more consistent data set, meaning that the results are more reliable and predictable.

4 Answer the Question

Questioning Strategies

- When analyzing the weights, do you just consider which feed gives heavier chickens? **No, you still have to consider how consistent the feed is.**

- When making a business decision with measures of center and variability, what else do you need to consider? **You also need to consider costs and decide if the better feed is worth the extra cost.**

Teaching Strategies

Have students circle key words in the questions so that they know which previous problems to use to help answer the questions. For part A, students should realize that *larger chickens* is a clue that they should look at their work of plotting the data and finding the mean and median. For part B, students should circle *less variability* and realize that they should use their work related to the box plot.

Journal

Have students write a journal entry in which they summarize how they used the measures of center and the measures of variability to decide which feed Farmer Fred should use. Have them justify their reasoning.

Research Options

Students can extend their learning by doing online research to show how the measures of center and the measures of variability are used to help people make business decisions.

3 Measures of Variability

A Find the lower quartile, upper quartile, least weight, and greatest weight of the chickens in pen A. Round to the nearest tenth if necessary.

> Ordered data set:
>
> 4.8, 4.9, 5.1, 5.2, <u>5.5, 5.6</u>, 6.2, 6.4, 6.4, 6.6, 6.7, 7.5, 7.5, 7.6, <u>7.7, 7.9</u>, 8.1, 8.1, 8.1, 8.3
>
> Least value = 4.8
>
> Greatest value = 8.3
>
> Lower quartile = $\frac{5.5 + 5.6}{2} \approx 5.6$
>
> Upper quartile = $\frac{7.7 + 7.9}{2} = 7.8$

B Make a box plot of the data for pen A.

Pen A – Premium Star

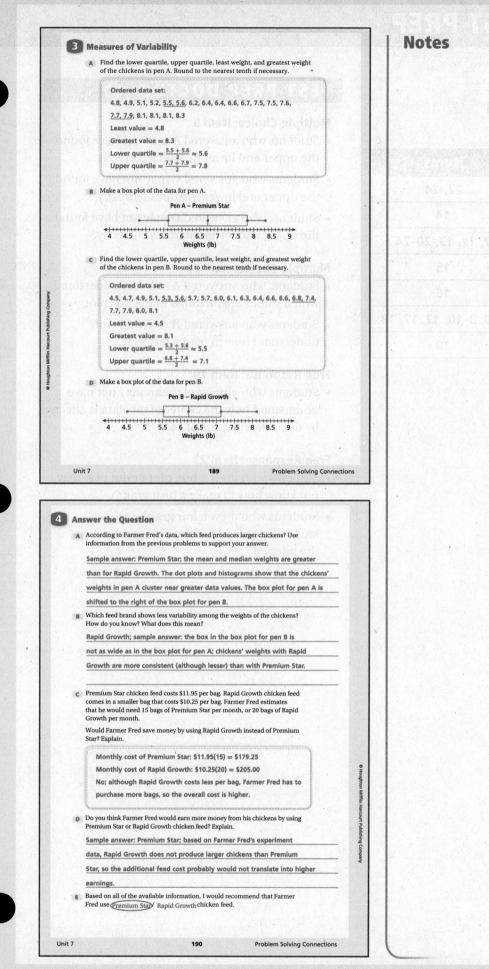

Weights (lb)

C Find the lower quartile, upper quartile, least weight, and greatest weight of the chickens in pen B. Round to the nearest tenth if necessary.

> Ordered data set:
>
> 4.5, 4.7, 4.9, 5.1, <u>5.3, 5.6</u>, 5.7, 5.7, 6.0, 6.1, 6.3, 6.4, 6.6, 6.6, <u>6.8, 7.4</u>, 7.7, 7.9, 8.0, 8.1
>
> Least value = 4.5
>
> Greatest value = 8.1
>
> Lower quartile = $\frac{5.3 + 5.6}{2} \approx 5.5$
>
> Upper quartile = $\frac{6.8 + 7.4}{2} = 7.1$

D Make a box plot of the data for pen B.

Pen B – Rapid Growth

Weights (lb)

4 Answer the Question

A According to Farmer Fred's data, which feed produces larger chickens? Use information from the previous problems to support your answer.

Sample answer: Premium Star; the mean and median weights are greater

than for Rapid Growth. The dot plots and histograms show that the chickens'

weights in pen A cluster near greater data values. The box plot for pen A is

shifted to the right of the box plot for pen B.

B Which feed brand shows less variability among the weights of the chickens? How do you know? What does this mean?

Rapid Growth; sample answer: the box in the box plot for pen B is

not as wide as in the box plot for pen A; chickens' weights with Rapid

Growth are more consistent (although lesser) than with Premium Star.

C Premium Star chicken feed costs $11.95 per bag. Rapid Growth chicken feed comes in a smaller bag that costs $10.25 per bag. Farmer Fred estimates that he would need 15 bags of Premium Star per month, or 20 bags of Rapid Growth per month.

Would Farmer Fred save money by using Rapid Growth instead of Premium Star? Explain.

> Monthly cost of Premium Star: $11.95(15) = $179.25
>
> Monthly cost of Rapid Growth: $10.25(20) = $205.00
>
> No; although Rapid Growth costs less per bag, Farmer Fred has to
>
> purchase more bags, so the overall cost is higher.

D Do you think Farmer Fred would earn more money from his chickens by using Premium Star or Rapid Growth chicken feed? Explain.

Sample answer: Premium Star; based on Farmer Fred's experiment

data, Rapid Growth does not produce larger chickens than Premium

Star, so the additional feed cost probably would not translate into higher

earnings.

E Based on all of the available information, I would recommend that Farmer Fred use (Premium Star) Rapid Growth chicken feed.

COMMON CORE CORRELATION

Standard	Items
CC.6.SP.2	22, 24
CC.6.SP.3	14
CC.6.SP.4	7, 11, 13, 20–24
CC.6.SP.5a	15
CC.6.SP.5b	16
CC.6.SP.5c	1–6, 8–10, 12, 17, 18
CC.6.SP.5d	19

TEST PREP DOCTOR ✚

Multiple Choice: Item 5

- Students who answered **A** may not have found the upper and lower quartiles correctly.
- Students who answered **C** may not have found the upper and lower quartiles correctly.
- Students who answered **D** may not have found the upper and lower quartiles correctly.

Multiple Choice: Item 13

- Students who answered **A** may not understand which values are included in the box plot.
- Students who answered **B** or **C** may not understand how to read a box plot.

Free Response: Item 19

- Students who answered **mean** may not have understood how the center of the data is affected by the outlying value of 14.

Free Response: Item 23

- Students who drew a **box plot** or **dot plot** may not know how to make a histogram.
- Students who drew a **bar graph** may not know that each bar of the histogram covers the interval.

© Houghton Mifflin Harcourt Publishing Company

Name _____ Class _____ Date _____

MULTIPLE CHOICE

Members of the school science club collected canned food for a food drive. The numbers of cans collected by 8 club members are shown. Use these data for 1–7.

Cans Collected

4	10	5	11	15	7	3	9

1. What is the mean number of cans collected?
   A. 8   C. 10
   B. 9   D. 11

2. What is the median number of cans collected?
   F. 8   H. 10
   G. 9   J. 11

3. What is the upper quartile?
   A. 5   C. 10.5
   B. 7   D. 11

4. What is the lower quartile?
   F. 3   H. 5
   G. 4.5   J. 6

5. Which expression gives the interquartile range?
   A. 5 − 4   C. 13.5 − 5
   B. 10.5 − 4.5   D. 15 − 3

6. What is the mean average deviation?
   F. 3.25   H. 8
   G. 6.5   J. 26

7. What would be the leftmost and rightmost points on a box plot of these data?
   A. 3 and 15   C. 4.5 and 10.5
   B. 4 and 9   D. 6.5 and 8

Use the box plot for 8–13.

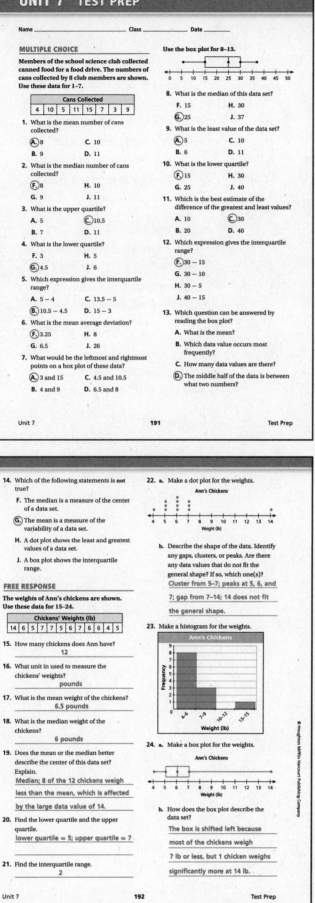

8. What is the median of this data set?
   F. 15   H. 30
   G. 25   J. 37

9. What is the least value of the data set?
   A. 5   C. 10
   B. 6   D. 11

10. What is the lower quartile?
    F. 15   H. 30
    G. 25   J. 40

11. Which is the best estimate of the difference of the greatest and least values?
    A. 10   C. 30
    B. 20   D. 40

12. Which expression gives the interquartile range?
    F. 30 − 15
    G. 30 − 10
    H. 30 − 5
    J. 40 − 15

13. Which question can be answered by reading the box plot?
    A. What is the mean?
    B. Which data value occurs most frequently?
    C. How many data values are there?
    D. The middle half of the data is between what two numbers?

---

14. Which of the following statements is **not** true?
    F. The median is a measure of the center of a data set.
    G. The mean is a measure of the variability of a data set.
    H. A dot plot shows the least and greatest values of a data set.
    J. A box plot shows the interquartile range.

FREE RESPONSE

The weights of Ann's chickens are shown. Use these data for 15–24.

Chickens' Weights (lb)

14	6	5	7	7	5	6	7	6	6	4	5

15. How many chickens does Ann have?
    12

16. What unit in used to measure the chickens' weights?
    pounds

17. What is the mean weight of the chickens?
    6.5 pounds

18. What is the median weight of the chickens?
    6 pounds

19. Does the mean or the median better describe the center of this data set? Explain.
    Median; 8 of the 12 chickens weigh less than the mean, which is affected by the large data value of 14.

20. Find the lower quartile and the upper quartile.
    lower quartile = 5; upper quartile = 7

21. Find the interquartile range.
    2

22. a. Make a dot plot for the weights.

Ann's Chickens

   b. Describe the shape of the data. Identify any gaps, clusters, or peaks. Are there any data values that do not fit the general shape? If so, which one(s)?
   Cluster from 5–7; peaks at 5, 6, and 7; gap from 7–14; 14 does not fit the general shape.

23. Make a histogram for the weights.

Ann's Chickens

24. a. Make a box plot for the weights.

Ann's Chickens

   b. How does the box plot describe the data set?
   The box is shifted left because most of the chickens weigh 7 lb or less, but 1 chicken weighs significantly more at 14 lb.

Correlation of *On Core Mathematics Grade 6* to the Common Core State Standards

Ratios and Proportional Relationships	Citations
CC.6.RP.1 Understand the concept of a ratio and use ratio language to describe a ratio relationship between two quantities.	**pp. 113–116, 135–138**
CC.6.RP.2 Understand the concept of a unit rate *a/b* associated with a ratio *a:b* with $b \neq 0$, and use rate language in the context of a ratio relationship.	**pp. 119–122, 135–138**
CC.6.RP.3 Use ratio and rate reasoning to solve real-world and mathematical problems, e.g., by reasoning about tables of equivalent ratios, tape diagrams, double number line diagrams, or equations. a. Make tables of equivalent ratios relating quantities with whole number measurements, find missing values in the tables, and plot the pairs of values on the coordinate plane. Use tables to compare ratios. b. Solve unit rate problems including those involving unit pricing and constant speed. c. Find a percent of a quantity as a rate per 100 (e.g., 30% of a quantity means 30/100 times the quantity); solve problems involving finding the whole, given a part and the percent. d. Use ratio reasoning to convert measurement units; manipulate and transform units appropriately when multiplying or dividing quantities.	**pp. 117–118, 119–122, 123–126, 127–130, 131–134, 135–138**

The Number System	Citations
CC.6.NS.1 Interpret and compute quotients of fractions, and solve word problems involving division of fractions by fractions, e.g., by using visual fraction models and equations to represent the problem.	**pp. 7–10, 29–32**
CC.6.NS.2 Fluently divide multi-digit numbers using the standard algorithm.	**pp. 3–6, 29–32**
CC.6.NS.3 Fluently add, subtract, multiply, and divide multi-digit decimals using the standard algorithm for each operation.	**pp. 11–14, 15–18, 19–22, 29–32**
CC.6.NS.4 Find the greatest common factor of two whole numbers less than or equal to 100 and the least common multiple of two whole numbers less than or equal to 12. Use the distributive property to express a sum of two whole numbers 1–100 with a common factor as a multiple of a sum of two whole numbers with no common factor.	**pp. 23–26, 27–28, 29–32**
CC.6.NS.5 Understand that positive and negative numbers are used together to describe quantities having opposite directions or values (e.g., temperature above/below zero, elevation above/below sea level, credits/debits, positive/ negative electric charge); use positive and negative numbers to represent quantities in real-world contexts, explaining the meaning of 0 in each situation.	**pp. 37–38**

CC.6.NS.6 Understand a rational number as a point on the number line. Extend number line diagrams and coordinate axes familiar from previous grades to represent points on the line and in the plane with negative number coordinates. a. Recognize opposite signs of numbers as indicating locations on opposite sides of 0 on the number line; recognize that the opposite of the opposite of a number is the number itself, e.g., $-(-3) = 3$, and that 0 is its own opposite. b. Understand signs of numbers in ordered pairs as indicating locations in quadrants of the coordinate plane; recognize that when two ordered pairs differ only by signs, the locations of the points are related by reflections across one or both axes. c. Find and position integers and other rational numbers on a horizontal or vertical number line diagram; find and position pairs of integers and other rational numbers on a coordinate plane.	pp. 37–38, 45–48, 51–54
CC.6.NS.7 Understand ordering and absolute value of rational numbers. a. Interpret statements of inequality as statements about the relative position of two numbers on a number line diagram. b. Write, interpret, and explain statements of order for rational numbers in real-world contexts. c. Understand the absolute value of a rational number as its distance from 0 on the number line; interpret absolute value as magnitude for a positive or negative quantity in a real-world situation. d. Distinguish comparisons of absolute value from statements about order.	pp. 39–42, 43–44, 51–54
CC.6.NS.8 Solve real-world and mathematical problems by graphing points in all four quadrants of the coordinate plane. Include use of coordinates and absolute value to find distances between points with the same first coordinate or the same second coordinate.	pp. 45–48, 49–50, 51–54

Expressions and Equations	Citations
CC.6.EE.1 Write and evaluate numerical expressions involving whole-number exponents.	**pp. 59–62, 77–80**
CC.6.EE.2 Write, read, and evaluate expressions in which letters stand for numbers. a. Write expressions that record operations with numbers and with letters standing for numbers. b. Identify parts of an expression using mathematical terms (sum, term, product, factor, quotient, coefficient); view one or more parts of an expression as a single entity. c. Evaluate expressions at specific values of their variables. Include expressions that arise from formulas used in real-world problems. Perform arithmetic operations, including those involving whole-number exponents, in the conventional order when there are no parentheses to specify a particular order (Order of Operations).	**pp. 63–66, 67–68, 69–72, 77–80**
CC.6.EE.3 Apply the properties of operations to generate equivalent expressions.	**pp. 73–76, 77–80**
CC.6.EE.4 Identify when two expressions are equivalent (i.e., when the two expressions name the same number regardless of which value is substituted into them).	**pp. 73–76, 77–80**
CC.6.EE.5 Understand solving an equation or inequality as a process of answering a question: which values from a specified set, if any, make the equation or inequality true? Use substitution to determine whether a given number in a specified set makes an equation or inequality true.	**pp. 85–88, 101–104, 105–108**
CC.6.EE.6 Use variables to represent numbers and write expressions when solving a real-world or mathematical problem; understand that a variable can represent an unknown number, or, depending on the purpose at hand, any number in a specified set.	**pp. 63–66, 77–80, 85–88, 101–104, 105–108**
CC.6.EE.7 Solve real-world and mathematical problems by writing and solving equations of the form $x + p = q$ and $px = q$ for cases in which p, q and x are all nonnegative rational numbers.	**pp. 89–92, 93–96, 105–108**
CC.6.EE.8 Write an inequality of the form $x > c$ or $x < c$ to represent a constraint or condition in a real-world or mathematical problem. Recognize that inequalities of the form $x > c$ or $x < c$ have infinitely many solutions; represent solutions of such inequalities on number line diagrams.	**pp. 101–104, 105–108**
CC.6.EE.9 Use variables to represent two quantities in a real-world problem that change in relationship to one another; write an equation to express one quantity, thought of as the dependent variable, in terms of the other quantity, thought of as the independent variable. Analyze the relationship between the dependent and independent variables using graphs and tables, and relate these to the equation.	**pp. 97–100, 105–108**

Geometry	Citations
CC.6.G.1 Find the area of right triangles, other triangles, special quadrilaterals, and polygons by composing into rectangles or decomposing into triangles and other shapes; apply these techniques in the context of solving real-world and mathematical problems.	pp. 143–146, 147–150, 151–154, 167–170
CC.6.G.2 Find the volume of a right rectangular prism with fractional edge lengths by packing it with unit cubes of the appropriate unit fraction edge lengths, and show that the volume is the same as would be found by multiplying the edge lengths of the prism. Apply the formulas $V = l\,w\,h$ and $V = b\,h$ to find volumes of right rectangular prisms with fractional edge lengths in the context of solving real-world and mathematical problems.	pp. 159–162, 167–170
CC.6.G.3 Draw polygons in the coordinate plane given coordinates for the vertices; use coordinates to find the length of a side joining points with the same first coordinate or the same second coordinate. Apply these techniques in the context of solving real-world and mathematical problems.	pp. 155–158
CC.6.G.4 Represent three-dimensional figures using nets made up of rectangles and triangles, and use the nets to find the surface area of these figures. Apply these techniques in the context of solving real-world and mathematical problems.	pp. 163–166
Statistics and Probability	**Citations**
CC.6.SP.1 Recognize a statistical question as one that anticipates variability in the data related to the question and accounts for it in the answers.	pp. 175–178, 187–190
CC.6.SP.2 Understand that a set of data collected to answer a statistical question has a distribution which can be described by its center, spread, and overall shape.	pp. 175–178, 179–182, 183–186, 187–190
CC.6.SP.3 Recognize that a measure of center for a numerical data set summarizes all of its values with a single number, while a measure of variation describes how its values vary with a single number.	pp. 179–182, 183–186, 187–190
CC.6.SP.4 Display numerical data in plots on a number line, including dot plots, histograms, and box plots.	pp. 175–178, 183–186, 187–190
CC.6.SP.5 Summarize numerical data sets in relation to their context, such as by: a. Reporting the number of observations. b. Describing the nature of the attribute under investigation, including how it was measured and its units of measurement. c. Giving quantitative measures of center (median and/or mean) and variability (interquartile range and/or mean absolute deviation), as well as describing any overall pattern and any striking deviations from the overall pattern with reference to the context in which the data were gathered. d. Relating the choice of measures of center and variability to the shape of the data distribution and the context in which the data were gathered.	pp. 175–178, 179–182, 183–186, 187–190